S0-AJQ-520

لماذا الإسلام هو إختيارنا؟

WHY ISLAM IS OUR ONLY CHOICE

by

Muhammad Haneef Shahid

Publishers & Distributors:

Publishers & Distributors
DAR AL-HADYAN
Riyadh, Saudi Arabia

AL-ATTIQUE
INT'L ISLAMIC PUBLICATIONS
Toronto Ont. Canada

© **ALL RIGHTS RESERVED**

جميع حقوق الطبع محفوظة

No part of this book may be reproduced or utilized in any form or by any means, electronic or mechanical, including photocopying and recording or by any information storage and retrieval system, without written permission of the publisher.

Copyright   : All rights reserved
First Edition Printed in   : 1997
Printing Supervised by   : M. R. Attique
Printed at   : Riyadh

© Dar Al-Hadyan for Publishing & Distribution, 1997

King Fahd National Library Cataloging-in-Publication Data

Shahid, Muhammad Hanif

Why Islam is our only Choice
... p., ... cm.
ISBN: 9960-9148-4-4
1. Islam, General Principles   1. Title

211 dc   1651/18

Legal Deposit no. 1651/18
ISBN: 9960-9148-4-4

Published By:

Dar Al-Hadyan   مكتبــة دار الهــديان
Publishers & Distributors   للنشــر والتوزيــع
P.O. Box 15031, Riyadh   ص ب ١٥٠٣١ الرياض ١١٤٤٤
Saudi Arabia - 11444   المملكة العربية السعودية
Tel.: 4631685 Fax: 4470266   ت/٤٦٣١٦٨٥ فاكس/٤٤٧٠٢٦٦

Canada:

Al-Attique International Islamic Publications
288 - Westmoreland Ave. Toronto Ont. Canada
Tel.: (416) 516 3856 Fax: (416) 516 4066
E-MAIL quran @ Istar. ca

Publisher's Note

In the name of Allah, the Beneficent, the Merciful. Most Praise be to Allah, the Lord of the worlds. The blessings and peace be upon the Apostle of Allah, his family, his companions, successors, and all those followed the right path until the Last Day of Judgment.

"WHY ISLAM IS OUR ONLY CHOICE" compiled by Muhammad Haneef Shahid is scholarly research contains the relevant information about our Muslim brethren who embraced the true religion of Allah. This title reveals the truth to those generally understood Islam in its narrowest context, and elaborate its meaning to the fact that submission and obedience to the will and order of Allah, what the Quran teaches to all mankind, and messages of Islam and its qualities. The true believers and sincere servants of Allah from all corners of the world, regardless their race, color, tribe, creeds and nationalities, who embraced Islam, tell their true tales and share their real experience in this book. To be more precise this title reveals to the common denominator is that they all embraced Islam through their long search for the truth religion of Allah the Glorious and Exalted, their various kinds of hurdles and hindrances, giving us their own reasons and accounts of their long life-journeys. There are 50 multi-faceted Muslim personalities, including a state president, doctors, professors, journalists, scientists, millionaire, Bishops, and political powerful leaders, are shared their views in this tremendous work.

This title, aims at presenting a true picture of those doctrines to a true truth-seeker. By reading this compiled research book corresponds to the conviction that the more scientific and religious studies advance, the more the scholars and thinkers, scientists and professionals who are still within the fold of different religions and doctrines, will agree with Islam. This book should prove to be a very valuable asset to all including both Muslims and Christians, and will be an effective tool for Muslim propagators in our efforts to invite them to Islam, God Willing.

We, DAR AL-HADYAN - as always its motto is to enlighten the insight of mankind with the LIGHT OF ALLAH and the light of the true FAITH, and we hope is that the Non-Muslim will accept the truth and bear witness to the Oneness of Allah and the Muhammad is His slave servant and Messenger (may peace and blessings be upon him).

Yours brother in Islam,

M. R. ATTIQUE
Publisher, Dar Al-Hadyan, Riyadh
16/06/1418H - 17/10/1997G.

Foreword

IN THE NAME OF ALLAH, THE MOST GRACIOUS,
THE MOST MERCIFUL

When Brother Sheikh Muhammad Haneef Shahid kindly asked me to write a Foreword to the SECOND VOLUME of his serialized work "WHY ISLAM IS OUR ONLY CHOICE", I could not help seize this opportunity and act upon it immediately. This is really a great honour with which I would like to be associated, at least for two reasons. First of all, this work in its entirety is encyclopedia in the sense that it attempts to trace the truth about the true religion, Islam, in its historical and everyday life settings. Secondly the work contains a mine of information about our Muslim brethren who have reverted to Islam through their laborious search and Godly guidance. No one can envy the scholarly effort and hard work exerted by Br. Muhammad Haneef. I can only offer him my sincerest congratulations for his academic research which will prove significant in the cause of Islam.

The true meaning of the"Islam" itself is misconceived and misrepresented by various people in different places of the world. It is generally and widely known that Islam is the religion of the Muslims who reside in some parts of Asia and Africa. Some people even go to the extent of creating names such as Mohammedanism and Mohammedans to stand for Islam and Muslims, respectively. To most people, however, Islam is the religion that started 1417 years ago in Arabia. Some of these ideas are right, but some are not. The truth of the matter is that Islam is generally understood in its narrowest context. In its widest sense, however, Islam means the submission and obedience to the order of Allah, the only Almighty God, and his messengers the last of whom is Prophet Muhammad (PBUH). Defining the religion of Islam, Br. Abu Ameenah Bilal Philips states:[1]

---

[1] Philips, Abu Ameenah Bilal, THE TRUE RELIGION, Dammam: Islamic Daawa and Guidance Center, n.d., pp. 1-3. Brother Bilal is a revert to Islam

a

"The first thing that one should know and clearly understand about Islam is what the word "Islam" itself means. The religion of Islam is not named after a person as in the case of Christianity which was named after Jesus Christ, Buddhism after Gotama Buddah, Confucianism after Confucius, and Marxism after Karl Marx. Nor was it named after a tribe like Judaism after the tribe of Judah and Hinduism after the Hindus. Islam is the true religion of "Allah" and as such, its name represents the central principle of Allah's religion; the total submission to the Will of Allah "God". The Arabic word "Islam" means the submission or surrender of one's will to the only true God worthy of worship "Allah" and anyone who does so is termed a "Muslim". The word also implies "peace" which is the natural consequence of total submission to the will of Allah. Hence, it was not a new religion brought by Prophet Muhammad (PBUH) in Arabia in the seventh century, but only the true religion of Allah re-expressed in its final form.

Islam is the religion which was given to Adam, the first man and the first prophet of Allah, and it was the religion of all the prophets sent by Allah to mankind. The name of God's religion, Islam was not decided upon by later generations of man. It was chosen by Allah himself and clearly mentioned in His final revelation to man. In the Quran, the final book of divine revelation, Allah states the following:

"This day have I perfected your religion for you, completed My favour upon you, and have chosen for you Islam as your religion" (Noble Qur'an 5:3)

"If anyone desires a religion other than Islam (submission to Allah) (God) will never be accepted of him" (Noble Qur'an 3:35)

"Abraham was not a Jew nor yet a Christian but an upright Muslim" (Noble Qur'an 3:67)

b

No where in Bible will you find Allay saying to Prophet Moses's people or their descendants that their religion is Judaism, nor to the followers of Christ that their religion is Christianity. In fact, Christ was not even his name, nor was it Jesus! The name of "Christ" comes from the Greek word Christos which means the anointed. That is, Christ is a Greek translation of the Hebrew title "Messiah". The name "Jesus" on the other hand, is a Latinized version of the Hebrew name Esau.

Thus, the above statement by Br. Bilal leads to two important questions: the universality of Islam and the inborn inclination to worship Allah, our Almighty Lord. Regarding the first question, Br. Bilal explains: [1]

"Since the consequences of false religion are so grave, the true religion of Allah must be universally understandable and attainable, not confined to any people, place or time. There can not be conditions like baptism, belief in a man, as a saviour etc., for a believer to enter paradise. Within the central principle of Islam and its defination, (the surrender of ones's will to God) lies the roots of Islam's universality. Whenever man comes the realization that Allah is one and distinct from his creation, and submits himself to Allah, he becomes a Muslim in body and spirit and is eligible for paradise. Thus, anyone at anytime in the most remote region of the world can become a Muslim, a follower of God's religion, Islam by mercly rejecting the worohip of creation and by turning to Allah alone. It should be noted however, that the recognition and the submission to Allah requires that one chooses between right and wrong and such a choice implies accountability. Man will be held responsible for his choices, and as such, he should try his utmost to do good and avoid evil. The ultimate good being the worship of Allah alone and the ultimate evil being the worship of His creation

---

[1] Op. Cit., pp. 11f

c

along with or instead of Allah. This fact is expressed in the final revelation, i.e. Quran, as follows :

"Verily those who believe, those who follow the Jewish (Scriptures), the Christians and the Sabians and any who believes in Allah and the last day, and work righteousness, shall have their reward with their Lord; They will not be overcome by fear nor grief." (Noble Qur'an 2:62)

On the question of natural inclination of worship, Br. Bilal illuminates : [1]

"The question which arises here is, 'How can all people be expected to believe in Allah given their varying backgrounds, societies and cultures?" For people to be responsible for worshipping Allah they all have to have access to knowledge of Allah. The final revelation teaches that all mankind have the recognition of Allah imprinted on their souls, a part of their very nature with which they are created.

In Surah Al-A' raf, Verses 172-173; Allah explained that when He created Adam, He caused all of Adam's descendants to come into existance and took a pledge from their saying, Am I not your Lord? To which they all replied, "Yes, we testify to it." Allah then explained why He had all the mankind bear witness that He is their creator and only true God worthy of worship. He said 'That was in case you (mankind) should say on the day of Resurrection, "Verily we were unaware of all this." That is to say, we had no idea that You Allah were our God. No one told us that we were only supposed to worship You alone. Allah went on to explain 'That it was also in case you should say, 'Certainly it was our ancestors who made partners (with Allah) and we are only their descendants; will You then destroy us for what those liars did?" Thus, every child is born with a natural

---
[1] Op. Cit., pp. 13f

d

belief in Allah and an inborn inclination to worship Him alone called in Arabic the 'Fitrah''. If the child were left alone, he would worship Allah in his own way, but all children are affected by those things around them, seen or unseen. The Prophet (PBUH) reported that Allah said, 'I created my servants in the right religion but devils made them go astray''. The Prophet (PBUH) also said, 'Each child is born in a state of 'Fitrah', then his parents make him a Jew, Christian or a Zoroastrian'' (Collected by Al-Bukhari and Muslim)... So, just as a child submits to the physical laws which Allah has put in nature, his soul also submits naturally to the fact that Allah is his Lord and Creator.

The university of Islam is repeatedly referred to in the Holy Qur'an, which contains all the essential, basic guidelines of the monotheistic religion regarding worship, good manners and behaviour, learning and knowledge, science and technology, and human interactions and transactions, etc. Thus Islam is not only a religion of worship alone, but also it is a way of life in which religious beliefs and social life intertwine; and in which religion and scientific development are interwoven and they never clash. In his book, [1]Dr. Maurice Bucaille expresses this fact more lucidly. He states :

'The Qur'an follows on from the two Revelations (Torah and Gospels) that preceded it and is not only free from contradictions in its narration, the sign of the various human manipulations to be found in the Gospels, but provides a quality all of its own for those who examine it objectively and in the light of science i.e. its complete agreement with modern scientific data... In view of the level of knowledge in Muhammad's day, it is inconceivable that many of the statements in the Qur'an which are connected with science could have been the work of a man. It is, moreover,

---

[1] The Bible, the Qur'an and Science, Lahore: Kazi Publications, 1979, pp. 251f.

e

perfectly legitmate, not only to regard the Qur'an as the oa Revelation, but also to award it a very special place, on account of the guarantee of authenticity it provides and the presence in it of scientific statements which, when studied today, appear as a challenge to explanation in human terms."

The teaching of Islam and its qualities appeal both to the human mind and heart at the same time. Notions such as loving God Almighty, the brotherhood of all mankind, equality of all people, simplicity and moderation of the faith, peace and reasoning, among others, can inspire any person to revert to Islam. Indeed this reversion is an ongoing process, and it has been there since time immemorial. So, it is no surprise or strange to meet Muslims in all corners of the world. Also it is not strange at all to meet people who have reverted to Islam coming from different backgrounds, age groups, sexes, colours, creeds and beliefs, and different nationalities.

"WHY ISLAM IS OUR ONLY CHOICE", volume I and II are written for the purpose of shedding light on this area of research which have been neglected and hardly been scholarly studied. Brother Muhammad Haneef is setting a good model to redress the balance and study this very important area rather thoroughly. The tools of research he is using, such as Questionnaires, interviews, personal communications and a thorough scanning of old and new literature on the subject, will enable him to reach his goal in the long run, insha Allah (SWT). No doubt that his comprehensive approach and occasional statistical analysis add a special value to this project. In particular, Vol. II of WHY ISLAM IS OUR ONLY CHOICE is of a very widely varied nature, in terms of time, place and rank. To be more precise, this volume contains information about personalities who reverted to Islam at their own will. Although each person has his own story to tell, the common denominator is that they all accepted Islam through their long search for the truth and the true religion of Almighty Allah the one who 'begets not, nor was He begotten; And there is none co-equal or comparable unto Him" (Noble Qur'an 112:3-4).

f

The journeys of the reversion to Islam are not easy and they all are fraught with various kinds of hurdles and danger. The participants in this volume have given us their own accounts of their journeys very faithfully, though occasionally very briefly. Amongst our participants there are 37 gentlemen and 13 ladies. They include a president of a state, physicians, professors, journalists, scientists, a millionaire, a first Muslim Englishman, a first American Captain (Chaplain) in U.S. Armed Forces, Bishops, a U.S. Mayor, among other highly professional leaders, too. This is largely why I am honoured to be in the company of the faithfuls. I am very pleased to have read their given accounts in manuscript form before going to the press. I am sure that the readers will share the joy I had when I was going through each chapter of this book. I must confess that the poem entitled "The Brothers in Islam (this volume), written by the late Lord Headley (1855-1935), is very interesting and joyful to read and I would like to share with the readers some of the ideas expressed in it.

"East meets West in the Universality of Islam

It has been said we could not meet

Or join in prayers for further grace

Together reach Thy mercy seat

Or mingle praise in the same place.

O Heavenly Father, Thou hast shown

To us, Thy loving faithful sons,

How Brotherhood has quickly grown

Insep'rable while time still runs.

In all the ages of the past,

In all the future years to come,

g

Thy Name alone can bind us fast,

Whilst we can say, "Thy Will be done"

Great Allah, Lord, Our God, Our King,

Who knowest what for us is best,

We praise Thy Name and loudly sing

The fusion of the East and West.

To conclude, the present volume of WHY ISLAM IS OUR ONLY CHOICE is now ready for publication. Brother Muhammad Haneef has to be finally congratulated for his ceaseless effort and zeal for the service of Islam. One may assume that this type of research is done by a group of researchers; but to realize that this is a single individual's work is in itself quite an achievement indeed. May I pray to Allah Almightly to help him bring out the rest of the volumes he is planning to produce in the very near future, with comprehensive indexes. Ameen!

Muhammad Hasan Bakalla
Professor
Department of Arabic,
College of Arts,
King Saud University,
Riyadh, Saudi Arabia.
20 Ramadan, 1417 H.
(29th January, 1997)

h

Contents
****

Chapter One

Men at the threshold of Islam

i

iii

iv

Chapter Two

Women at the threshold of Islam

The Truth prevails eventually!

****

Ibn 'Abbas reported : Dimad came to Mecca, he belonged to the tribe of Azd Shanu'a, and he used to protect the person who was under the influence of charm. He heard the foolish people of Mecca say that Muhammad (PBUH) was under the spell. The following 'dialogue' took place between Dimad and the Prophet Muhammad (PBUH) :

(Upon this Dimad said: "If I were to come across this, Allah might cure him at my hand." (He met him and said : Muhammad (PBUH) I can protect (one) who is under the influence of charm, and Allah cures one whom He so desires at my hand. Do you desire (this)" ?

Upon this the Messenger of Allah (PBUH) said: "The Praise is due to Allah, we praise Him, ask His help; and he whom Allah guides aright there is none to lead him astray, and he who is led astray, there is none to guide him, and I bear testimony to the fact that THERE IS NO GOD BUT ALLAH, HE IS ONE, HAVING NO PARTNER WITH HIM, AND THAT MUHAMMAD IS HIS SERVANT AND MESSENGER".

(Now after this) Dimad said: "Repeat these words of yours before me," and Messenger of Allah (PBUH) : Repeated these words to him thrice.

Dimad said : "I have heard the words of soothsayers and the words of magicians, and the words of poets, but I have never heard such words as yours, and they reach the depth (of the ocean of eloquence). Bring forth your hand so that I should take 'Oath of Fealty' to you on ISLAM. So he took an oath of allegiance to him.

The Messenger of Allah said : "It (this allegiance of yours) is on behalf of your people too.

Dimad said: "It is on behalf of my people too" [1]

At the Feet of Muhammad!
****

The well-known British Poet, Rudyard Kipling (1865-1936) in his famous 'Ballad of East and West', said :
Oh! East is East
And West is West,
And Never the Twain
Shall meet!
Maulvi Bashir Pickard, a devout Mulsim (after accepting Islam) commenting 'East is East; said :
'Kipling's 'never' has oft been refuted :
God made the East, God made the West;
Behold! they blend at His behest. [2]
Dr. Ameen Neville J. Whymant (Ph.D. of Oxford), who entered the fold of Islam and became a staunch Muslim, refuted Kipling when he wrote the following poem in praise of our Noble Prophet (PBUH), namely 'At the feet of Muhammad' [3].

The stars shine clear o'ver the desert wide,

----

[1] Dimad was at once convinced that these utterances of the Holy Prophet Muhammad (PBUH) could not be the driveling of an insane man. There was a conviction of the Oneness of the Lord in his words and this rational and sacred idea of Divinity could not be conceived by an insane mind especially when it was overlaid by so many superstitions of material and disfigured gods of idolatry.
Reference : Sahih Muslim, translated by Prof. Abdul Hameed Siddiqi. Lahore, Sh. Muhammad Ashraf, 1976, Vol. 2 page 411 (Chapter CCCIX)

[2] Islamic Review, November 1923 (11:11), page 387
[3] Islamic Review, November-December 1934 (22:11-12), page 412

The moon smiles down in peace
And the gossamer veil of eventide
Gives night from day release
And on my ear fall words so fragrant and sweet:
At the feet of Muhammad East and West meet.

The Yogi and Swami, Rishi too,
Bow to Allah the One,
And Christian and Buddhist and Hindu
Unite when day is done,
Together to pray and together repeat:
At the feet of Muhammad East and West meet.

While clearly the Mosque lamp is burning
Their voices whisper low,
In the tongue of Romance and Learning,
The Truths that all men should know.
Then let us arise and the new Message Greet:
At the feet of Muhammad East and West meet.

INTRODUCTION

In the name of Allah, the Most Beneficent, the Most Merciful!

When we study the Noble Qur'an thoroughly, regarding the Covenants, we come to the 'Covenant' of the Prophets', which the Creator of the Universe, Allah, the All-Mighty, took from the Prophets. The Noble Qur'an says:

"Behold! God took the Covenant of the Prophets, saying : I give you a Book and Wisdom; then comes to you an Apostle, confirming what is with you; Do ye believe in him and render him help". God said: "Do ye agree, and take this my Covenant as binding on you?" They said: "We agree." He said: "Then bear witness, and I am with you among the witnesses." If any turn back after this, they are perverted transgressors". (Noble Quran 3: 81-82)

From the above-mentioned 'Covenant of the Prophets', it is crystal clear that all the Prophets not only agreed to believe in Prophet Muhammad (PBUH), as 'Seal of the Prophets', but also promised to render help to him.

So, according to the 'Covenant of the Prophets', their followers are bound to believe in the Apostleship of Prophet Muhammad (PBUH) - and in the finality of his Prophethood, because all the Prophets are parental brothers and they brought with them one and the same message, which is Islam. Not to speak of men, all the creatures in the heaven and on earth have, willing or unwillingly, bowed to the Will of Allah, i.e. accepted Islam. The Noble Quran, referring to this fact, says:

"Do they seek for other than the 'Religion of God? -- while all creatures in the heavens and on earth have, willing or unwilling, bowed to His Will accepted Islam, and to Him shall they all be brought back." (Noble Quran 3:83)

Unlike the Christians and Jews, it is part of belief of the Muslims to believe not only in the 'Oneness of Allah', but also in all the Scriptures revealed from Allah and all the Prophets i.e. Abraham, Ismail, Isaac, Jacob, Moses, Jesus, etc., Allah, the Most Beneficent, the Most Merciful, addressing the Holy Prophet Muhammad (PBUH) declares :

"Say: 'We believe in God, and in what has been revealed to us and what was revealed to Abraham, Ismail, Isaac, Jacob, and the Tribes, and in (the Books) given to Moses, Jesus, and the Prophets, from their Lord: We make no distinction between one and another and to God do we bow our will (in Islam)". (Noble Qur'an 3:84)

As we have already stated that 'Islam is the Religion of Allah' which has, from Hazrat Adam to the Holy Prophet Muhammad (PBUH) been preached and if any body believes in any other religion and resists Islam, it will not be accepted. Allah, the Omnipotent and Omnipresent, makes this fact clear when He says in the Noble Qur'an :

"If anyone desires a religion other than Islam (submission to God), never will it be accepted of him, and in the Hereafter he will be in the ranks of those who have lost (all spiritual good)". (Noble Qur'an 3:85)

Islam means to 'bow to the Will of Allah' or to 'surrender to His Will' and when a person declares His faith in 'Tawhid' (Oneness of Allah), in the final 'Prophethood of Prophet Muhammad (PBUH), and all the holy 'Scriptures' revealed to the previous Prophets, he becomes a 'Muslim'. As all the Prophets brought the Message of Islam, so the first message of every Prophet to his people according to the Noble Qur'an was:

"Serve God, you have no God other than Him'
(Noble Qur'an 7:59,65,73,85)
"You shall not serve any but God".
(Noble Qur'an 11:26)
"O ye who believe! believe in God and His Apostle".

xi

(Noble Qur'an 4:136)

As mentioned before, all the Prophets were Parental brothers[1] in Islam and their message was one and the same. Prophet Nuh was the first messenger sent by Allah to warn his people. In this respect, the Noble Qur'an says:

"He said: O my people, truly I am a clear Warner to you, worship Allah, fear Him and obey me". (Noble Quran Surah Nuh 71:1-3)

Prophet Hud warning his people said:

"Do not worship except Allah. In-deed do I fear for you from the punishment of a great day".

(Noble Qur'an Surah al-Ahqaf 46:21)

Likewise, Prophet Salih told his people thus:

"O my people! I had indeed conveyed to you the message of my Lord and advised you, but you do not like advisors". (Noble Quran Surah al A'raf 7;79)

According to the Noble Qur'an Prophet 'Ibraheem was not a Jew, nor was he a Christian, but he was one inclining towards Right, submitting to Allah; and he was not of the polytheists". (Noble Quran Surah Ale Imran 3:67)

They were Prophet Ibraheem and his son Isma'il who while raising the foundations of the 'House of Allah' prayed for the advent of Prophet Muḥammad (PBUH) thus:

"Our Lord! make of us Muslims, bowing to Thy (Will), and of our progeny a people Muslim, bowing to Thy Will; and show us our places for the celebration of (due) rites: and turn unto us (in Mercy); for Thou are the Oft-Returning, Most Merciful".

"Our Lord! send amongst them an Apostle of their own, Who shall rehearse Thy Signs to them and instruct them in Scripture and Wisdom, and sanctify them: for Thou

---

[1] Narrated Abu Huraira: I heard Allah's Messenger (PBUH) saying : "I am the nearest of all the people to the son of Mary, and all the Prophets are paternal brothers, and there has been no Prophet between me and him (i.e. Jesus)". (Sahih Bukhari, Vol. 4, Hadith No. 651)

are the Exalted in Might, the Wise". (Noble Quran 2:128-129)

Many verses in the Noble Qur'an order adherence to the 'Religion of Abraham' in answer to the claims of the Jews and Christians that theirs is the preferred way. Allah Subhana hu wa Taala ordered Prophet Muhammad (PBUH) to hold to the 'True Religion' that was taught by Prophet Ibraheem: The Noble Quran says:

"Then We revealed to you (O Muhammad) to follow the way of Ibraheem, inclining to the Right (i.e. Truth)".
"The Religion of your father, Ibraheem, - it is He (i.e. Allah) Who has called you Muslims (in submission to His Will) formerly and in this (Scripture) so that the Messenger (Muhammad) may be a witness over you, and you may be witness over the people". (Noble Quran 16:123; 22:78).

And the Torah confirms that Moses did bear the sort of witness that, according to the Quranic account, he was charged to bear. The Bible reports him to have said:

"A Prophet like me will the Lord, your God, raise up for you from among your kinsmen; to him you shall listen. This is exactly what you requested of the Lord, your God, at Horeb, on the day of the assembly, when you said; "Let us not again hear the voice of great fire anymore, lest we die". And the Lord said to me. "This was well said. I will raise up for them a Prophet like you from among their kinsmen, and will put My Words into his mouth; he shall tell them all that I commanded him. If any man will not listen to My Words which he speaks in My Name, I Myself will make him answer for it". (Deuteronomy, 18: 15-19)[1]

---

[1] Islamic Order. Special Number vol. 4, no. 1, 1982. page 11

The New Testament, likewise, reports Jesus to have borne witness to the primordial covenant and to have discharged his obligation by making the following pronouncement :

"Nevertheless I tell you the Truth; it is expedient for you that I go away; for , if I go not away the Comforter will not come unto you, but if I depart, I will send him unto you. And when he is come, he will reprove the world of sin, and of righteousness, and of judgment". (John, 16:7-8)

"I have yet many things to say unto you, but ye cannot bear them now. Howbeit when he, the Spirit of Truth, is come, he will guide you into all Truth; for he shall not speak of himself; but whatsoever he shall hear, that shall he speak; and he will shew you things to come". (John 16:12-13)[1]

According to the English translation of the Gospel of Barnabas, published by the Oxford University Press:

"Then said the priest: "How shall the Messiah be called, and what sign shall reveal his coming?" Jesus answered: "The name of Messiah is admirable, for God himself gave him the name when he had created his soul, and placed it in a celestial splendour, God said: "Wait Mohammad: for thy sake I will create paradise, the world, and a great multitude of creatures, whereof I make thee a present, insomuch that whoso shall curse thee shall be-cursed. When I shall send thee into the world I shall send thee as my messenger of salvation, and thy word shall be true, insomuch that heaven and earth shall fail, but thy faith shall never fail." Mohammad is his blessed name." Then the crowd lifted up their voices, saying: "O God, send us the messenger:

---

[1] Islamic Order. Special Number vol. 4, no. 1, 1982. page 12

xiv

O Mohammad, come quickly for the salvation of the world". (pp. 113-114)[1]

Regarding 'Seal of Prophets', there is most famous Hadith of the Prophet Muhammad (PBUH) quoted in Sahih Bukhari and Muslim which reads thus:

"Myself and the other Prophets are like a beautiful castle in which one brick is missing: people go around and see it and wonder about the beauty of the building except for the missing brick. I am the one who fills the missing brick. I am the one who completes the building and ends the line of the Prophets".[2]

So from the above-mentioned verses of the Holy Qur'an and Hadith of the Noble Prophet Muhammad (PBUH), it is crystal clear and there is not an iota of doubt that the teachings of all the Prophets are one and the same, the Holy Quran is the "Word of Allah" and our Noble Prophet Muhammad (PBUH) is the 'Last of the Prophets' (i.e. Seal of the Prophets), hence it is obligatory to all human beings to obey Allah, the Creator of the Universe and His Apostle. The Holy Qur'an, at various places says:

"Whoever obeys the Messenger has obeyed Allah".

(Holy Qur'an Surah Al-Nisa 4:80)

In other words, he who obeys the Apostle of Allah, obeys Allah, and he who does not obey the Messenger of Allah, dis obeys Allah. The duty of our Noble Prophet Muhammad (PBUH) was to proclaim the 'Message' (the Noble Qur'an), which he did quite successfully, on the contrary he was not responsible for their affairs. Addressing the Noble Prophet Muhammad (PBUH) Allah says:

"O Messenger (Muhammad) ! Proclaim (the Message) which has been sent down to you from your Lord. And if you do not, then you have not conveyed

---

[1] Islamic Order. vol. 4, no. 1, 1982 page 13
[2] Summarized Sahih al Bukhari Arabic - English. Tr Dr. M.M. Khan. Maktaba Dar us Salam, Riyadh, 1994 page 696 , Chapter 30:1475 (The Last of all the Prophets) Narrated by Jabir Bin 'Abdullah

His Message. Allah will protect you from mankind. Verily, Allah guides not the people who disbelieve". (The Holy Quran Surah Al-Ma'idah 5: 67)

Allah even enjoins upon the 'People of the Book' (Jews and Christians) not only to obey the teachings of 'Torah', the 'Gospel', but also the Holy Quran. Addressing the Noble Prophet Muhammad (PBUH), Allah says :

"Say (O Muhammad)! "O People of the Scripture (Jews and Christians)! You have nothing (as regard guidance) till you act according to the Torah, the Gospel, and what has (now) been sent to you from your Lord (the Quran)". Verily, that which has been sent down to (Muhammad) from your Lord increases in many of them their obstinate rebellion and disbelief. So be not sorrowful over the people who disbelieve". (Holy Quran Surah Al-Ma'idah 5:68)

It is worth mentioning that the Holy Quran confirms the 'Torah' and the 'Gospel' whereas the "People of the Book" do not accept the Holy Quran as "Word of Allah". In this regard, Allah, the Omni-Potent, says:

"And We have sent down to you (O Muhammad) the Book (this Quran) in truth, confirming the Scriptures that came before it and Mohayminan (trustworthy in highness and a witness) over it (old Scriptures)." (Holy Quran Surah Al-Ma'ida 5:48)

Likewise, the 'Scripture', i.e. the 'Torah' and the 'Gospel' confirm the 'Word of Allah' (the Holy Quran). The Holy Quran in this respect says :

"And verily, it (the Quran, and its revelation to Prophet Muhammad) is (announced) in the Scriptures (i.e. the Torah and the Gospel) of former people." (Holy Quran Surah Ash-Shu'ara 26:196)

The Holy Quran is 'Well-guarded' (56:78) and 'Inscribe' in Al-Lauh Al-Mahfûz (The Preserved Tablet) (86:22) and not only

Allah bears witness to the Holy Quran but also His Angels do the same. The Holy Qur'an says:

"But Allah bears witness to that which He has sent down (the Quran) unto you (O Muhammad), He has sent it down with His Knowledge, and the Angels bear witness. And Allah is All-Sufficient as a Witness".
(Holy Quran Surah Al-Nisa 4:166)

In short, keeping the 'Covenant of the Prophets' in view which Allah, the Creator of the creation took from them; that all the Prophets are parental brothers; that they were sent down by Allah with the same Message (i.e. Islam); that they were all 'Muslims' (they all bowed to the Will of Allah), so their followers are bound to obey them all. As all the Muslims believe in all the Messengers of Allah, whether Moses or Jesus and also in the holy Scriptures, i.e. Torah and the Gospel, the 'People of the Book', accordingly, are bound to believe in the Holy Quran and the Noble Prophet Muhammad (PBUH). Addressing the Noble Prophet Muhammad (PBUH), Allah invites the 'People of the Book' thus:

"Say (O Muhammad): "O People of the Scripture (Jews and Christians): Come to a word that is just between us and you, that we worship none but Allah, and that we associate no partners with Him, and that none of us shall take others as lords besides Allah! Then, if they turn away, say : "Bear witness that we are Muslims". (Holy Quran Surah Al-Imran 3. 64)

The people who enter the 'Religion of Allah', are undoubtedly fortunate and Allah has promised 'Reward' for them in this world and in the Hereafter.

Hazrat Ibn Masud said: We entered the room of Ayesha to meet the Holy Prophet at the time of his death. He stared at us and began to shed tears and said :

"Welcome to you, may God grant you long life. May He give you refuge. May He help you. I give you my last instructions to fear God. I give you my last advice as a Warner of God. Don't show pride over the dwellers of towns and cities and over God. Death is near. I shall have to return to God, to Sidratul Muntaha (farthest lote tree), to my resting place: Paradise, and the full Fountain. Take my words to your people and to those people who enter your Religion after me. Salam and God's mercy on my behalf." [1]

It is heartening to note that the 'Religion of Allah' is fast-growing not only in U.S.A but also throughout the world. According to Arab News (October 2, 1996), an American researcher at the world famous Harvard University has found that Islam is the fast-growing Religion in the United States.

Of the more than 5 billion people in the world, 1.1 billion are Muslims. While the largest proportion, 69.2 percent, live in Asia, China has only 20 million Muslims in a population of 1.2 billion.

Asia	760 million
Africa	300 million
Europe	32 million
North America	5.5 million
Latin America	1.3 million
Oceania (inc. Australia & Pacific islands.	0.4 million

World Total	1.099 billion[2]

A new chapter was opened in the history of United States and in the History of Islam, when for the first time the White House celebrated 'Eid al Fitr' and Mrs. Clinton invited nearly 200 Muslim families and delivered a speech on Islam. Giving details of this great event, the Islamic Horizons (May/June 1996, p. 21) writes:

"This week, for the first time in American history, the White House hosted a celebration of an Islamic holiday. It was long over-due. To mark the end of the

---

[1] Imam Gazzali's Ihya ul ulum id din, (book iv), New Delhi, Kitab Bhavan, 1976 page 482.
[2] Islamic Horizon. Nov.-December 1996 Vol. 25 no. 6, page 19.

holy month of Ramadan, the most important holiday of the year, I welcomed 200 men, women and children (and even some sleeping babies) from across to the Indian Treaty Room of the Old Executive Building.

There were prayers and speeches, and a feast of traditional dishes, including meat dumplings, pita bread, hummus, baba ganoush, tabbouleh.

Like I billion other Muslims around the world, these American Muslims had just finished fasting from sunrise to sundown for 30 days. Ramadan is a special time for families, when parents and their children practice self-discipline and deny themselves of food and water to gain greater compassion for the poor.

As I shared in this historic celebration of joy, love and family life, I could not help thinking of how we, as a society, too often mischaracterize Islam and those who adhere to its teachings.

The reality is that the vast majority of the estimated 4 million Muslims in the United States are loyal citizens whose daily lives revolve around work, family and community.

People who find spiritual guidance and sustenance in ISLAM represent all walks of American life. ... I am proud to be an American. And I am proud to be an American Muslim. I am grateful that my daughter has had a chance to study Islamic history in high school, certainly not an option for my generation. In fact, Chelsea was so enthusiastic about the course that when we travelled to South Asia together last year, she provided a running commentary on everything we did and say."

It was the same occasion (Ramadan's iftar) that CAIR Communications Director Ibrahim Hooper presented Mrs. Clinton with a copy of the Holy Quran. (Saudi Gazette 20th September, 1996). This event proved so useful that it provided Mrs. Clinton an opportunity to come into contact with Islam. Mrs. Hillary Clinton made the following remarks in a speech read out by the U.S. Cultural Attache in Riyadh, at 'Islam and the West', Symposium which was organized as a part of the annual Janadriya festival. She said that she has become an eager student of Islam in recent years, and noted: "I thought of how Western society too often mischaracterizes ISLAM and those who adhere to its teachings". (Arab News; March 12, 1996).

It is worth-mentioning that another chapter was opened in the history of the United States when Attorney Lateefah Muhammad received the oath at the Investiture Ceremony of Mayor and Council in Tuskegee, Alabama. She became the First Muslim for the position of City Council Person and also the First Attorney ever elected to public office in this historic city. Lateefah Muhammad, displaying the high intelligence and articulateness that helped her cause greatly in the election, in her first public speech as an elected official introduced her family, her husband, Jamal, her son Karriem, her sister, Dorothy, and asked her mother seated in the audience to stand for recognition. (Saudi Gazette November, 11, 1996).

Unlike the First Part in this series, this part (which is the Second Part) consists of 50 personalities. It is divided into Two Chapters. Chapter One covers 37 male personalities whereas Chapter Two covers 13 female personalities who entered the fold of Islam. The book includes Bishops, Doctors, Professors, Journalists, Army Officers, Engineers, Sportsmen and Barons. It includes the 'Reversion stories' of Captain Abdul Rasheed Muhammad, Islam's First Captain (Chaplain) in the U.S. Armed Forces, Prof. Abdul Ahad Daud, B.D., formerly Bishop of Urmiah, Brother Abu Bakr, formerly Martin Bishop John Mypopol, Charles Mustafa Bilal, formerly Charles Edward Jenkins, First Muslim Mayor of Kountze, Texas, Dwight Muhammad Abdul Qawi, formerly Dwight Braxton, a former World Lightweight and Cruise-Weight Champion, Brother Greg Noakes, Editor of the Washington Report on Middle East Affairs, Lord Headley Al-Haj

El-Farooq, Sir Rowland George Allanson-Winn, British Baron, Sir Jalal ud din Lauder Brunton British Baron, Muhammad Alexander Russell Webb, First American Muslim, Dr. Aminah Coxon, Dr, Ayesha Abdullah, Maryam Jinnah, wife of Quaid-i-Azam Muhammad Ali Jinnah, and Sarah Jeseph, Editor Muslim Youth Magazine. In short, the book includes persons from all walks of life who profess nearly all the famous religions.

It is our first and foremost duty to thank all brothers who lent us a helping hand by providing either material or valuable suggestions. Among them are Brother Syed Khalil-ur-Rahman, Syed Arif Manmood Bukhari, Pervaiz Aslam Burki, Nazir Ahmad Naseem Uddin, Mahmood Alam, Mustata Hashim, Abdul Mateen, Abdur Rasheed and others. Our special thanks are due to Dr. M. M. Siddiqui who devoted his precious time and gave priceless advices. We are thankful to our son Engineer Muhammad Azhar Saeed Chaudhry who helped us during the compilation and proof reading of the manuscript.

We feel grateful to brother Omer Bin Abdullah, Editor-in-Chief, Islamic Horizons (USA) for his cordial help and cooperation not only in supplying addresses of brothers and sisters who have entered the fold of Islam, but also material in this respect. Not only this, he has very kindly allowed us to reproduce material from the Islamic Horizons with due acknowledgement of the source.

Our thanks are due to brother Salim Karim, editor, the Message for his kind help and cooperation in our project and his best and sincere wishes, and for the permission to reproduce and reprint articles from his esteemed journal 'The Message'. Moreover, he has been very kind to supply us addresses of brothers/sisters who embraced Islam quite recently in England.

It will be injustice on our part if we do not express our sincere thanks to brother ·Aslam Abdullah, Editor-in-Chief, of 'The Minaret', Los Angeles, USA for rendering us material, help, and guidance.

Besides this, we are thankful to brother Captain Abdul Rasheed Muhammad, Islam's first Captain in the US Armed Forces; brother Charles Mustafa Bilal, First Muslim Mayor of Kountze, Texas, U.S.A., brother Daud Robert Matthews of King Saud University, brother Greg Noakes, Editor of the Washington Report on Middle East Affairs, Dr. Hassan Nakata of Japan, Dr. Kamal H. Ali of U.S.A., brother Qasim S. Nohara, Dr. Aminah Coxon of U.K., Ms. Dr. Khaula Hassan Nakata of Japan, in particular and other brothers and sisters in Islam in general for their cooperation in answering to our questionnaire and their sincere wishes for the success of our project. May Allah bestow His bounties and favours upon all of them! Ameen!

We also feel most grateful to Dr. Muhammad Manazir Ahsan, Director, The Islamic Foundation, Leicester, U.K., for his cordial help and guidance in this sacred project. May Allah bless him and bestow His favours upon him. Ameen!

Last but not the least, we would like to thank from the core of our heart brother Abul Hassan Ateeq, Proprietor Maktaba Dar-ul-Hadyan, Riyadh who is known to us for the last 15 years and who has undertaken the responsibility of the publication of this valuable book. May Allah bestow His bounties and favours upon him and accept this humble offer!

At the end, we must admit that this is our humble effort for the cause of Islam and we thank Allah, the Most Gracious, Most Merciful, Who gave us the strength, patience and health to finalize this project. Any sort of advice and suggestions will be highly appreciated. We pray to Allah with this supplication

"I only desire reform so far as I am able, to the best of my power. And my guidance cannot come except from Allah, in Him I trust and unto Him I repent". (Holy Quran Surah Hud 11:88)

6th December, 1996   Muhammad Haneef Shahid
                                                              King Saud University, Riyadh

Why I embraced Islam !

Prof. Abd l'Ahad Dawud, B.D., formerly Bishop of Urmiah, born in 1867 was a well-known personality. Before embracing Islam, his name was Rev. David Benjamin Keldani, a Roman Catholic Priest of the Uniate - Chaldean - Sect. He entered the fold of Islam after thorough and deep study and several discussions and interviews with the Sheikh ul Islam Jamal ud din Effendi and other Ulemas. About his 'Reversion to Islam', Prof. Dawud writes :

"My conversion to Islam cannot be attributed to any cause other than the gracious direction of Almighty God. Without this Divine guidance all learning, searching and other efforts to find the truth may even lead one astray. The moment I believed in the Absolute Unity of God, His Holy Apostle Muhammed became the pattern of my conduct and behaviour."

I have not the slightest intention, nor desire to hurt the religious feelings of Christian friends. I love Christ, Moses and Abraham, as I do Muhammad and all other holy Prophets of God".[1]

Prof. Dawud has a lesson for the Christians and he stresses upon them by saying :

"I must remind Christians that unless they believe in the Absolute Unity of God, and renounce the belief in three persons, they are certainly un-believers in the true God. Strictly speaking, Christians are polytheists, only with this exception, that the gods of the heathen are false and imaginary, whereas the three gods of the Churches have a distinct character - is the one true God, but the son is only a Prophet and servant of

---

[1] Yaqeen International, 22nd Sept. 1988, Page 118.

God, and the third person one of the innumerably holy spirits in the spirits of the Almighty God".
After embracing Islam, Prof. Dawud, devoted his life for its cause and wrote a lot on Christianity and Islam. His most outstanding and valuable contribution is 'Muhammad in the Bible'. This book comprises 21 articles which were published in the Islamic Review (London) in a complete series entitled: Muhammad in the Old Testament and Muhammad in the New Testament. This series ran into nine installments and was published in the Islamic review in June 1928 (Vol. 16:6); July 1928 (16:7); August 1928 (16:8); September 1928 (16:9); November 1928 (16:11); December 1928 (16:12); February 1929 (17:2); March 1929 (17:3); July 1929 (17:7); and Muhammad in the New Testament in the same journal in November 1929 (17:11); January 1930 (18:1); March + April 1930 (18:3,4); May 1930 (18:5); September 1930 (18:9); October 1930 (18:10); November 1930 (18:11); January 1931 (19:1); February 1931(19:2); March + April 1931 (19:4+5); August 1931 (19:8) respectively.

Recently, these articles have been published in the form a book under the title 'Muhammad in the Bible' by the Presidency of Shariyah Courts and Religious Affairs Doha, Qatar (3rd ed. in 1980 which is available with us). H.E. Abdul Rahman Abdullah Al-Mahmoud, Vice President, wrote a few lines for this book, where as the 'Foreword' is written by some unknown, 'X.X.'. The strange thing which caught our attention is that on the back page of the Title the same 'note' has been reproduced as it was published in the Islamic Review's February 1929 (Vol. 17:2) issue which runs :

"Professor Abdul 'Ahad Dawud, B.D. the writer of the present series of articles entitled "Muhammad in the Old Testament", which will be followed by the two

2

other equally erudite series, under the headings of "Muhammad in the New Testament", and "Muhammad in the Besorah". 1

This note by the editor of the Islamic Review speaks itself the reality. It is alarming that there is no mention in the book that it is based on the series of articles which were published in the Islamic Review. Strange enough, the compiler did not change the above-mentioned editorial note. As a matter of fact, there must have been a mention of the Islamic Review and full bibliographical reference in the book, keeping in view the copyright act.

The same thing has happened in connection with the same book which has been published by Abul Qasim Publishing House, Jeddah, K.S.A. This book is the true copy of the series of articles published in the Islamic Review and the same 'editorial note' has been given without any slight change. It is worth-mentioning that in the print line 'Copyright', 'All rights reserved', 'No part of this publication may be reproduced', etc., is given. Under these circumstances, one can easily understand whether 'Copyright act' has been violated or not!

Prof. Dawud made clear the purpose of writing this valuable and historical series thus :

"I propose, through this article and the ones which will follow it, to the best of my ability and by the help and grace of Allah to show that the doctrine of Islam concerning the Deity and the last great Messenger of Allah is perfectly true and confirms to the teaching of the Bible". 2

---

1 Islamic Review. February 1929, Vol 17, No. 2, Page 40.
2 Islamic Review. June 1928, Vol. 16, No. 6, Page 196-197.

After this introduction, we would like to reproduce the biographical sketch and the 'Reversion to Islam' story of Prof. Dawud for the benefit of our esteemed readers.

We earnestly hope that by reading this thought-provoking and soul-inspiring 'journey to Islam' of Prof. Dawud, our brothers and sisters will be inspired, Insha Allah! -Editor.

'ABDUL D'A'UD is the former Rev. David Benjamin Keldani. B.D. a Roman Catholic priest of the Uniate-Chaldean sect. He was born in 1867 at Urmiah in Persia; educated from his early infancy in that town. From 1886-89 (three years) he was on the teaching staff of the Archbishop of Canterbury's Mission to the Assyrian (Nestorian) Christians at Urmiah. In 1892 he was sent by Cardinal Vaughan to Rome, where he underwent a course of philosophical and theological studies at the Propaganda Fide College, and in 1895 was ordained Priest. In 1892 Professor Da'wu'd contributed a series of articles to The Tablet on "Assyria, Rome and Canterbury", and also to the Irish Record on the "Authenticity of the Pentateuch." He has several translations of the Ave Maria in different languages, published in the Illustrated Catholic Missions. While in Constantinople on his way to Persia in 1895, he contributed a long series of articles in English and French to the daily paper, published there under the name of The Levant Herald, on "Eastern Churches." In 1895 he joined the French Lazarist Mission at Urmiah, and published for the first time in the history of that Mission a periodical in the vernacular Syriac called Qala-La-Shra'a', i.e. 'The Voice of Truth." In 1897 he was delegated by two Uniate-Chaldean Archbishops of Urmiah and of Salmas to represent the Eastern Catholics at the Eucharistic Congress held at Paray-le-Monial in France under the presidency of Cardinal Perraud. This way, of course, an official invitation. The paper read at the Congress by 'Father Còngress, called 'Le Pellerin" of that year. In this paper, the Chaldean Arch-Priest (that being his

4

official title) deplored the Catholic system of education among the Nestorians, and foretold the imminent appearance of the Russian priests in Urmiah.

In 1888, Father Benjamin was back again in Persia. In his native village, about a mile from the town, he opened a school gratis. The next year he was sent by the Ecclesiastical authorities to take charge of the diocese of Salmas, where a sharp and scandalous conflict between the Uniate Archbishop, Khudab'ash, and the Lazarist Fathers for a long time had been menacing a schism. On the day of New Year 1900, Father Benjamin preached his last and memorable sermon to a large congregation, including many non-Catholic Armenians and others in the Cathedral of St. George's, Khorov'abad, Salmas. The preacher's subject was 'New Century and New Men." He recalled the fact that the Nestorian Missionaries, before the appearance of Islam, had preached the Gospel in all Asia; that they had numerous establishments in India (especially at the Malabar coast), in Tartary, China and Mongolia; and that they translated the Gospel to the Turkish Uighurs and in other languages; that the Catholic, American and Anglican Missions, in spite of the little good they had done to the Assyro-Chaldean nation in the way of preliminary education, had split the nation already a handful - in Persia, Kurdistan and Mesopotamia into numerous hostile sects; and that their efforts were destined to bring about the final collapse. Consequently he advised the natives to make some sacrifices in order to stand upon their own legs like men, and not to depend upon the foreign missions, etc.

The preacher was perfectly right in principle; but his remarks were unfavorable to the interests of the Lord's Missionaries. This sermon hastily brought the Apostolique Delegate, Mgr. Lesne, from Urmiah to Salmas. He remained to the last a friend of Father Benjamin. They both returned to Urmiah. A new Russian Mission had already been established in Urmiah since 1899. The Nestorians were enthusiastically embracing the religion of the "holy" Tsar of All Russias!

5

Five big and ostentatious missions - Americans, Anglicans, French, Germans, and Russians - with their colleges, Press backed up by rich religious societies, Consuls and Ambassadors, were endeavouring to convert about one hundred thousand Assyro-Chaldeans from Nestorian heresy unto one or another of the five heresies. But the Russian Mission soon outstripped the others, and it was this mission which in 1915 pushed or forced the Assyrians of Persia, as well as the mountaineer tribes of Kurdistan, who had then immigrated into the plains of Salmas and Urmiah, to take up arms against their respective Governments. The result was that half of this people perished in the war and the rest expelled from their native lands.

The great question which for a long time had been working its solution in the mind of this priest was now approaching its climax. Was Christianity, with all its multitudinous shapes and colours, and with its unauthentic, spurious and corrupted Scriptures, the true Religion of God? In the summer of 1900 he retired to his small villa in the middle of vineyards near the celebrated fountain of Chali-Boulaghi in Digala, and there for a month spent his time in prayer and meditation, reading over and over the Scriptures in their original texts. The crisis ended in a formal resignation sent in to the Uniate Archbishop of Urmiah, in which he frankly explained to Mar (Mgr.) Touma Audu the reasons for abandoning his sacerdotal functions. All attempts made by the ecclesiastical authorities to withdraw his decision were of no avail. There was no personal quarrel or dispute between Father Benjamin and his superiors; it was all a question of conscience.

For several months Mr. Dawud - as he was now called - was employed in Tabriz as Inspector in the Persian Service of Posts and Customs under the Belgian experts. Then he was taken into the service of the Crown Prince Muhammad 'Ali Mirza as teacher and translator. It was in 1903 that he again visited England and there joined the Unitarian Community. And in 1904 he was sent by the British and Foreign Unitarian Association to carry on an educational and enlightening work among his country people. On

6

his way to Persia he visited Constantinople; and after several interviews with the Sheikh-ul-Islam Jemal-ud-Din Effendi and other Ulemas, he embraced the Holy Religion of Islam. - Editor.

'My conversion to Islam cannot be attributed to any cause other than the gracious direction of Almighty God. Without this Divine guidance all learning, searching and other efforts to find the truth may even lead one astray. The moment I believed in the Absolute Unity of God, His Holy Apostle Muhammad became the pattern of my conduct and behavior.

I have not the slightest intention, nor desire to hurt the religious feelings of Christian friends. I love Christ, Moses and Abraham, as I do Muhammad and all other holy Prophets of God.

Qur'an, in 3:83 says: 'We believe in Allah and what has been revealed to us and what has been revealed to Abraham and Ishmael and Isaac and Jacob and the tribes, and what was given to Moses and Jesus and to the Prophets from their Lord; we do not make any distinction between any of them, and to Him do we submit."

TO CHRISTIANS

My writings are not intended to raise a bitter and therefore, useless dispute with the churches, but only invite them to a pleasant and friendly investigation of this all-important question with the spirit of love and impartiality. If the Christians desist from the vain attempt of defining the essence of the Supreme Being and confess His absolute Oneness, then the union between them and the Muslims is not only probable but extremely possible. For once the Unity of God is accepted and acknowledged, the other points of difference between the two faiths can more easily be settled. It would be a mere waste of time here to refute those who ignorantly or maliciously suppose the Allah of Islam to be different from the true God and only a fictitious deity of Muhammad's own creation. If the Christian priests and theologians know their Scriptures in the Original Hebrew instead of in translations as the Muslims read their Qur'an in its Arabic text, they would clearly see that Allah is the same ancient Semitic

7

name of the Supreme Being who revealed and spoke to Adam and all the Prophets.

Allah is the only self-existing, knowing, powerful Being. He compasses, fills every pace, being and thing, and is the source of all life, knowledge and force. Allah is the unique Creator, Regulator and Ruler of the universe. He is absolutely One. The essence, the person and nature of Allah are absolutely beyond human comprehension, and therefore, any attempt to define His essence is not only futile, but even dangerous to our spiritual welfare and faith for it will certainly lead us into error.

The Trinitarians branch of the Christian Church, for about seventeen centuries, has exhausted all the brains of her saints and philosophers to define the essence and the person of the Deity and what have they invented. All that which Athanasiuses, Augustines and Aquinases have imposed upon the Christians 'under the pain of eternal damnation" to believe in a God who is, 'the third of three'! Allah, in His Holy Qur'an condemns this belief in these solemn words:

"They are certainly unbelievers, who say God is the third of three, for there is no God but the One God and if they refrain not from what they say, a painful chastisement shall surely be inflicted on such of them as are unbelievers". (Qur'an 5: 73)

The attributes of God are not to be considered as distinct and separate divine entities of personalities, otherwise we shall have, not one trinity of persons in the God-head, but several dozen of trinities. An attribute until it actually emanates from its subject has no existence. We cannot qualify the subject by a particular attribute before that attribute has actually proceeded from it and is seen. Hence, we say 'God is Good" when we enjoy His good and kind action but we cannot describe Him - properly speaking - as God is goodness, because, goodness is not God, but His action and work.

The first verse with which St. John Gospels commence was often refuted by the early Unitarian writers, who rendered its true readings as foilows; 'In the beginning was the word and the word

8

was with God; and the Word was God's." It will be noticed that the Greek form of the genitive case 'theou" i.e. "God's" was corrupted into "Theos"; that is, "God," in the nominative form of the name! It is also to be observed that clause, "In the beginning was the word" expressly indicates the origin of the word which was not before the beginning! By the "word of God" is not meant a separate and distinct substance, coeval and co-existent with the Almighty, but an expression and proclamation of His knowledge.

Christian Formula

The Christian auspicatory formula: "In the name of Father and of the Son, and of the Holy Ghost," does not even mention the names of God! And this is the Christian God! The Christians Trinity in as much as it admits a plurality of persons in the Deity, attributes distinct personal properties to each person; and make use of family names similar to those in the pagan mythology, cannot be accepted as a true conception of the Deity.

Allah is neither the father of a son, nor the son of a father. He has no mother, nor is He self-made. The belief in "God the Father and God the Son and God the Holy Ghost" is a flagrant denial of the unity of God, and an audacious confession in three imperfect beings who, unitedly or separately, cannot be the true God.

Then we are told that each person of the trinity has some particular attributes which are not proper to the other two. And these attributes indicate - according to human reasoning and language - priority and posteriority among them. The Father always holds the first rank and is prior to the Son. The Holy Ghost is not only posterior as the third in the order of counting but even inferior to those from whom he proceeds. Would it not be considered a sin of heresy if the names of the three persons were conversely repeated ?

The truth is that there is no mathematical exactitude, no absolute equality between the three persons of the Trinity. If the Father were in every respect equal to the son or the Holy Spirit, as the unit I is positively equal to another figure I, then there

9

would necessarily be only one person of God and not three, because a unit is not fragment or fraction, nor a multiple of itself.

The Truth

The very difference and relationship that is admitted to exist between the persons of the Trinity leaves no shadow of doubt that they are not equal to each other nor are they to be identified with one another. The Father begets and is not begotten; the Son is begotten and not a father; the Holy Ghost is the issue of the other two persons; the first person is described as creator and destroyer; the second as savior or redeemer, and the third as Life-giver.

Consequently none of the three is along the Creator, The Redeemer and the Life-giver. Then we are told that the second person is the word of the first person, becomes man and is sacrificed on the cross to satisfy the justice of this father and that his incarnation and resurrection are operated and accomplished by the third person.

In conclusion, I must remind Christians that unless they believe in the absolute Unity of God, and renounce the belief in the three persons, they are certainly unbelievers in the true God. Strictly speaking, Christians are polytheists, only with this exception, that the gods of the heathen are false and imaginary, whereas the three gods of the Churches have a distinct character, of whom the Father - as another epithet for Creator - is one true God, but the son is only a Prophet and servant of God, and the third person one of the innumerably holy spirits in the service of Almighty God.

10

"I have found a peace of mind which I never experienced before"

When Abdul Ahad Halford formerly Rev. Phillip Halford, studied at a Church of England theological College between 1945 to 1946, he had virtually no contact with Muslims in the areas where he later served as a priest.

Abdul Ahad who later embraced Islam and became very active in Dawah gradually began experiencing a total change in his life in the seventies when he took a job after developing splayed ligaments which made prolonged walking difficult.

Over the next years he came into contact with a number of Muslims and began to study the Holy Qur'an and books about Islam.

'It was a result of this change of work that I believe the first seed was sown with which Allah in his mercy led me to the true path of Islam', recalls Abdul Ahad who now works with the Islamic Propagation Center International (IPCI) in Birmingham, United Kingdom.

Abdul Ahad said in 1988 he preached what turned out to be his last Sermon in a Christian Church. 'During those first days of November Allah made it clear to me that my duty was to submit and bow my will to Islam'.

A year later his wife also embraced Islam which he said made him very happy. 'I have no regrets, for I have found a peace of mind which I never experienced before'.

Inspired by the example of Sheikh Ahmad Deedat of South Africa, IPCI was set up six years ago to present Islam to non-Muslims in the most effective way and to educate Muslims about Islam and

11

comparative religion", says its Secretary-General, Shamshad Khan.

Over the past years IPCI has been distributing the Holy Qur'an free to schools, colleges, universities and public libraries as well as hospitals and prisons nationwide. It published, printed and distributed books, pamphlets and other Dawah material and placed ads in national and international newspapers in the cause of Dawah and Islam (A.N.)[1]

****

[1] Islamic Review (WAMY) No. 38, June 1994, page 9
Why I embraced Islam?

12

Islamic Teachings are clear and appeal to common sense. In Qur'an there is no ambiguity or contradiction. Every thing is logical and rational

These are the words of brother Abdul Kareem formerly Garry Aherad who is a youngman of 27 years and hails from Langka, Lupon, Deveo Oriental, the Philippines. He belongs to a Catholic family. He got his education from Lupon school of Fisheries. Being brought up in Catholic environment, he had certain misunderstandings. He was still at school when Allah guided him through a Muslim friend who gave him a book entitled: " Islam; the Religion of All Prophets'. After reading this book, his misunderstandings and misconceptions were gone. Finally, convinced with the belief in 'Monotheism' and impressed by the Islamic Teachings, he entered the fold of Islam on the 5th of February, 1984. It is heartening to note that after a period of three years of his reversion to Islam, through his continuous efforts and preaching his family members accepted Islam. May Allah bless them all.

Before embracing Islam, brother Abdul Kareem was not satisfied with the doctrine of 'TRINITY', belief in 'Mediation' and concept of 'Original Sin'. It is note worthy that Islam condemns and rejects all these doctrines and concepts. With the courtesy of Saudi Gazette we present his 'Voyage to Islam' to our readers. - Editor. 1

As already mentioned, ABDUL KAREEM (previously known as Gary Aharad), 27, hails from Langka, Lupon, Davao Oriental, the Philippines. He got his education at the Lupon school of

---

[1] Saudi Gazette, 18th March, 1996. Page 8.

13

fisheries and comes from a catholic family background. He arrived in Saudi Arabia on August 14, 1995. Since then he is working as a family driver of his sponsor Muhammad Asim Naqshabandi in Jeddah.

Q. What made you decide to convert to Islamic?

A: First of all, Islamic teaching are clear and appeal to commonsense, going deep into heart. The Qur'an is only one without undergoing, even slightly, any change, even after passing 1,400 years. From chapter 1 to chapter 114, there is no contradiction or ambiguity in it. Everything is logical and relational.

Besides, the belief in monotheism is also logical. God is only One, Almighty. Why should He have wife or son. We human beings need them because the wife looks after her husband when he is tired and wishes to rest. Similarly, a man rears his offspring so that when he grows old and becomes weak, his offspring who by then becomes strong and youthful may look after him. God never tires. He does not want rest or sleep. So, why should He have wife or children.

Moreover, Islam is a complete code of life. It guides us from the cradle to the grave. How should we treat our parents, brothers, and sisters, our teachers, friends and our neighbours. It grants us our rights and assigns us our duties. It is not confined to mosques, nor is it the name of practicing a few customs of birth and death, or marriage or festivals. Rather, it guides us in all aspects of life. It has its own economic, political and social setup. It tells us what to eat, drink and wear and what not.

In the Bible, we find so many contradictory verses. Jesus said "Never did I say them anything of other than what I was commanded to say, that is worship God who is my Lord and your Lord". Then how do Christians justify worshipping Jesus ?

There is not a single statement throughout the Bible, in all its 600 Volumes of the Protestant version, or in the 73 Volumes of the Roman Catholic versions, where Jesus claims to be God or the he says to worship him. According to the Biblical teachings, Jesus

14

did not come to destroy the laws brought by earlier prophets and he continued preaching the same guidance which had been preached by his predecessors. In a nutshell, the aim of the prophet's message was to establish a proper relationship between man and God and between man and man.

Moreover, Christians have mediation between man and God, but in Islam there is no mediation. You, do not need to go to a priest to confess or repent to him. In Islam, every Muslim has direct contact with God, no matter how weak, poor or ignorant he is. In Islam, everything is simple and logical; the first life, then death, then the day of judgment, and then the second life. So, Islam looks at the first life as an examination period for man.

After the first life, the day of judgment is similar to the day of announcing the result of the examinees. The second life is the time when each examinee enjoys or suffers from the outcome of his deeds during the test period.

Q. How do you feel now after embracing Islam ?

A. Of course happy, because there is no concept of original sin. Our parents, Adam and Eve, committed a mistake and only they were responsible for what they committed. God forgave them. The matter ends there. We do not inherit their mistakes, therefore, we can't be held responsible for what they did. We are responsible only for our deeds. Enjoying good and forbidding bad is our duty, individually and collectively, and we have to discharge it and we would be held responsible for it in the Hereafter.

Moreover, my misunderstanding is gone off that since God has killed His 'son' and accepted the sacrifice of his life as an atonement to pardon the sins of all mankind. The impeachment by God in the hereafter makes me responsible and careful about my activities in this life.

Q. Where does your journey to Islam begin from ?

A. When I was in the Lupun School of Fisheries, I had a Muslim friend who gave me a book *Islam the Religion of All Prophets* There I read about Jesus Christ mentioned as one of messengers of Islam.

But in my (earlier) religion, Jesus is a God. The book said: A Muslim is a non-Muslim if he does not believe in Jesus Christ (pbuh) as a slave and messenger of God. I became very curious to know this. So, without wasting any moment, I went to my neighbour - a Revert to Islam. I asked about his reversion to Islam. He informed me that Islam means complete submission to the will of God, and it is the way of life. Even Virgin Mary, the mother of Jesus (pbuh), has been honoured by the Qur'an, and he read the verses : Behold, the angels said, "O Mary! God hath chosen thee and purified thee. Chosen thee above the women of all nation. O Mary! worship thy God devoutly: prostrate thyself and bow down (in prayer) with those who bow down, (Qur'an 3: 42,43)

He said take note that the last word's in verse 42: Chosen thee above the woman of all nations. Such an honour is not given to Mary even in the Bible. And he said let me ask you one thing. Did Jesus ever claim to be God or said that he is our Lord and we should worship him. I said he did not say like that.

Finally, convinced with the belief in monotheism and that Jesus was nothing more or less than a slave and prophet of God, I embraced Islam on February 5, 1984 in my province Davao oriental.

Q. Have your family members also embraced Islam ?

A. Yes, my family members have embraced Islam when I started preaching Islamic beliefs and teaching to them. I tried to remove their misunderstandings about the trinity and confusion which the present day Christianity creates and after three year of my conversion they came to the fold of Islam.

Q. Your plan as a Muslim in future?

A. The Prophet (PBUH) said: "Convey from me, even a single verse". This hadith is my future planning. I want to propagate Islam through my conduct as well as my tongue. Also I have a plan to make even a small Islamic propagation centre in my province for this purpose.

****

16

Islam is rational and avoids extremist of all kinds!

The following thought-provoking and soul-inspiring 'Road to Islam' anecdote of Abdullah Adiyar formerly Adiyar who was born in 1935 to an Atheist and Stalinist father has changed the minds of a number of Hindus and brought them to the 'Straight path' i.e., Islam. Brother Abdullah never went to Hindu temple for idol worship. Later he joined the DK Movement which was started as a protest against worshipping idols, casteism and Brahminism. He graduated, Tamil being his main subject. He was a staunch advocate of the 'No God, No God, at all' theory pronounced by DK leader E.V. Rama Swamy.

Mr. Adiyar was the editor of 'Murasoli', a Tamil daily published by Murosoli Trust, Madras, India. The newspaper was started in 1960 and was the mouthpiece of DMK: Dravida Munnetra Kazhgam. Afterwards, Mr. Adiyar edited another daily newspaper namely Nee Toli for a number of years till in 1975 it was banned and Mr. Adiyar arrested under Security Act under Emergency imposed by Ms. Indra Ghandi, former Prime Minister and he was put into the jail. During his stay in jail, he studied different religions from a comparative point of view. His Christian wife who was a school teacher gave him a copy of the Bible. But it could not satisfy him, especially it could not answer the questions like 'What is death? and 'What is the reason of creation'? Thereupon, he studied Hinduism and at last, Islam. It was the Holy Qur'an that satisfied his quest for truth and gave answers to his questions. Later on, he read the 'Seerat of the Noble prophet Muhammad (PBUH) and prepared extensive notes and it were these notes which became the basis of 17 article series published

17

in a Tamil Daily under the title 'Kadilikkum Islam' (I love Islam). These articles were, later, translated into Urdu, Sindhi, and Hindi and finally published in book form. General Muhammad Zia ul Haq, former President of Pakistan, invited brother Abdullah Adiyar as 'Guest of honour' on the inauguration ceremony of the Sindhi version of his book published by Sindhi Adab Melo.

Brother Maqbool Ahmed Siraj interviewed brother Abdullah Adiyar which was published in Riyadh Daily1 and Muslim World League Journal. With the courtesy of both of these valued media organs, we present the story of brother Abdullah Adiyar's 'Reversion to Islam'.

It is note worthy that brother Abdullah Adiyar has reverted nearly 3000 people to Islam. Among the noteables are :

1. Mr. Kodikkal Chellappa, former District Secretary of Communist Party of India, presently Kodikkal Sheikh Abdullah.
2. Zamindar/land owing aristocrat from Utter Pradesh.
3. Veer Abdur Rahman, a collegue of Dr. Ambedkar and presently Muhammad Bilal.
4. Swami Anand Bhiku, Tamilian Burmese monk and his present name is Muhammad Mujeebullah.

Till 1987, Abdullah Adiyar was merely known by his only name Adiyar that stood alone. His conversion to Islam proficed it with a prefix Abdullah. Adiyar edited *Murasoli*, the powerful daily mouthpiece of the former ruling Dravida Munnetra Kazhgam (DMK) for 17 years. His next tenure as editor of daily Nee Toli ended abruptly in 1975 when it was banned and Adiyar arrested

---

[1] Riyadh Daily 15th December, 1995, page 7
See also Saudi Gazette. May 10, 1996. Page 7

18

under Maintenance of Internal Security Act (MISA) under Emergency imposed by Prime Minister Indira Ghandi. He was tortured in the jail and his abdomen was torn by brute jail authorities. It was during this period that Adiyar studied various religious scriptures. Adiyar studied various religious scriptures. Adiyar says with tearful eyes that with a bruised body and wounded soul he was almost hearing the footsteps of death.

It was in these moments that his Christian wife Thayammal, a school teacher, delivered him a copy of Bible. 'But Bible did not provide me the answer. The atheist in me was looking for answers to questions like "why death? What is reason for creation?" Quest led him to the Vedas and finally the Qur'an. The Qur'an provided the answer i.e. Khilafat to establish the rule of God on the Earth and explore the hidden truth of nature. "Then I read the books on the Life of the Holy Prophet (PBUH) took extensive notes and compared him with other religious personalities of the world."

The notes later became the basis of 17-article series in a Tamil Daily entitled *Nan Kadilikkum Islam* (I love Islam). This brought him into interaction with activists of Islamic movement in Madras culminating into declaring his entry into the fold of Islam. The articles were translated into Urdu and from there onto Sindhi (in Pakistan) and Hindi in Northern India. He was guest of honor of President of Pakistan General Muhammad Zia ul Haq at the release ceremony of the Sindhi version by Sindhi Adab Melo.

Born to an atheist and Stalinist father in Tirupur in 1935, Adiyar says he never went to a Hindu temple for idol worship. He joined the DK (Dravida Kazhgam movement, which started as a protest against idol worship, casteism and Brahminism) as a student leader and did graduation with Tamil as the principal subject. He was a staunch advocate of the 'No God, No God at all" theory propounded by DK leader E.V. Ramaswamy

The people who have embraced Islam in recent days include Kodikkal Chellappa, former district secretary of Communist Party of India. He is now Kodikkal Sheikh Abdullah. Veerabhadranam, a colleague of Dr. Ambedkar is now Md. Bilal. Swami Anan

Bhiku, a Tamilian Burmese monk who had converted to Buddhism has now embraced Islam. His new name is Md. Mujeebullah.

Abdullah Adiyar is a noted Tamil author, journalist playwright Adiyar who embraced Islam in 1987, today heads the Islamic Dawa centre at Madras. He is currently planning an Islamic program for Satellite Television aimed at 60 million Tamil speaking people in Tamil Nadu, Sri Lanka, Malaysia, Singapore and the expatriates in the Gulf countries. Devoted to the cause of promotion of Islam, Adiyar is exploring the talent and resources for the said program. The 60-year old author who has made name in Tamil literary world through his 120 novels and over a dozen plays besides his widely red columns in numerous Tamil dailies feels that Islam has a wide appeal among Tamil masses due to its promise of egalitarian society and message of social equality. He finds in Islam a reflection of the teachings of great Tamil sages of yore who worked at levelling out the wrinkles of the society.

Mr. Abdullah Adiyar recently spoke to journalist Maqbool Ahmed Siraj expounding views on Islam. Excerpts from the interview in the centre are as follows :

Q. Though you were known admirer of Islam, you were never keen on joining its fold till 1987. Then what led you to embrace Islam?

A. It was a queer turn of events for me. I knew my booklet entitled Nan Kadilikkum Islam or its Urdu version *Islam jis se mujhe ishq haqi*, was being widely read. It had drawn a surge of response. But that there was not for becoming a Muslim. I knew Islam required one to be strictly disciplined, what with controls and taboos extending into the very core of social life, personal traits and even dietary habits. But all that changed on a sunny humid afternoon in 1987 when a Zamindar (land-owning aristocrat) from Uttar Pradesh walked into my office in Madras. The man had embraced Islam after going through the Hindi version of my booklet Nan Kadilikkum Islam. He found me sunk in my chair with cigarette pressed between the fingers and an open

20

whisky bottle on the table. He stood aghast at the sight. I had the least idea that my booklet would move somebody to embrace Islam. Similarly the man burst into tears on seeing me in company of vices. His ideal lay shattered before him. That night was the night of revolution for me. I could not sleep all through the night and at the end vowed never to touch the bottle. My conscience began prodding me to turn to Islam and in the end I was guided by Allah to adopt Islam as my faith.

Q. What aspect of Islam fascinates you so much?

A. Islam is rational and avoids extremism of all kinds. It is against celibacy and asceticism. It also offer numerous concessions. It exhorts its followers to be *Ummatan Wasatan* (the middle people).

Q. What is your precept of image of Muslims or Islam in Tamil masses?

A. As far as I see Muslims and their faith have a place of honour, in the heart of Tamil masses. Islam's image is a positive one. Tamil literature goes back nearly 1000 years. They have thousands of formats. Maulvi Umar Pullaver wrote the great Seerah Puranam. The tradition continues to this day. Kavikko Abdur Rahman and Prof. Md. Mehta are among the most Prominent poets. Tikar Abdul Khader is a known prose writer. Muslims in Tamil Nadu are generally referred as "Bhai" a very respectable term. (Rowthers justice) is a popular proverb in Tamil Nadu which speaks of high esteem in which Muslims are held. (Rowther is how Muslims are referred to in Tamil language).

Dravidian culture is such that communalism has not affected the masses. Muslims have even developed their exclusive vocabulary in Tamil literature.

Q. Why mass conversions to Islam have become a phenomenon in Tamil Nadu?

A. It is universal phenomenon. The former untouchables are upset at the treatment of the upper castes. the leaders of the DK movement E.V. Ramaswamy had warned that these people who are now categorized as Scheduled Castes (Scs), would remain

21

slaves in Hinduism and appeal to them to leave out its fold to get salvation.

But it seems the roots of rebellion from enslavement go deeper into Tamil culture.

The great sages of Tamil people preached equality, the very antithesis of Brahminism. The great Tamil saint Thiruvalluvar had struck at the roots of Varnashrama (caste system) and held that everybody is equal by birth. (He said *Perappu Okkum, Ella Veerukkum*: (people are identified by the deeds). Tamil literature is based on the philosophy of "One God, on family".

Q. What are the objectives before the Islamic Dawa Mission?

A. It's chief objective is to promote Islam through Dawa. It also sympathizes with Dalits (the *mustadafeen* or the dispossessed).

Islam has immense appeal for the Dalits in Tamil Nadu. Several important public figures have embraced Islam. The intelligence agents question me if I had converted 3000 persons in Tamil Nadu? And how can I convert 3000 persons ? And how could I prevent if people want to embrace the religion of salvation. It's none of my business to convert people. The Hidaya (guidance) is purely from Allah's hands.

****

22

Parapsychological research and spiritual treatment of man in the light of the Holy Qur'an, convinced me of the scientific Truth of Islam.

These were the words uttered by Dr. Abdullah J. Alisen, formerly Dr. Arthur J. Alison who entered the fold of Islam. Dr. Abdullah Alison is the head of the Department of Electrical and Electronics Engineering in a British University. He worked for six years as the Chairman of the British Parapsychological and Spiritual Studies Society and studied comparatively in that position. While attending an International Scientific Conference in Cairo, on 'Medical Miracles in the Qur'an', he declared his conversion to Islam.

He has published several studies in parapsychology. He attended the conference with Dr. Yahya-Mushrefi, a Professor at the Oxford University Institute of Psychology.

While writing a paper for the conference, his major goal was to study parapsychology and spiritual medicine in the light of the Holy Qur'an. The results were surprisingly outstanding and very convincing as to the nature and condition of 'sleep and death' as well as other related phenomena. With the result, he 'discovered Islam'.

He is of the opinion that the Muslims have failed to demonstrate the scientific reality of Islam to the people of other religions.

Abdullah Alison, urged Western scientists to get acquainted with Islam which "addressed both intellect and sentiments at the same time."

Several Western scientists who happened to study the Qur'an when their academic research warranted it ultimately embraced Islam finding it purely scientific and technological theories.

The British scientist said he worked for six years as the Chairman of the British Parapsychology and Spiritual Studies Society.

23

This position, he said, led him to a deep study of different religions and philosophies, including Islam.

Declaring his conversion to Islam at the international conference on medical miracles in the Qur'an held in Cairo, Alison said he was attending the conference in his capacity as a researcher in parapsychology.

Since he has published several studies in parapsychology, he was invited to the conference which he attended with Dr Yahya Al-Mushrefi, a professor at the Oxford University Institute of Psychology.

Dr. Alison's research deals with the relationship between sleep and death which, he said, was based on substantial studies with electrical and electronic instruments, his main area of specialization. He said that while writing the paper for the Cairo conference, his major goal was to study parapsychology and spiritual medicine in the light of the Qur'an.

The results were surprisingly outstanding and very convincing as to the nature and condition of sleep and death as well as other related phenomena, said Dr. Alison. "My joy knew no bounds as the results of my study were so convincing and thus, I discovered Islam," he added.

While preparing his paper for the Cairo conference, Dr. Alison said he stopped at a verse of the Qur'an which meant:

"It is God who takes the souls (of men) at death and those that die not (He takes) during their sleep. Those on whom He has passed the decree of death, He keeps back (from returning to life), but the rest, He sends (to their bodies) for a term appointed." (Al-Zumar)[1]

To throw more light scientifically on this section of the Qur'an, Dr.Alison worked with Dr. Al-Mushrefi and managed to prove scientifically that sleep and death are one single process as stated in the above quoted verses of the Qur'an.

He said his experiments have shown that 'something goes out of human body when man or woman is asleep and returns later which

---

[1] Holy Quran 39:42. Editor.

24

makes him awake. But with death, that "something" does not return. "And that is what the Qur'an says in very clear words". Dr. Alison added "I'm convinced of what the Qur'an says."
"Muslims will have to make greater efforts to spread Islam and make it more understandable to non-Muslims", said Dr. Alison. "The people of the West listen to voice of intellect". (Islamic Voice, India)
****

Unlike the Bible, the Holy Qur'an has only One version without any change even after fourteen centuries!

Islam is a fast growing religion in the Philippines. People who hail from the Philippines and reside in the Middle East are embracing Islam rapidly. Philippinos who are working in the Kingdom of Saudi Arabia outnumber in entering the fold of Islam. According to a recent report 1 " there are some 14 different ethnic groups professing the Islamic faith and Muslims comprise about 5% of the total population of the Philippines. More than 50,000 Muslims live in North of the country. There are some persons professing the Baha'i Faith2. 94% of the populations are Christians; 84.1% Roman Catholic, 6.2 belong to the Philippines Independent Church and 3% are Protestants. An estimated 43,000 are Buddhists. Animists3 and persons professing no religion number approximately 400,000".

Brother Abdullah Valencia, formerly Wilfredo Valencia who hails from the Philippines, was born on 30th January, 1960 and was brought up in a Catholic family. During his study of the Bible, he came to know that it has different versions, and the Christians are divided into various sects, which follow different versions of the Bible. Finding out the differences in

---

[1] The Europe Yearbook 1992. Vol. 2., pages 2161, 2162

[2] A beliver in Bahaism; a modern religion developed originally in Iran from Babism, that stresses principles of universal brotherhood, social equality, etc. New World Dictionary, page 104

[3] The doctrine that all life is produced by a spiritual force separate from matter; the belief that all natural phenomena have souls independant of their physical being; a belief in the existence of spirit, demons, etc. New World Dictionary, Simon, New York, 1980. page 55

various versions of the Bible, he came to the conclusion that it was not a 'DIVINE BOOK', on the contrary, it had been totally distorted , which made impossible for him to differentiate between right and wrong.

During his stay in the Kingdom of Saudi Arabia, he happened to read the Holy Qur'an and was astonished to find that unlike the Bible it had only one version, without any change even after 14 centuries. Islamic teaching and beliefs are clear and appeal to a common man who has some common sense. On the contrary, Christianity is deprived of such teachings of high morality.

Brother Abdullah Valencia was dissatisfied with the Christian dogmas such as 'born sin', 'Trinity' and that a priest or a nun has to remain unmarried throughout his or her whole life.

Being disgusted with these Christians beliefs, he studied Islam. Consequently, he entered the fold of Islam in October 1994 at the Islamic Education Foundation in Jeddah.

Brother Fozzil A. Ghazali interviewed brother Abdullah which was published in the Saudi Gazette1 and with the courtesy of this esteemed newspaper we represent this soul-inspiring and thought-provoking interview for the general benefit of our Muslim and non-Muslim brothers with the hope that it will help moulding the character of those who have common sense and reason - Editor.

ABDULLAH Valencia hails from Manila, the Philippines. He obtained a degree in civil engineering from the University of Nueva Caceres, Naga City, in 1989. He came to Saudi Arabia in 1991 on the Sponsorship of Al Khereiji Corporation and since then

---

[1] Saudi Gazette, 19th January, 1996, page 7.

27

working with it as a construction store-keeper. Earlier, he had been working as a production assistant in the Ministry of Human Settlement in the Philippines.

Valencia was born in a Catholic family on January 30,1960 in Camarinasur in Bicol province. His previous name was Wilfredo Valencia. He embraced Islam at the Islamic Education Foundation in Jeddah in October, 1994.

Valencia was brought up according to his family religion. When he started studying the Bible, he knew that it has different versions. The Christians are divided into sects and factions such as Jehova's Witnesses, Born Again, Lglesia Ni Kristo, all having different versions of the Bible, claiming their version as the true version of the Bible. "The differences in different versions of the Bible made me sure that it was not the Divine Book, or if it was, it has been destroyed by now, making it impossible to distinguish right from wrong", said a dismayed Valencia.

With this in mind, Valencia came to the Kingdom and studied the Holy Qur'an. He was astonished to see that unlike the Bible, it was only one version without any change even after 14 centuries. All Muslims, irrespective of their nationalities, family backgrounds or social status, believe in the same book. "Its teachings and beliefs are clear and appeal to a common man who has a common sense. It does not impose anything from outside. Instead, it talks of those things which are inclined in human nature", he said. He cited the example of caring for teachers and parents, especially when they attain old age. One does not remain a Muslim in true sense if he goes to bed stomach-full and his neighbour sleeps hungry. This emphasis to care for the fellow human beings is one of the most distinguished features of Islamic teachings which we know when we ourselves go to bed without food or feel ourselves totally uncared for in our old age. Unfortunately, the present -day Christianity is deprived of such teachings of high morality. Moreover, Muslims are one wherever they live, whatever the language they speak, whatever the family back ground they hail from, Valencia observed.

Christians confess their sins to the priests for God's redemption thinking that they have been forgiven as if God is bound to forgive them even if they go on committing sins and indulging themselves in immoral activities. "That's why", he said, "We see the Christian world having alarming rates of crimes, always shooting up. Divorce, suicide, gambling, drug addiction and sexual abuse are prevailing in the Christian world". On the other hand, the Qur'an says that everyone is accountable for his activities in the hereafter. Even the prophets would be impeached by God about the responsibility they were assigned to discharge. This concept of impeachment makes a man very cautious and helps him mend his ways.

When asked why he cannot become a priest as he enjoys high status in the Christian society, Valencia replied a priest, or a nun, has to remain unmarried throughout her life. Marriage is considered something irreligious. How can something which is in human nature be irreligious ? How long can a priest, or a nun, suppress this instinct? asks Valencia. They secretly commit adultery to quench their biological urge. Unlike this, Islam lays too much emphasis on marriage and discourages a man or woman for a long time without specific reasons. Violation of these Islamic laws drags a man or woman in sexual anarchy shattering family cohesion. Muslim's faith remain incomplete unless they get married. This is natural which goes deep into the hearts and leads to the right destination without getting diverted or being astray.

Now, see the Bible. It openly says that Jesus (pbuh) has informed his followers about the advent of a prophet who will bring a book and complete his unfinished task. Muslims believe in Jesus as a human being and as a prophet as they believe in other prophets.

But, Christians do not believe in other prophets. Christians do not believe in Prophet Muhammad (PBUH) although it is in the Bible. The only reason behind it is the advent of the last prophet in the progeny of Ismail, the first son of Prophet Abraham (PBUH), and not in the progeny of Issaic, in whom progeny so many

29

prophets, including Jesus Christ, came. Perhaps they were expecting the last prophet also in the progeny of Prophet Issaic (PBUH). Here, developed jealousy and they advertendly don't believe in Islam, the religion brought and preached by Jesus (PBUH) himself.

Another reason of their refusal to Muhammad's (PBUH) prophethood is that they say that prophet Mohammed (PBUH) did not perform miracles as Jesus (PBUH) used to perform. But, that's wrong. The Qur'an is itself a miracle. How can an unlettered man start suddenly presenting a book whose language was parexcellence to the literary works of poets and orators of entire Arabia. The Qur'an challenged the non-believers to present even a single verse similar to that the Prophet (PBUH) was presenting. They tried, but failed.

Moreover, Prophet Muhammad (pbuh) divided the moon into two with his finger's point. This miracle was also observed by thousands of people. He also visited the hell and paradise in the Ascension (Meraj) and the situation of the both places he told is what is mentioned in the Bible.

****

30

Haj was the most fantastic experience of my life. Spiritually it was very fulfilling!

It was a privilege for us to read in the Saudi Gazette1 about Captain Abdul Rasheed Muhammad, Islam's First Captain in the U.S. armed forces. Brother Samy Baaghil interviewed brother Imam Muhammad who is serving Islam and his nation heart and soul. " I think the Army bringing in an Islamic Chaplain is a symbol of the increased sensitivity towards Islam". The armed forces have taken important steps to accommodate Muslim beliefs" , are the views of Imam Muhammad. Imam Muhammad is extending extra-ordinary services for the cause of Islam and Muslims in the U.S. Army. Talking about the historic day Imam Muhammad was commissioned, Islamic Voice wrote :

" It was a historic day at the Pentagon recently when Captain Abdul Rasheed Muhammad was commissioned as the first Imam or 'Chaplain' in the U.S. Army. As Col. Hereman Keizer, Executive Director of the Armed Forces Chaplains Board, said, this reflected the growing number of Muslims in the services over the past 10 years, and 'mirrors growth in U.S. society, where Islam is the fastest growing religion" 2.

In another report, citing the appointment of first Imam in the U.S. Navy, the same magazine wrote :

"In the Navy, Legalman First Class Malik Noel, who accepted Islam in 1988, is set to become its first Imam".[3]

It is heartening to note that the appointment of brother Imam Muhammad in the U.S. Armed Forces as 'First Imam' (Chaplain)

---

[1] Saudi Gazette. 24th July, 1995. Page 8.
[2] Islamic Voice. February 1994, page 21.
[3] Islamic Voice. October 1994, page 18.

31

on the sacred day, i.e. Friday, the 3rd December, 1993 was welcome in the USA in particular and in the Muslim world in general. Praising the US Armed Forces's decision regarding the appointment of brother Abdul Rasheed Muhammad as First Imam (Chaplain) Islamic Horizon in its 'Editorial' wrote :

"If we are to measure the accomplishments of Muslims in the United States in the last era, we must surely include the appointment of Abdul Rasheed Muhammad on Friday, December 3, 1993 as the first imam (Chaplain) of the U.S. military.

The function was held at the Pentagon Executive Dining Room with all the pomp and ceremony of a military engagement and the solemn and girded observance of a Muslim prayer, replete with Qur'an reading and shouts of takbir.

Has Islam finally "arrived" in American politics or have U.S. policy-makers wised up to the fact that Muslims are an integral part of the American society and are here to stay?

This significant recognition of the needs of 2500 Muslims in the U.S. military is a welcomed gesture from the government. It indicates a new attitude towards Muslims and Islam. With the recent signing of the Religious Freedom Restoration Act (RFRA), Muslims should strive even harder to ensure representation in different agencies of the government. Imam Abdul Rasheed Muhammad's appointment should be viewed as the stepping-stone to better things.

With all the excitement that this bestowal has brought to Muslims we realize that we are far from reconciling our political outlook. Like previous administrations, the Clinton administration also fails to understand the Muslim psyche. For instance, Clinton's recent meeting with the infamous Salman Rushdie, against the express wishes of his advisors, indicate grave short sightedness. However, we hope that through the appointment or election of Muslims to important positions in the government, the administration will begin to understand, recognize and grasp the Muslim point of view.

We congratulate Imam Abdul Rasheed Muhammad and wish him well."

Besides, brother Samy Baaghil, sister Bonne Lovelace, a freelance writer in Indianpolis, Indiana, interviewed Captain Abdul Rasheed Muhammad from a different angle which was published in the Islamic Horizons1. In 'My Journey to Islam', the first Imam in the U.S. Armed Forces, explains why he embraced the 'Religion of Allah' and his mission. This autobiographical 'Road to Islam' story appeared in the Arab News2, which has been published with the courtesy of Islamic Horizons. We feel great pleasure in presenting them all together for the benefit of our esteemed Muslim and non-Muslim readers, and we do hope that these informative, thrilling, soul-inspiring and thought-provoking interviews will help moulding the character of those who are in pursuit of 'Truth', Insha Allah! - Editor.

Another Chapter in Islamic history was written on December 3, 1993, when Captain Abdul Rasheed Muhammad became the first commissioned Islamic Military Chaplain (Imam) in the United States Army.

Currently stationed at the 28th Combat Support Hospital, 44th Medical Brigade in Fort Bragg, N.C., Capt. Muhammad is officially listed as a chaplain to all soldiers, both Muslim and Non-Muslims, and serves as a "social worker", responsible for developing programs, providing guidance, and creating opportunities for persons of other religious groups to practice their faith, even those without a designated faith.

Imam Muhammad began his military career as a supply specialist (1982-1985), in addition to being an Islamic lay leader and delivering Friday Khutbahs to enlisted service members and

---

[1] Islamic Horizons May/June 1995, page 46.
[2] Arab News 17 April, 1996, page 12.

officers stationed at both Fort Lee and Fort Belvoir in Virginia. Outside the Army, Muhammad served as an Imam and counselor to the Muslim community in Ann Arbor and Ypsilanti, Michigan, as well as being an Imam and advisor on Islamic affairs in Buffalo and the Greater Western New York area, working with Muslim youth and Muslim prisoners.

In May of 1994, Muhammad marked one of the highest points in his life, performing the Hajj. "It was the most fantastic experience of my Life...", said Muhammad. "Spiritually it was very fulfilling." Muhammad, who converted to Islam in 1973, met with King Fahd of Saudi Arabia, as well as other dignitaries at a banquet in Mina to which he was invited by the Muslim World League.

Although there is no established religious clergy in Islam, Muhammad suggests that there will be a need for other Military Imams in the near future, in accordance with the U.S. Army's policy of not requiring enlistees to state a religious preference, there are estimates of 10,000 Muslims in uniform. Only 1,492 are officially listed in military records; however, the discrepancy in numbers is due to many soldiers having converting to Islam during the Desert Storm and the dedication of people such as Muhammad. "It is up to the Muslims to come forward and openly acknowledge their faith," says Muhammad.

According to Army records, Islam and Muslims have been present in military as far back as the Civil War, when Egyptian animatrainers were used by the Union Army as camel guides in the southwestern United States. It wasn't until World I that Islam was officially recognized, and Muslim soldiers were issued military "dogtags" that identified them by their faith; those who fought in World War I were religiously listed as "other" because they were not within the only recognized faiths of Christianity or Judaism.

"I think the Army bringing in an Islamic chaplain is a symbol of the increased sensitivity towards Islam," says Muhammad, "the armed forces have taken important steps to accommodate Muslim beliefs."

As an Islamic Chaplain to Muslim soldiers, both male and female, some of the issues facing Muhammad include military leniency for beard growth, the wearing of Hijab and Kufis, modified uniforms for physical training, duties for Muslim women, special prayer areas, wedding ceremonies (Nikkahs), and burial services (Janazahs). On a recent visit to ISNA headquarters, Muhammad expressed hope for the development of M.M.R.E.s (Muslim Meals-Ready-to-Eat) by the IDF Halal Meat and Food Corporation. The IDF is a service of ISNA. The MMREs would be distributed to troops serving in military installations. Recently, Muslim soldiers serving in Haiti were given vegetarian MMREs.

Eventually, Muhammad hopes that correct exposure about Islam and Muslims will cause Americans to rethink their negative views and afford Islam the same respect as that of Judaism and Christianity. ".. we [Muslims] have to do our part of the mainstream; As Islam is exposed more, people will recognize and respect the whole idea of difference of opinion, and hopefully they will realize how we are all the same... we will worship the same God."

Muhammad holds a Bachelor of Science degree in Anthropology from New York State University, A Masters of Science degree in Counseling Education from San Diego State University and a Masters Degree in Social Work from the University of Michigan. He and his wife Saleemah have six children.

I came to Islam by choice in June 1973. My conversion to Islam, like my wife's and that of many other Muslim Americans of African descent, came by way of the Nation of Islam (NOI), inspired by the teachings of Elijah Muhammad. Although the misrepresented Islam out of ignorance, his concept of social change and economic independence is of merit. This was the movement that was much needed among the so-called Negro or blackman of America. This message was best articulated by Malcolm X and Malik El- Shabazz.

My attraction for this message aside, I always maintained a personal resistance to accepting man as the Creator. But I, like many others in my community in Buffalo, NY, had never been exposed to the real Islam. It was not until Imam Warithuddin Muhammad became the new leader of NOI shortly after his father, Elijah Muhammad's death. It was during this period in 1975, that we, the now former followers of the teaching of NOI, began the gradual study of Qur'an in its pure form, and the sunnah of Prophet Muhammad (peace be upon him). Even Louis Farrakhan (the self-proclaimed inheritor of Elijah's teachings), accepted the new teachings or the direction of the community as did most of the over 250,000 NOI adherents.

Unlike Farrakhan and a few others who chose to leave the new community, I remained and travelled through this spiritual change as it transformed into the World Community of Islam in the West to the American Muslim Mission and finally the American Muslim Community.

I was born in Myron Maxwell. Although I always respected and usually obeyed my parents, I felt a need for change in my religious expression. Surprisingly, unlike many other decisions, choosing Islam was not so difficult. The difficult part, however, was adopting my Muslim name. I believed doing so personally necessary.

After finishing my undergraduate studies in anthropology in Brockport, NY, I travelled west to San Diego State University for my graduate studies in anthropology.

It was at Masjid Muhammad in southeast San Diego that I met my future wife, Saleemah R. Abdullah in spring 1978. We were married shortly in a double wedding ceremony at the campus. Saleemah, like myself comes from a Christian (Lutheran) background. She is the only Muslim in her family.

Another choice I made was to join the US Armed Forces in September, 1982. My decision to enlist at that time was based upon my desire to further the spread of Islam beyond the local community. I initially enlisted as chaplain assistant but later

36

transferred to another area when I experienced internal conflict with some duties this job entailed. Although controversial to some, my decision to join the US Army in 1982 was a personal choice. I always believed that Allah watches out for the sincere person. My choice, thus, was not separate from or unique to my personal conviction as a Muslim. I have remained sincere in my faith, even prior to accepting Islam, that Allah truly protects the sincere believer.

My appointment as American Armed Force's first Imam (chaplain) was a fulfillment of a life time goal. My work as army chaplain included helping soldiers and their families with their problems such as marital and family problems and moral issues.

As a former social worker, I have always enjoyed meeting the many challenges of human problem-solving. My current responsibilities as imam/chaplain allow me the opportunity to utilize all the professional skills that Allah has enabled me to inquire over the past 20 years.

September has become an auspicious month for Muslims in North America because they get the opportunity to come together for the ISNA Annual Convention. I have good news to give that very soon, Insha Allah, Fort Bragg will get contonment masjid capable of accommodating some 300 Muslims.

This was the outcome of the proposal I had forwarded to my installation commander. My request included a proposal that a masjid be built at Fort Bragg within the next five years. I am grateful to Allah that this proposal has been accepted because I had made it a priority for 1995.

As Muslims in the military, we want to use our God-given intelligence and not our emotions as we continue striving to establish our Islamic way of life in the US Armed Forces. As Muslim American Soldiers, we do not see our mission differently, as related to the establishment of Islam in the West, from that of the Companions of Prophet Muhammad (pbuh).

We firmly believe this religion is not restricted to any people or nation, region, or period in human history. It is therefore, this level

37

of acceptance and understanding of our Islamic faith that will enable us to ultimately be successful examples of Muslims in uniform.

As Muslims we must come to accept the fact that America was never intended to be a nation dominated by any particular race, religion, or creed. As it was my individual choice to accept Islam, without compulsion, it is also our choice as Muslim Americans to determine that influence we will allow our faith to have within the United States.

****

38

Why Dr. Abdur Rahman Barker embraced Islam ?

Muhammad Haneef Shahid

Dr. Abdur Rahman Barker was a well - known Orientalist, linguist, writer, research scholar and preacher. He was born to a well-to-do but learned family which hailed from Washington. His father, who was an educationist, worked against a higher position in the education department. He paid special attention to Barker's education. As a result, Mr. Barker got higher education. In 1951, he got Fulbright Scholarship and went to India in connection with research work on the historical, cultural and linguistic background. After five year's stay in India, he returned to U.S.A. Thereafter, he went to Canada and worked on the comparative study of religions under the guidance of famous orientalist Smith. He got his Ph.D. of which his topic was "Red-Indians".

During his educational career, he had the opportunity of learning nearly ten languages. Besides English, he learned Arabic, Persian, Urdu, Balouchi, Pushto, French, German, Greek, Sanskrit, etc. In 1959, he visited Pakistan on the recommendation of Ford Foundation to do research work on 'Modern Urdu Language.' He worked as the Head of Department in the Punjab University, Oriental College, Lahore. During his service in Pakistan, he compiled a book in Urdu namely 'Mehfil' which includes selections of the Urdu poets whom he had the pleasure of listening in poetical recitations (Mushaira) held in Lahore.

The following is an interview of Dr. Barker with Mr. Altaf Hasan Qureshi which was published in Urdu Digest, Lahore. We have rendered it into English

39

and feel much pleasure in presenting to our esteemed readers.

Question : Why did you embrace Islam?

Answer : "My father did not believe in religion. Once, when I asked him about God, he replied : "What I can tell you about God, I have never met him? Moreover, I do not need him because every think is available to us in abundance". My father's reply did not satisfy me. Consequently, I started comparative study of different religions. I had the opportunity of studying deeply and thoroughly the sacred books of Judaism and Christianity. I did not find anything except difference, disorder and confusion.

In my opinion their historical value and position was doubtful. I could not think of studying Islam in those circumstances and in that state of affairs, because people's general view about Islam was that it was the creed of mad and insane people, who just attack the cities, kill the innocent people, plunder and make the women folk their slaves. Obviously, I was not ready to be called a savage at any cost at that time. Later on, when I visited India, I had the chance of meeting Hindu Scholars. I studied Hinduism, but I found dearth of permanent values in Hinduism. On the other hand, there was such a confusion and chaos and complexity that I felt very much upset and disturbed. Later on, I found some Hindus in the southern part of India. According to their religious belief, six real brothers could marry a single woman and strange enough they still believed in the teachings of Mahabharath. Knowing all this I was very much upset mentally as well as spiritually, because it was quite unreasonable, and did not appeal the mind. In this perplexed situation, I met a Muslim youth through whom I underwent a radical change. Though he belonged to a Muslim family, but he was influenced by Communism. Eventually, I developed friendly relations with him. He invited me to his house. He told me that his father was a devotee of Islam. When we reached his house, his father received me with open arms. He had a very charming magnetic-like personality. I was

40

impressed by him, because he was a symbol of love, sincerity and truth.

He told me some of the basic principles of Islam in a very simple, vivid and clear manner, which I felt very weighty. We exchanged a number of visits. He gave me some books written in English. It included the translation of the Holy Qur'an by Muhammad Marmaduke Pickthall. I started reading the Holy Qur'an and opened Surah Al-Kausar (S.cviii: 108) Small but beautiful sentences pierced into my heart like arrows. Their melodies had a very sweet but everlasting effect in my ears. They were so magical that I repeated the verses un-intentionally. I went on reading them again and again, I felt as if I was drinking the water of immortality. I was even ready to believe in the true teachings of the Holy Qur'an, but there were some doubts in my mind. They were about the Prophethood of the Holy Prophet, position of women in Islam and lawful and unlawful issues which that pious man removed in a very reasonable and philosophical manner. In fact, I had found the Truth and unknowingly I pronounced the "Kalima-e-Tawhid". I was so happy that I could not express my feelings in words.

When I went to United States, I was a changed man. The first question my father asked me was: "Do you still drink wine?" I replied in the negative by saying: "It is forbidden in Islam". On hearing this, he was very much pleased and said : "My son! The religion which forbids wine must be true". Time passed by. I felt that it was rather difficult for me to live as a Muslim in un-favourable society. I was quite dis-satisfied with my meaningless life and I decided to end it. One day, in this perturbed state of mind, I went to sleep. During my sleep, I had a nightmare in which I found myself staggering in darkness. But, at last, I found some rays of light which was source of satisfaction and peace of mind. When I woke up, I found myself quite content and satisfied. Eventually, I came to the conclusion that it was the light of 'Islam' and it was the only religion which guarantees success and eternal peace.

41

Question : Our next question was : "Please shed some light on the negative attitude and hatred found in the American people against Islam".

Dr. Barker replied : "There are many reasons for this, but the main reason is the Crusades. The Christians have not forgotten the defeat they faced at the hand of the Muslims. Out of revenge, they thought different ways and means through which they spread misleading propaganda against Islam. They depicted the character of the Muslims in such a manner as if they were un-civilized, beasts, savages and cruel who knew only to plunder, kill and make the women folk their slaves.

Secondly, Modern Christianity is so hollow and lifeless that no reasonable person is going to accept it as his religion. On the contrary, Islamic teachings are so convincing and appealing and reasonable. To divert attention from this, Islam was distorted and misrepresented so that intellectual Christian community may not be attracted to it.

Thirdly, Islam has never been presented to the American people according to their aspirations and social behaviour. I am fully confident if Islam is presented to the American people in a particular way, majority of the people will welcome it because they are searching for the truth eagerly.

In fact, the American people have a quite different temperament. They value the historical position of anything before believing it. In other words, they judge the authenticity on historical basis. Accordingly there is a dire need of transforming the valuable and unique researches done by the Muslim Traditioners into English. It should be made clear to the West that Islamic treasure of knowledge is more authentic, definite and convincing that no other religion in the world can compete with it. The fundamental principles of Muslim jurisprudence made by the Traditioners and Muslims Jurists are more reasonable and unchangeable.

After proving the historical authenticity of the Holy Qur'an and the Traditioners of the Holy Prophet, the next important step to

42

be taken is that such books should be written in English in which basic references are particularly given. The Westerners and American people are very much impressed if basic references and bibliography are given. For example, if any valuable book is published but it does not contain references and bibliography, it is not given any consideration and importance.

Another factor which needs special attention is that the islamic teachings, which deal with the day to day life of the people i.e. social, cultural, and ethical, should be popularized and made public. The fundamental characteristics of the social life of the Holy Prophet dealing with cleanliness, purity, simplicity, piety, purification, social justice, etc., should be presented to the public with full details. The West is badly in need of spiritual satisfaction and peace of mind. It really, needs such a religion which can guarantee confidence, love, brotherhood, tranquality, toleration and moderate living. I am fully confident, Islam can provide all this.

It should be made clear that Islam's economic system not only provides spiritual purity, enlightenment and ethical values but also it guarantees the society wholesome welfare and economic development. It is the need of the day that through Islamic Readers, Islam's basic teachings should be made available and within every person's reach in their mother tongue.

****

43

It was through my research that I was inspired by Islam and its beliefs and was not forced by anybody".

Hereunder is the first hand account, (i.e. autobiography) of 'Reversion to Islam' of brother Abu Bakr formerly Martin (Bishop John Mypopol). How this Bishop reverted to Islam? Mr. Ghalib Jonker, Religious Editor of the Saudi Gazette, writes thus :

" A Bishop of the Church who converted to Islam? this sounded too good to be true, and I decided to accompany Saudi Gazette reporter Atif Al-Ghamdi to meet this legend of Tanzania. Coming face to face with Abu Bakr was almost a " Doctor Livingstone, I presume scenario. To say that I was impressed with the former Bishop, is an understatement. Listening to him caused a renewed surge of Islamic committment and steadfastness which comes from being inspired, like Abu Bakr inspires. I left with visions of a new Africa where Islam, moderation and good will reign supreme".

Brother Abu Bakr was born on 22nd December, 1936, in Bilosa in the Eastern Province of Tanzania in a family of staunch Lutherans and believers of the Church. Like all other Christians, he was also baptized1 a Lutheran in 1938 and was named Martin. So he was brought up in the environment of the Church. After high school education he intended to join police force but his parents wanted him to become a priest. His father being himself a priest, and one of the leaders of the church, wished to see him a priest at any cost.

---

[1] "Our religion is the Baptism of God; and who can baptize better than God? And it is He Whom we worship".
(Surah Al-Baqarah 2: 138)

44

Consequently, on 17th February, 1960, he joined as a Trainee Pastor, with the result he learned a great deal of Christianity and its teaching. In 1973, he was appointed acting Bishop due to the death of the Bishop. In 1983, he went to Germany to get Master's degree and from there, he went to Kenya where he had the first encounter with Islam. He read about Islam and studied a translation of the Holy Qur'an. He had a number of questions in his mind which his teachers declined to answer. One of the question was : " Why was Jesus Crucified?" The others being " Lord's atonement and Jesus Christ being Son of the Lord" . After getting his Master's degree came back to Tanzania and took over the post of Bishop. He was leading a 'Paradise-like' life having all kinds of facilities at his disposal.

An un-usual incident took place in brother Abu Bakr's life. One day he met our Noble Prophet(PBUH) of Islam. His wife woke him and told him that he was murmuring about some prophet of Islam. It was incredible and un-believable for him. In fact, the truth had dawn on him through our Noble Prophet (PBUH). As brother Abu Bakr had knowledge of the Bible and the Holy Qur'an, so Allah, Most Gracious, Most Merciful, guided him:

" And that those on whom knowledge has been bestowed may learn that the (Qur'an) is the truth from thy Lord, and that they may believe therein, and their hearts may be made humbly (Open) to it; for verily God is the Guide of those who believe, to the Straighty Path". (Surah Hajj 22:54).

As a result of this guidance, brother Abu Bakr went to pray in the Mosque, even though, he was in his priestly robes, and met Sheikh Ahmarah and embraced Islam at his hands. After his 'Reversion to

45

Islam', brother Abu Bakr had to face a severe test which he never foresaw. His world was totally changed. He lost his job, home and belongings. His wife and four children left him for good. But, inspite of all this, he remained steadfast, resolute and firm in his belief. And Allah, the All-Mighty, has given glad tidings for such people :

" Be sure we shall test you with something of fear and hunger, some loss in goods or lives or the fruits (of your toil), but give glad tidings to those who patiently persevered, -- Who say, when afflicted with calamity : " To God we belong, and to Him is our return" :- They are those on him (descend) blessings from God, and Mercy and they are the once that receive guidance". (Surah Al-Baqarah 2:155-157)

Sheikh Ahmarah provided him with all kinds of facilities. He also gave him a plane ticket to Zambia on his request. During his travel, brother Abu Bakr, happened to meet a nun, who showed sympathy and keen interest in him and shared his experiences. Later on, she also entered the fold of Islam and got married. Presently, they are residing in Durban, South Africa and leading a happy life. With the courtesy of the Saudi Gazette1, we wish to reproduce this heart-rending, soul-inspiring and thought-provoking story for the benefit of our esteemed readers. - editor.

My name is Abu Bakr John Mypopol. This is my Islamic name. I was born on December 22, 1936, in a village known as Bilosa in the Eastern Province of Tanzania. I was baptized a Lutheran in 1938, when I was just 2 years old, and was given the name Martin. My parent were very staunch Lutherans and believers of the Church. They brought me up in the environment of the Church. I was the third child in a family of ten.

---

[1] Saudi Gazette, 24 May, 1995, page 17.

When I completed high school, I thought of joining the police force. But my parents were pressuring me to become a priest. I opted to become a police man.

My father, who was a priest, was constantly advising me to take up priesthood, telling me that though he had other sons, he was keen to see me as a priest. And since he was one of the leaders of the Church, he said that it would be best for me to become a priest of that Church.

So, on February 17th, 1960, I joined as a trainee pastor. It was here that I learned a lot about Christianity, and its teachings. In 1973, I was sent to Germany for my degree course, and in the same year I was appointed acting Bishop. Our Bishop had passed away, and I happened to be the Church administrator at that time.

In 1983, I was sent to Germany again, this time for my Masters. It was around this time that something made me turn towards Islam. From Germany I was sent to attend a meeting in Kenya which was to discuss ways and means to Christianize east Africa, which is pre-dominantly Islamic. The subject of our agenda was how to counter Islam, and our organisation had spent about $ 52 million for this project.

By then I had read a few pamphlets on Islam, and had come across a translation of the Holy Qur'an. There were many questions to be answered and I asked my teachers but they were unable to answer them. I had to re-read the Bible to see if I could answer them myself. One of the questions was "Why was Jesus Crucified?" I wanted to give the Biblical point of view, not the human point of view. Nobody had answered it.

One of my teachers said that in the Bible, God has illustrated what crucifixion and the cross was. The Lord punishes anyone found guilty of any crime and he is condemned to death. If you hang him on the cross, it means that he is cursed by God. So, if you tell that Jesus was crucified for man's sins, it does not make sense since it is the curse of God. But when you question them the teachers tell you to follow what they tell you. It means that we

47

should agree with what they say, though it could be without any meaning.

The other questions were pertaining to the Lord's atonement and Jesus Christ being the Son of the Lord. I did not have good answers for these questions and that is when I wanted to know more about Islam. I started reading many books and after my Masters degree I returned to Tanzania and took over my position as Bishop and forgot about the past. But, there was something which was always making me feel guilty, the materialism of human beings. The position which I was holding was good, with wonderful facilities more like paradise, and to leave such a position is quite difficult. But I used to keep thinking and had to take a decision.

According to the Bible, every man is created with reason, and his mission is to be fulfilled. My position was doubtful, and I was not content with my self. So I kept on reading and came across the book God is One, which tells us that nothing material is attributed to God since He Himself clearly says that there was nobody before me, nor will there be anyone after me, and I am the only God.

In the Bible, when Jesus was asked, he also mentions that he has come down to fulfill the mission given to him by the Lord, The Lord of Moses. So it is quite clear that there is just one Lord, and to whom everyone should believe. Anyway I resumed my duties as usual, and one day I had a dream, and was woken by my wife. She said that I was murmuring about some Prophet of Islam. It was difficult for me to believe since it is well known that the Truth is often revealed thus.

Anyway, I rested that day, which was a Saturday and after I got up, I ate and made a trip to the town. I had brought some things for the house, and while returning it was time for the Magrib Prayer. I suddenly decided to visit a mosque even though I was in my priestly clothes. When I entered the Mosque premises the people who had come for prayer were surprised and they

48

asked me what I wanted. I told them that I wish to pray with them.

They said I was welcome to discuss anything with them. I told them that I wanted to meet Sheikh Ahmarah, who used often call me son. He is no more and may Allah bless him. When I met the Sheikh, I told him that I wish to embrace Islam. He thought I was joking, but I told him that I was quite serious. He asked me to take off my shoes and wash myself though he did not use the word ablution, being under the impression that I would not know what it meant. I removed my shoes and put them in my car. While everybody watched I washed my self starting with my left hand. When the Sheikh took me inside and told one of his assistant that they had a guest. He asked me to stand behind him, in the back row for prayer.

We completed the prayer, after which the Sheikh asked the congregation to be seated. He asked them if they knew me. They all agreed in unison that they did know father Martin. When he told them about my wish to embrace Islam, and all present were quite happy.

He held my hand and told me to repeat the Kalema after him, which I repeated though I could not pronounce the words properly. When I had finished he told me that from then on I was a Muslim. I was quite surprised and asked him how I could become a Muslim without any studies. He explained that a person is taken into the fold first and then studies would follow.

You can start right away, he told me. We are to know that you believe in the Oneness of Allah, and the Prophethood of Muhammad, His messenger, and then comes the teachings. He addressed the congregation again, telling them that it was through my own research, that I was inspired by Islam and its beliefs, and was not forced by anybody.

When I addressed the congregation, one of those present casually mentioned that now since father Martin has converted to Islam majority of the people in Tanzania would follow suit, since I was an active member of the Church, and had quite a large following.

Abu Bakr's real test of faith started after his conversion 8 years ago. Difficulties beset him which he never foresaw. But he remained resolutely firm in his commitment. His job, home and belongings were taken away from him. His wife and four children left him. He was left absolutely without support, but he did not care. The Sheikh of the Mosque provided him with accommodation at a Hotel, and he was given a plane ticket to Zambia, and eventually to Durban, South Africa, where he had settled before coming to Mecca for Haj.

Abu Bakr, in the course of his travel from Tanzania to Zambia, met a nun who took a keen interest in what he experienced. She eventually converted to Islam and he married her. They are at present residing in Durban, South Africa.

****

50

Allah
opened my heart to Islam!

This is the story of 'Journey to Islam' of brother Abu Usamah Idris Ahmed Yusuf. He is the Imam in Seychelles Mosque, ever since the first Mosque was opened officially in Seychelles about twelve years ago. The Muslims had to depend on the services of overseas Imams. There were five Imams who served before brother Abu Yusuf. Four of them hailed from Mauritius and one from Pakistan. It is a happy news, that at last, the Muslims have finally managed to obtain the services of a local Imam and that is brother Abu Yusuf.

Brother Abdul Jalil Mollabux who arrived from Mauritius four years ago to take up his post as the fifth Imam of Sheikh Mohammad Bin Khalifa Al Nahayan Mosque left Seychelles with his family on the 26th December, 1994 on the completion of his contract.

We produce here the 'Conversation story' of brother Abu Yusuf with the courtesy of Iqra. Editor.1

Ever Since the first Mosque was officially opened in Seychelles twelve years or so ago, we had to depend on the services of overseas Imams. Actually, we had five - four hailed from Mauritius and one from Pakistan. But we are pleased to record that we have now finally managed to obtain the services of local Imam. He is brother Abu Usamah Idris Ahmed Yusuf.

Brother Idris was born in the fourth largest island of the Seychelles archipelago : La Digue in 1382 A.H. (1962 CE). He completed his preliminary education over there and then came over to Mahe to join the Hotel and Tourism School for a Diploma in Tourism.

---

1 Iqra (Annual) February 1995 (Ramadan 1415, page 13.

As he puts it; it was afterwards that "Allah opened my heart to Islam". He had a great to desire to study Islam. Thus in 1982, He embraced Islam on the hands of our first Imam, Maulana Abdul Bashir Bussurudy. Four years later, he obtained a scholarship from the Islamic University in Al-Madinah in the Kingdom of Saudi Arabia with the help of our beloved brother Dr. Nabil Yasin Al-Quarashi (May Allah reward him for his efforts). After spending two years at the Arabic language institution for non-Arabs speaking students, he obtained a diploma in Arabic. He had to spend another two years at the Islamic High School to secure a higher school certificate to be admitted at the Faculty of Shari'ah (Islamic Law) where he obtained his BA in Islamic Law last year.

During his eight years sojourn in Madinah, he had the opportunity of meeting some the greatest scholars of Islamic like Sheikh Al-Abani (who is one of the greatest authority in science of Hadith), Sheikh Abdul Aziz Bin Baz, Sheikh Al-Usaymin and a student of Sheikh Al-Abani, Alee Hasan Alee Abdul Hamid.

Brother Idris is married and has four children Salimah, Usamah, Hamza and Maymuna.

He officially took up his post as the sixth Imam of the Sheikh Mohammad Bin Khalifa Al-Nahayan Mosque in Victoria as from 1st January 1995. With the help of some other brothers, he is devoting his time teaching the men and boys while his wife, sister Safiyah with the help of other sisters is teaching the girls. Brother Idris also holds Taleem sections for the sisters on Saturdays.

We wish brother Idris and his family all the best for the future and assure him of our full cooperation. May Allah bless him and his family always. Ameen !

****

President of Gabon Al-Haj Albert Bernard Umar Bongo Accepts Islam !

September 1973 is a landmark in the history of Gabon in particular and in Islamic history in general because H.E. Al-Haj Albert Bernard Umar Bongo (born on 30th December, 1935) entered the fold of Islam in this month. It is worthy to note that on his 'Reversion to Islam' a befitting ceremony was held on that occasion, which was attended by a delegation of the Muslim World League, that was specially sent to congratulate him to present him a copy of the Holy Qur'an, a piece of the Holy Ka'aba's cover, some water of the 'Zamzam' and dates of Madinah al Munawwarah. Besides, the Secretary General of the Muslim World League sent a telegram to President Umar Bongo congratulating him and praying for him on this great occasion, and expressing the hope that his conversion will immediately benefit the Muslim community in that region. 1

It is heartening to note that the following persons declared their 'Reversion to Islam' when the President of the Republic of Gabon, H.E. Al-Haj Umar Bongo accepted Islam. We, from the core of our heart, congratulate our esteemed brothers and pray for them to Allah, the Al-Mighty, Most Gracious, Most Merciful, to bestow His bounties and favours upon them, Ameen ! (Editor)

1. Osman Slahou   2. Imaila Moubeigui

3. Mamadsu Mikala   4. Bassirou Bisselo

5. Odamau Moussadji   6. Mousourou Moussavou

7. Abdou Rahman Mombo   8. Abdou Salam Boussougou

---

[1] The Muslim World League Journal, December 1973, (vol. 1, no. 3) page 72.

9. Alpha Mdoumba

10. Ibrahim Nzigou

11. Hawa Bibalou

12. Djibrila Kounbila

13. Hamidou Mabika

14. Ibrahim Yembi

15. Djibril Boussa

16. Ibrahim Mandoukou

17. Aligou Mikala

18. Mamadous Mibika

19. Baubakar Mihiudou

20. Aliyou Nguiuili

21. Ibrahim Moussadji

22. Aliyou Mzougo

23. Mamadou Moubeyr

24. Omar Kouta

25. Boubakar Bouboyou

26. Osman Koumba

27. Osman Benguglie

28. Osman Moukagui

29. Djibril Mapaugou

30. Mamadou Moubibe

31. Abdoulaye Mamguegui

32. Abdou Salam Mboumba

33. Mustapha Moussavou

34. Adamou Moussaye

35. Osman Ngoma

36. Alpha Ngoumba

37. Abou Bakr Nzamakaka

38. Halidou Idou

39. Harouna Bendiakoue

40. Omar Saeko

41. Djibril Obame

42. Aboubakar Mapaugou

43. Mamadou Djoulde

44. Idrissa Bakinda

45. Mamadou Hilkala

46. Osman Ngoma

47. Aliyou Sabilou

48. Hawa Ibotsi[1]

About 60% of Gabon's population are Christian, mainly adherents of the Roman Catholic Church. About 40% are <u>animists</u>

---

[1]The Muslim World League Journal, June 1974, page 64

and fewer than 1% are Muslims[1]. According to another report the Gabon Republic is a West African Country, with a Population of 500,000, Muslims form 25% of the population[2].

In February, 1967, M'ba was re-elected to Presidency for a seven year term with Albert Bernard Bongo, previously deputy Prime Minister and Vice President. M'ba died in November and was succeeded by Bongo, then only 31 years of age. On 12th March, 1968, Bongo announced the formal constitution of one party Government. Al-Haj Bongo took office on 2nd December 1967 was elected on 25th February, 1973, re-elected in December 1979 and November, 1986. It is noteworthy that Gabon attained full independence on the 17th August, 1960 from France, so on 17th August is celebrated the Independence and Idul Fitr and Id-al- Azha are 'national holidays'.[3]

After his marriage to Josephine Kama in 1959, Al-Haj Bongo showed an interest in the Catholic religion of his wife but did not become a Christian. In September, 1973, he announced his 'Reversion to Islam', which he stated was a 'personal decision', and took the name of the Umar, later calling himself El-Haj, Umar after a pilgrimage to the Holy city of Mecca.[4] In the month of April 1978, President Umar Bongo paid a visit to the Kingdom of Saudi Arabia which lasted for four days. He held talks with HM King Khalid Bin Abdul Aziz. President Bongo also performed 'Umra' and was seen off by Prince Fawaaz Bin Abdul Aziz, Governor of Mecca Al-Mukarrima.[5]

****

---

[1] The Europa World Yearbook, 1992. vol. 1, page 1160.
[2] Yaqeen International, 22 Nov., 1973, page 159
[3] Historical Dictionary of Gabon, by D.E. Gardinier, 1981. page 44-45.
[4] Saudi Gazette, 27th April, 1978.
[5] The Europa World Yearbook 1992, Vol. 1, page 1154.

55

"My total submission to Allah has given me peace of mind and heart"

This is the 'Reversion to Islam' story of brother Ahmed Bilal Mana Lastas, a Phillippino who was brought up in a Christian family. Like other Christians who entered the fold of Islam, he was never convinced and satisfied with the concept of 'TRINITY'. He could never agree that Allah, Most Gracious, Most Merciful, and the Creator of the Universe, could have a son. According to brother Ahmed, as Allah created Hazrat Adam out of Clay, and without parents, the very creation of Hazrat Adam negates the concept of 'TRINITY'- God, His Son, and the Holy Spirit, God gives birth to none nor He was given birth by anyone.

When we study the Holy Qur'an, we find a number of verses which reject and negate the concept of 'TRINITY'. For example the Holy Qur'an says :-

" Say (O Muhammad) : " He is Allah, (the) One. Allah As -Samad (The Self-Sufficient, Master, whom all creatures need, He neither eats nor drinks). He begets not, nor was He begotten, and there is non co-equal or comparable unto Him" . (Surah Al-Ikhlas 112: 1-4)

Brother Bilal read thoroughly the writings of Muslim scholars like Syed Qutab, 'Syed Abul Al-Ala' Maududi. Allah, Most Gracious, Most Merciful, guided him to the 'Right Path!' He sought 'Light' from the Holy Qur'an and the traditions of the noble Prophet Muhammad (PBUH). He is deadly against all kinds of 'Systems' and 'Isms' as they are the creation of man, on the contrary, Islam is a 'Divine Religion, and its teachings are perfect. Brother Ahmed entered the fold of Islam about four years ago and, at present, he is 50 years old. He loves 'Adhan'- Calling people to prayer,

56

because his 'Adhan' has special appeal and attraction to his colleagues. He is called 'Bilal' by his friends after the name of Hazrat Bilal, a favourite companion of the Noble Prophet Muhammad (PBUH).

With the courtesy of Saudi Gazette, we feel pleasure in presenting the 'Journey to Islam' story of brother Ahmed Bilal.- Editor. 1

Ahmed Bilal Mana Lastas is a Phillippino who embraced Islam about 4 years ago.

Ahmed who is 50 years of age is considered a God fearing pious Muslim who loves calling to people for prayer. Since his *Adhan* (Prayer Call) has an special appeal, his colleagues call him Bilal, the companion of the Prophet, Peace be upon him, known for his attractive voice.

During an informal chat with *Saudi Gazzette* recently Ahmed, an autoparts expert working with Al-Jumea Co. the distributors of GM Vehicles in the Kingdom, explained why he became a Muslim and the impact of Islam on his life.

Ahmed was a Christian. He says that he was never convinced with the concept of 'TRINITY' in Christianity. He could never digest the belief that God could have a Son of Mary. He says God created Adam, the first human, out of clay. Adam was created without parents. The very creation of Adam out of clay negates the concept of 'TRINITY' - God, His Son and the Holy Spirit. Christianity is a religion of the past.

Now Ahmed believes that God gives birth to none nor He was given birth by anyone. He is beyond the confines of space, time and shape. He says he started reading books on Islam in 1982. "I have read books by great scholars like Syed Qutub and Sheikh Maududi. I sought light from the Qur'an, the books of the traditions of the prophet Muhammad (PBUH) i.e. Sahih Al-Bukhari, and Tirmidhi. I am of the conviction that Allah shows the true path to those who seek to correct themselves", he says.

---

1 Saudi Gazette, 8th April 1996 page 8.

Islam, he says, urges man to save himself and others from hell by his belief in the Oneness of God, the last prophethood of Muhammad (PBUH) good conduct and life after death.

Ahmed's entry into Islam was encouraged by his family and friends. His wife and children respect him as they used to in the past. "The reaction of my family and friends to my embracing of Islam deserves appreciation from one and all", he says.

Speaking about the changes brought about in his life after he embraced Islam, he said that faith lays great stress on uprightness. The concept of cleanliness is also emphasized. It is said that cleanliness forms half of the faith. It leads one to God. "My entering into Islam has prevented me from haraam (prohibited way of life", he says.

All systems and "Isms" are the creation of man. Many of these systems have already failed. The others will crumble soon. On the other hand, Islam is a Divine Religion. Its teaching are perfect. "My mind doesn't wander anymore. I know I have found the light of life in Islam. My total submission to Allah has given peace of mind and heart", Ahmed says.

He also says that the Islamic Da'wah (propagation) centres in the Kingdom are doing a great job in spreading the word of Islam. Allah will reward the Saudi Government for establishing Da'wah centres and also those who are working with dedication for them.

He expresses his thanks to Muhammad Amin Qavi and others who helped him with numerous books, like Towards Understanding Islam and Islam in the West, that help him greatly in his search for the truth.
****

58

The five daily prayers establish direct contact between man and his Creator. In them, I feel so much solace, patience and encouragement which I can hardly express in words.

These are the words of brother Ahmad Khan, who was previously a Hindu, named Hanumant Rao. He was born in 1952 to a Brahmin family of Hyderabad Deccan, India. Like other broadminded and learned Hindus, he accepted Islam in 1973 and took the Islamic name of Ahmad Khan. He was disgusted by the Hindu belief; the concept of 'AWA GAWAN' that when a person dies, his spirit transform itself into a better human being, or some animals, depending on his deeds in his previous life. Brother Ahmad was highly impressed by five times daily prayers, fasting and others marvellous Islamic teachings. He was also enchanted by the Islamic belief in the impeachment by Allah in the Hereafter

Presently, brother Ahmad Khan is working in the Indian Embassy School, Jeddah, as a music teacher.

With the courtesy of Saudi Gazette, we reproduce the 'Interview' of brother Ahmad Khan for our esteemed readers. Editor.1

AHMAD Khan, 43, is a music teacher in the Embassy of India School in Jeddah. He was born in a Brahmin family of Musicians in Hyderabad, India. He learnt music from Ustad Badri Nath and his Uncle who were both lecturers in the Government Music College in Hyderabad. He learnt how to play sitar for *ghazals* and carnatic style on Tabla from Pandit Shanta Prasad in Varanasi during 1970-74. During the 1970s he worked as musician with the All India Radio in New Delhi and Hyderabad. He is decorated with a number of awards from the state as well as the centre.

---

1 Saudi Gazette, 23rd February, 1996, page 7.

Ahmed embraced Islam in 1973. His previous name was Hanumanth Rao. He married a Muslim women and is blessed with three sons and three daughters. Five of his childrens are, Alhamdulillah, hafiz (memorisers of the whole Qur'an) and the sixth one, the youngest daughter, is busy in memorising the Qur'an.

"The five daily prayers establish direct contact between a man and his Creator. In them I feel so much solace, patience and encouragement which I can hardly express in words. I am in direct communication with my Lord. I ask for His forgiveness and whatever I want without exposing my sins to anyone else. This direct contact gives me a sense of self-respect and self-impeachment. For performing the prayers, I have to keep myself clean. The place where I perform the prayers must also be clean. The daily prayers purify man both physically and spiritually. This sense of cleanliness and humbleness are found only in Islam", says Ahmed.

"Besides, fasting develops fear of God which is essential to keep us away from sins. As there are several opportunities when we can deceive others, we can commit crimes when there is no one around. But, while fasting we do not take even a single drop of water when there is no one to watch us. This prevents us from committing sins".

He recalled an incident from the days of the Second Caliph, Omar Bin Khattab. Once, while on a night patrol, Omar overheard the conversation between a mother and her daughter. The mother was urging her daughter to mix water with the milk to make more money on selling it. The daughter told her mother that the Caliph had forbidden this. The mother said that the Caliph did not see them. But the daughter replied, "God is watching us. We can avoid the Caliph's punishment, but not God's". The Caliph was so happy with the daughter's reply that the next morning he performed nikah between her and his son.

The concept of Awa Gawan, the Hindu belief that when a person dies his spirit transforms itself into a better human being or

60

some animals, depending on his deeds in the previous life, never appealed to Ahmed. He wonders how is it possible that all the results of a person's deeds in his previous life come out just after his death. Sometimes it takes years, some times centuries.

If a man digs a well for human beings and animals, they benefit from it even several years after his death. What grade of human being will be he incarnate as in the "coming life" ? Similarly, if someone harms someone, its effects do not fade away quickly. "Which punishment will he deserve just after his death?" asked a dismayed Ahmed. "Therefore", he concludes, "A day must come when the world is totally destroyed. Work opportunity is seized from everyone and all must be impeached by God. Final punishment or reward should be announced then. This beleif in the impeachment by God in the Hereafter appeals to me, to all who have common sense", Ahmed says emphatically.

When asked about his association with the profession of music, Ahmed replied that he has been attached to it even before his conversion to Islam, when, in 1973, he embraced Islam, his parents threw him out of the house. All other family-members socially boycotted him. He was left with nothing except the clothes he was wearing, no money in his pockets, no one to provide him shelter. He spent nearly two years on the footpath of Moazzam Jahi market in Hyderabad. The only art which could earn bread for him was music and, thus, he remained attached to it.
****

What I learned of ISLAM changed my whole thinking and deepened my Faith?

These are views of brother Charles Mustafa Bilal, America's First Muslim Mayor of Kountze, Texas. We were lucky to read the interview of brother Bilal by brother Saeed A. Khotani which was specially written and published in the Arab News1. After getting the address of brother Bilal, we wrote detailed letter alongwith a 'questionnaire' and sent to him on 2nd July, 1995, requesting him to favour us with :-

1) His date of birth !
2) To shed some light on his educational background
3) To give some details of his family.
4) To give a few details of his previous religion.
5) To let us know the reasons of leaving his previous religion.
6) To tell us the circumstances which led him to embrace Islam.
7) And to let us know his views about : Islam; The Holy Qur'an;
8) The Noble Prophet Muhammad(PBUH); Fasting and Prayer.

Brother Bilal honoured us by sending answer to our questionnaire along with his remarkable achievements. It is note-worthy that though 99 percent of Kountze's residents are Christians, brother Bilal won the Mayoral election on 2nd May, 1992 with 51.9 percent votes, was re-elected on 7th May, 1994 with 55 percent votes. We feel honoured in presenting the remarkable, marvellous, and astounding achievements, answers to our questions, and soul-inspiring, heart-rending and informative interview for the benefit of our esteemed readers. - Editor.

---

[1] Arab News 28th June, 1995, page 12

It is worth mentioning that brother paid a visit to Indonesia and was a 'state guest'. Mr. Ann W. Richards, Governor of the State of Texas, while writing to brother Bilal on march 16, 1994, about his trip --- successful trip to Indonesia said :

"I understand that you have recently completed a successful trip to Indonesia. Ambassador Robert L. Barry of the United States Embassy in Indonesia wrote to tell me of your accomplishments during your visit. He said you were well received throughout your stay and that you were able to foster feelings of good will for the United States. Texas is lucky to have you among its leaders"

Brother Bilal intends to visit the Kingdom of Saudi Arabia and perform 'Umrah', but uptilnow, he has found no sponsor who can arrange his trip. We pray to Allah, Most Gracious, Most Merciful, to fulfill his pious ambition and aspiration, Ameen!

Talking about the interview by brother Saeed A. Al-Khotani, brother Bilal wrote to us in his letter on July 24, 1995 :

"Congratulation to you for the 36 books you have written in English and Urdu. Your book "Why Islam is our choice" have a great book title. Be sure to send me a copy.

I have received several letters of goodwill from people who have read my interview. Some of the readers are Americans that are working in Saudi Arabia.

News sources here in the United States have spoken highly of Saeed Al-Khotani interview with me in the Arab News. I hope the public like your book as well". (From letter written on October 27, 1995).

1. Please let me know about your date of birth ?
Answer :
My birth date is May 4th, 1948.

2. Please shed some light on your educational background?
Answer :
High School Diploma/Certificate of training in X-ray technology/Approz. One year of College/Numerous amount

63

of training in business and safety as Chief Executive Officer City of Kountze, TX.

3. Kindly give details of your family?

Answer :

My wife Theresa and I have (three daughters, Amina age 10, Ayeshah age 3, and Gabrielle age 7 months.

4. Please give a few details of your previous religion?

Answer :

My previous religion was Christianity. My family taught me to worship Jesus Christ as Lord and savior of the world. They told me that he had died for my sins and the only way I could Heaven would be through Jesus. My family members are strong faithful Christians.

5. Please let me know the reasons of leaving your previous religion?

Answer :

I had been searching for the truth to some of the un-answered questions I had concerning the Christian religion. Some of the things I learned from Christianity have placed doubt in my mind. For example;

Easter Sunday the so called resurrection of Jesus is celebrated with lies that rabbits lay eggs like the chicken.

Christmas December, 25 is the most popular day in America, the so called birthday of Jesus. Yet there are no records to verify his date of birth.

6. What were the circumstances which led you to embrace Islam?

Answer :

One day in the early 1970's I saw Muhammad Ali go to the corner of a boxing ring and pray. Ali later appeared on T.V. to tell the World that he would give up his boxing career or even his life before he would give up his religion (Islam). Those strong statements from Ali made me travel 150 miles to Houston, Texas to hear the honourable Elijah Muhammad speak on close circuit radio.

Imam W. Deen Mohammed' Muslim American spokesman, taught me the importance of Imam and the benefits of studying the Qur'an and the Sunnah of Prophet Muhammad ý(PBUH).

7. *What are your views about ?*
(a) Islam
(b) The Holy Qur'an
(c) Prophet Muhammad (PBUH)
(d) Fasting
(e) Prayer

Answer :

Islam Is a complete way of life. Islam is the Absolute answer to the ills of this world. Sunday here in America is a day when the Christians gather for congregational religious services. Sunday is also the most segregated time in America, when black people go to Their church and white people go to their church. Al-Islam bring people of all races, colors, and nationalities together for congregational religious services. Allah - u- Akbar !

The Holy Qur'an Is a guidance for those who fear Allah. It is like an owner's manual for the human beings. Surah 2 ayat 28 in the Qur'an Allah says, how can ye reject the faith in Allah? Seeing that ye were without life, and He gave you life; then will He cause you to die,, and will again bring you to life; and again to Him will ye return.

So you see, brother Shahid no matter what condition your life is in, the Qur'an can strengthen our faith.

Prophet Muhammad (PBUH_ Is the perfect role model given to us from Allah. In his farewell address, Prophet Muhammad (PBUH) said, **"You must know that every Muslim is the brother of another Muslim. You are equal. You are members of one common brotherhood."**

Fasting Gives us the power to self restrain and discipline ourselves.

Prayer Changes things. There is power in prayer.

65

ACHIEVEMENTS

Elected mayor of Kountze, Texas...........................5/2/92.
first Muslim mayor in USA.
First African American in South East Texas.
Invitation to the senate in vocation honouring Imam W.Deen Muhammad.
Muslim American spokeman for human salvation in Washington D.C. ....2/6/92.
Grand jury commissioner appointed by judge Earl B. Stover
....8/13/92
88th judicial district representing Hardin and Tyler counties.
(can choose any four people to serve on the grand jury)
built Kountze first city park...................................* 1992 *
Community service award presented by redeemed church of God in Christ Kountze, Texas 12/19/92
First appeal granted to any city by the Texas department of housing and community affairs...............................1/7/93
Volunteer sponsor at the De Quincy Louisiana state prison since 1979.
Texas department of criminal justice/Gib Lewis state prison 2-24-95.
Certificate of recognition for volunteer service to the pastoral team.
South east Texas leadership advisor committee member appointed by U.S.attorney Mike Bradford representing Harden, Jefferson and orange county.....................1994
letter of invitation to visit Saudi Arabia from the royal embassy of Saudi Arabia for Hajj...........................5/2/94
First U.S. mayor to receive an official invitation from the Consulate general of the republic of Indonesia and the Amanah magazine owner Mr. Lukman Umar to visit

Indonesia (10 days visit) ....August 19, 1993
Call the Adhan at the grand masjid in Jakarta, Indonesia, the only foreigner ever to do so.
parade of personalities certificate of appreciation presented by zion temple church of god in Christ port Arthur, Texas 11-6-93
CNN visit kountze , Texas to interview mayor Charles Bilal on his achievements as mayor of Kountze, Texas....1994
Jcpenney golden rule award for promoting volunteerism in Texas 1994
$250-000 grant received from the Texas department of housing and community affairs..............................1994.
$156,000 grant received from the Texas department of Housing and Community Affairs for home improvement to persons with low income.....................................1994
Appointed members of the world council of the mayors by the honourable mayor Johnny Ford, Tuskegee, Alabama founder of the national conference of black mayor in Washington D.C...April 28, 1994
Boys Scott Honorary member appointed by mayor Evlyn lord Beaumont, Tx.
Muhammad Ali (boxing champion) visit Kountze to start funds for a youth center   19th March, 1994.
Re-elected Mayor of Kountze, Texas with 55% of votes.May 7, 1994

   Charles Bilal has the distinction of being the first elected Muslim mayor of a U.S. city-he is the mayor of Kountze in southeast Texas. The county seat (center location) of Hardin County, Kountze houses a small Muslim community. A majority of them, according to Bilal embraced Islam after listening to the lecture of boxing champ Muhammad Ali during his visit to the city on March 19, 1994.

Born on May 4, 1948, Bilal became interested in Islam in early 1970s after he saw Ali pray while in the ring. He was also influenced by American Muslim leader Elijah Muhammad and Imam Warithuddin Muhammad.

In this exclusive interview with Arab News, Bilal says he embraced Islam when he found answers in the Qur'an for some of the questions concerning Christianity that had been troubling his mind. After accepting Islam, he changed his name from Charles Edward Jenkins to Charles Mustafa Bilal. "I had to face rejection from my family and friends", he said. Bilal believes that the Prophet Muhammad (PBUH) had set an example for everyone of us to follow and govern his life - regardless of his race, color, or nationality. "According to my knowledge, Islam is the only religion which attacks racism head on. In the Qur'an Allah says He created tribes and nations not to hate but to know each other", he said.

"What I learn of Islam changed my whole thinking and deepened my faith. I learnt how to restraint myself. I also knew that only Allah can forgive you your sins. The Qur'an gives you more knowledge about Allah's power, grace and mercy", he said.

The ancestors of the so-called black people who are now living in the U.S. were forcefully brought to America from Africa. Our ancestors' names and religion (Islam) were taken away. Now that the same people, once identified by slave names given by their masters, and then chose to call themselves African Americans, are now identifying themselves by their Muslim names. "The same people, at one time here in America, was deprived of their religious rights. They are now openly declaring: 'There is no god but Allah and Muhammad is His messenger'" Bilal said and urged Muslims to study the history of the African American Muslims and include it in the curriculums of schools and universities in the Islamic world.

Bilal sounded optimistic about the future of Islam and Muslims in the United States. "There are well over six million Muslims in the United States. Times are good now for U.S. Muslims. Islam's truthful teachings attract Americans to that religion", he said. Changes in Bilal's lifestyle encouraged some people to embrace and study Islam. Schools and members of the Christian community invited him to be their guest speaker on Islam.

Asked to comment on the anti-Muslim stereotypes used by Western people, Bilal said they are the result of misconceptions about Muslims. "I'm quite hopeful that intensive propagation will help remove these misconceptions to a great extent," he added.

Replying to a question on the implications of his election to a public office, the Muslim mayor said "People like to choose the best for public offices. If a Muslim could get elected thrice to a public office here in southeast Texas, it can happen again in any part of the United States."

Though 99 percent of Kountze's residents are Christians, Bilal won the mayoral election on May 2, 1992 with 51.9 percent votes, re-elected on may 7, 1995 with 55 percent votes. Bilal is now aspiring to become an ambassador.

Asked whether he faced any difficulties in performing the rituals of Islam, the mayor said, "No, I will not allow anything to compromise my religion." Bilal opens his council meetings with Al-Fatiha (the introductory chapter of the Qur'an). " I try as hard as I can to make decisions based on the teachings of Islam when it does not interfere with the American Political structure", he said.

CNN crew visited Kountze to interview Bilal after his success and achievements as the first Muslim mayor in southeast Texas.

According to Bilal, helping people individually is one of the best ways to improve the condition of a society. "I read the book "Islam : Unity and Leadership" in which (page 54) the author Warithuddin Muhammad describes how Prophet Muhammad built up the community," he said.

Islam, the mayor says, is the fastest growing religion in America. People of all races including whites are converting.

However, he emphasized the need for intensifying the Dawa work. "By nature everyone is a Muslim. Some people believe what they have heard about Muslims. And some times their source of information would be non-Muslims. This is why it is so important for us to propagate the religion," Bilal said.

Islam has made great changes in the lives of people in America, he says. "I believe the Muslim community in America will continue to grow and have a good impact on the future of the country," he said. The Muslim Journal, has played a big role in disseminating the message of Islam in America in the last twenty years, he said and urged Muslim to subscribe to the journal (Address : 910 W. Van Buren, Suite 100 Chicago, Illinois 60607). "This journal will help you keep updated with the progress of Muslims in America," he said.

American Muslims need more Islamic schools and mosques, he said. The majority of Muslim children is attending public schools.

"The more Islamic schools we have, the greater will be the chances for Muslim children to grow and educate themselves in an Islamic environment", he said. Sister Clara Muhammad school is the first and most popular Islamic school in the U.S. It was started in the early 1970s, he said.

The mayor said Muslims in America were also in need of an Islamic bank as well as improved ways and means of distributing Islamic literature for propagating Islam in the country. "We have to pool our resources to achieve these goals, joining together for our common causes like other religious organizations," he said and hoped the Muslim world would support these Islamic projects.

"We hope that Allah would help us build a mosque in the city before the end of this year," he said. Bilal travels 30 miles to offer Jumua prayers at a mosque in Beaumont, Texas.

The mayor spends most of his spare time teaching youth about Islam. "I also sponsor the program of teaching Islam to inmates of Texas and Louisiana prisons."

Asked whether his Islamic activities created dissatisfaction among non-Muslims, he said : "That's a good question. I believe

70

that Allah blessed me with this position because of my faith in Him. Yes, there will be dissatisfied people, some of them are from our own Muslim community. But I keep myself surrounded by people who keep me positively motivated. Some of these people are Christians."

"Here in America we need to improve our efforts in teaching the people about Islam. As I have said, times are good for Muslims, and these good times have made many of us complacent and slackened our efforts in the direction of dawa," he said. "Let's work harder in following the example of Prophet Muhammad (PBUH)," Bilal concluded.

****

71

In Islam, the idea that you can pray straight to God without going through Prophet Muhammad (PBUH) appeals to me !

Mr. Chinedu Nwoko is a Nigerian Millionaire who was awarded 'Finet Club Award' for professionalism in 1993. He has become a major force in Business, with a large financial empire as the biggest of Nigerain Millionaires. He is quite young of 32 years. He has risen to the top in a very short span of time and with enviable clan. He is one of the Partners of 'Pascalides & Co.'. He took his Bachelor's Degree from Keela and a Master's Degree in Law from King's College, London. He is one of the 10 or so African solicitors in England & Wales and of this unique few, he alone is a solicitor in the city of London.

By dint of his legal profession, he travels to all parts of the world. He wrote a book, namely 'You, the police and criminal Law Procedure in England and Wales', published by Linas International (UK) Ltd. This book has won great fame for him.

God, the Al-Mighty, guided him and he is fortunate to embrace Islam though his entire family had been Christian.

On the day he received that 1993 Finet Club Awards for professionalism, the citation mentioned his potential for becoming a major force in business, with as large a financial empire as the biggest of Nigerian millionaires. If the point raised eyebrows because he is only 32 years, the congenial London audience that witnessed the remarkable ceremony soon saw that it was indexed on an existing record of solid personal achievements. For Chinedu Nwoko has risen to the top in so short a span of time and with enviable clan that one will not doubt that the mountain is his destination in legal profession. This young partner of Pascalides and Co. who took a Bachelor's degree from Keele and a Master's degree in Law from King's College, London, is one of the ten or so African solicitors in England and Wales. And of this Unique few, he alone is a solicitor in the city of London.

Mr. Nwoko's legal profession sends him to all parts of the globe in the search of evidence and the defense of clients. And talking about clients, his stature becomes etched in the greater profile when it is disclosed that he counts Dr. Nnamdi Azikiwe, Air commodore Emeka Omeruah, as some of the many prominent personalities for whom he acts as solicitors. Even if individuals are taken out of the matter, the fact that the Nigeria High Commission, the Nigeria Port Plc and the Nigeria National Shipping Lines are among his clients makes the same point, not to talk of non-Nigerians, and other organizations for whom he holds brief.

Mr. Nwoko has just written a book published by his Linas International (UK) Ltd. titled "You, The Police and Criminal Law Procedure in England and Wales". It is a book long overdue. For in well-written and easy to understand prose, it discusses issues like arrest, detention and questioning, police searches, legal aids, the jury system, immigration procedures and other topics which any visitors to the United Kingdom will find it invaluable.

Given its theme, it is little wonder that in rare unison both the police and those anxious to extricate themselves from the grip of the law have been stampeding for copies. Not to talk of the general readers interested in edification. But why did Nwoko write the book? Simply as a service to those who step into avoidable problems on account of ignorance. Still he is into a second book, for a different reason- entertainment. It is a work of crime fiction due out shortly.

As a character in Chinua Achebe's Arrow of God has said a family is great because in it you find people who fit all notions of existence. His entire family had always been Christian. He was duly baptized. But he was never really into it. In maturity, he tried to raise some questions about it all but drew answers that left him unsatisfied. Still the intellectual quest for spiritual satisfaction egged him on.

Four years ago he discussed with some friends of his who were Muslims and they encouraged him to read the Qur'an "In Islam, the idea that you can pray straight to God without going through prophet Muhammad (PBUH) appeals to me. Islam hasn't painted

73

the picture of a Caucasian God and a black devil", he says. "But people should be free to follow whichever faith they like. I have not sought to convert my wife by force. And although I expect my children to become Muslims like me, at the last word it will boil down to what their choice is. Islam happens to be the faith most agreeable to me."

Chinedu Nwoko has not taken a Muslim name. "That is not the meaning of worship", he says. He doesn't any reason why his becoming a Muslim should cause any controversy. "If my great grandfather could abandon his traditional African religion to embrace Christianity before the turn of the century, why should it be anathema if today I chose, as I have done, to become a Muslim"?1

****

---
1 Islamic Future. November 1994, No. 42, page 10.

How I came to Islam?

Brother Daud Robert Matthews, formerly David Robert Matthews, was born on the 27th July, 1938 in Caterham, Surrey, U.K., and brought up as an Anglican (Church of England). He is a well read and qualified person. Being a Britisher, he has full command over English. He is HNC-Applied Physics. He is an international figure. He is member of the Institute of Nuclear Engineers (1970); ACM: Association of Computer Machinery (1982); Member Institute of Electronic and Electrical Engineers(1983); Member New York Academy of Sciences (1993); MENSA (1993); INTERTEL (1994); Fellow of the British Institute of Management (1983), British Computer Society (1984) and Chartered Engineer (1995). He has been named to the Dictionary of International Biography (1994) and Who's Who in the World (1983) due to his brilliant career and services. In 1968 around the age of thirty years, he joined a High Energy Physics Laboratory. In 1974, he got a job with the University of Petroleum and Minerals, Dhahran Saudi Arabia, where he served upto 1986 and in the same year he moved to Riyadh and has been serving in the Computer Centre of the King Saud University.

His voyage to Islam started at the age of twenty-three. He spent about eight years without a formal religion from the age of 23 years to about 30 years. He has a vast comparative study of Roman Catholicism, Judaism, Shintoism, Budhism, Hinduism, Taoism, Confucianism, Swedenborgenism and Islam.

After a deep and thorough study of Islam and meetings with Indian, Pakistani, Iranian and locals,

75

he came to the 'Right Path' and embraced Islam in March 1970 at Oxford, U.K.

While in Oxford, he had meetings and discussions with sister Anis who was doing her M.Phil. They understood each other. After finishing her M.Phil. she went to Pakistan. Brother Daud visited Pakistan the met the family of sister Anis. After mutual understanding, they got married in 1973. They are living a very happy and peaceful life. Brother Daud performed Haj twice in 1974 and 1978 respectively.

We had the privilege of meeting brother Daud and it was upon our request that he supplied the above-mentioned information. Now we feel much pleasure in presenting brother Daud's story: 'How I came to Islam' for our esteemed readers - Editor.

I was brought up as an Anglican (Church of England), baptized, confirmed, choir-boy etc. I went to church regularly, communion and evening service. When I came back from National Service, I began to have doubts as to what it was that I really believed.

I Found :

I could not understand the concept of Christian God, nor the Divinity of Jesus. I questioned the concept of inherited sin. The whole heirachy (theocracy) of the Christian Church seemed to be unnecessary. These doubts, or questions not only persisted they got stronger. I found when we stood and faced the alter to say the creed, that I was actively debating within myself as to whether I believed it. I came to the conclusion that if I continued to go to church I was a hypocrite; also that I would not find "God" in the Church. I stopped going to Church. I had discussed these points with the Vicar(s) and was told "You have to believe, my son. If you continue with these arguments then you will be in danger of stepping outside the Church, that is, an heretic."

I then concluded, I don't even know if there is a God. Let me be responsible for my own actions and let me try to help those less fortunate than myself. this became my "way of life."

I then spent some eight years without a formal religion from the age of about 23 years to about 30 years old. I discussed with anyone I could what it was they believed and what they found of value in their religion. I even read a few books. I came in contact with Roman Catholicism, Judaism, Shintoism, Buddism, Hinduism, Toaism, Confucianism, Swedenborgenism and then **Islam.** None of these seemed to be what I was looking for.

Then in 1968 around age of 30 years, I joined a High Energy Physics Lab. There were people living in the senior hostel there from India, Pakistan and Iran as well as the locals. After dinner, we used to discuss politics and /or religion. Something someone said about Islam caught my interest. I went to Oxford, the nearest City, and asked in the information Bereau if there was a mosque in Oxford. They gave me the name of someone who might be able to help. He turned out to be an Englishman who had embraced Islam some twenty years previously. My comment to him was, "I do not know if I can be a Muslim, but without information I will never know."

I arranged to visit him two evenings a week to discuss Islam. After some six months I was following him in the prayer, fasting and giving Zakat. Then I started going to the Mosque.

I had one doubt in my mind, "Would I want to go away from a new religion?"

One night I couldn't sleep and in my mind came, "O you who believe, go not away from the right path, the path that leads to 'A' the One God, Lord of all creation." Shivers went up and down my spine. I sat up, switched on the light and wrote it down. In the morning I analyzed it. The doubts ceased. I had found peace. The struggle within me to find whatever it was, was over. Then I started on the path of Islam. I formally said the declaration of faith March, 1970, having practiced 18 months or so.

We had still continued the discussion in the hostel. When Islam was discussed, I found a girl and myself were on a wavelength of our own. We understood and had a deeper meaning in what we were saying than even those listening and taking part could understand. (Someone referred to it as a joining of the minds.) I was not a young boy, but reasonably mature. Anyway this lady finished her M.Phil and went back to Pakistan. I used to write to her, of my experiences in Islam and of mutual friends. After a year or so, I was invited to meet her family in Pakistan. I went over, got on well with her family, proposed and we were married. That was 1973. It was her original comment that had interested me in Islam.

In 1974 I got a job with the University of Petroleum and Minerals, Dhahran, Saudi Arabia, and in 1986 moved here to Riyadh.

How did Islam effect my life: It gave it a sense of purpose , vector as opposed to scaler; and also, it brought more discipline.

My brother's and sister's accepted me as I am. We have no problems, and the family is quite close. My mother is now 90 years old. Unfortunately, none of them have embraced Islam.

Well, I could go on and on, but I think this is enough for now. If you have questions or if you would like further clarification, please do ask. Peace; - Daud.
****

It is just a 'Miracle' how a 'Book' (the Holy Qur'an) written in primitive days contains all the events of today and also events of the future which we cannot understand as yet!

The following is the 'Reversion' to Islam' story of brother Dawood who is seventeen years old and hails from a Christian Catholic family to Italy. Brother Dawood accepted Islam in 1994. Before embracing 'the Religion of Abraham', i.e. Islam, he was totally ignorant about it. It was during his primary school days when, he, at first, heard about Islam through a Muslim friend. Through discussion and discourse, he learnt about the Islamic Religious festivals and Islamic teachings. When he read more about Islam he came to the conclusion that Islam was meant for him, and the more he learned about it, the more he was happy. Reading the Holy Qur'an and the Hadiths (Traditions) of the Noble Prophet Muhammad(PBUH) was the main influence for his becoming 'reverted back to Islam'. In short, in his own words, Allah, the Creator of the Universe, guided him to the 'Right Path' at an early age for which he is very grateful to Him.

With the courtesy of Iqra (Ramadan 1416 AH) and Ramila Chanisheff (RC) of Australian Muslim News, we feel much pleasure in presenting his 'Interview' for the general public - Editor.1

R.C. When was the first time you heard about Islam?

D. I first heard about Islam when I was in primary school, as my friend was a Muslim. He used to talk to me about Islam and traditions of Prophet Muhammad(S.A.W). I was interested as he did not celebrate Christmas and Easter, so I asked him to explain to me the celebrations they had and also the reasons why they

---

1   Iqra, Ramadan 1416 A.H. Page 39 (with reference to Australian Muslim News)

79

did not celebrate these religious festivals. I would defend my religion from his arguement but whatever he told me about his religion made so much more sense, so I wanted to find out more about this interesting religion. My friend took me to the Mosque and also to visit other Muslim friends and Imams who talked to me. I then read more about Islam and the Muslim's 'way of life'.

R.C. **What was your first impression about Islam and the Muslims?**

D. Before I understood about true meaning of Islam and the Muslims, I was ignorant about Islam and was therefore easily taken in by what the media portrayed about the religion. It seemed like they were men with beards, and little white caps, and the women were covered from head to toe. They were the terrorists from the Far East, and it seemed like they were aliens, a complete different kind of human beings. I did not even know that there were white Muslims from here in Australia, America and from U.K.

R.C. Why did you decide to become a Muslim ?

D. When I learned more about Islam through my friends, I just knew that this religion was meant for me. The more I learned about it, the more I was happy with the answers to all my questions, about the history of Islam, the way of life in Islam, the future of Islam. The Qur'an was written more than 1400 years ago. Nothing in the Qur'an has changed since then, not even a single full stop. Yet it contains the knowledge of the present moment, science, and the future. It is just a miracle how a Book written in primitive days contains all the events of today and also events of the future which we cannot understand as yet. Islam is not just a religion, but a way of life, so this part of Islam appealed the most to me. When I could not answer all the questions that my friends threw at me about my religion, I was so surprised I could not answer any of it, but he could, and Islam could answer all the questions I was looking for. Reading the Qur'an and the Hadiths was the main influence for my being converted back into Islam.

80

RC. What kind of difficulties did you overcome as you converted to Islam?

D. The Major difficulty was my parents, as they are strong Catholics. It is very hard for them to accept that I had given up the religion that they so strongly believe in. My parents are religious, and go to Church often and celebrate the events throughout the year. They believe what they hear and see on television and in the papers, they believe that Islam is a very violent religion with all the wars going on around the world at the moment. I don't blame them for thinking this way but I believe that if you want to know more about something you should go looking for it rather than listening to the media or what other people have to say. What is going on around the world is not what Islam encourages, it is only what human beings fight for. Islam is a very peaceful religion and to find out about it you have to visit the Mosque, talk to the Imams, and also to the community leaders. I believe you should never judge anything without finding more about it yourself. I have explained all this to my parents but they are so set in their ways that they will not listen to me. When I converted to Islam it was very hard to hide this fact from my parents. As I knew that they would be totally against it. It was after about four months when my father had to hear it from me so he gave me an ultimatum, either leave Islam and stay home or pack up my bags and leave. So I chose Islam and left. I now live with my friend and his family who has taken me in as one of their own Allhamdullilah. I thank Allah for showing me the right path and also the right people to explain to me the true, and one and only religion I believe in.

R.C. How did you find socialising with your non-Muslim friends?

D. When I was still a Christian I was not interested in going out, nightclubbing or partying at all. Deep inside me I felt it was wrong to get into drugs and drinking. I would go out with my friends but did not get involved much into the activities. I do not feel as if I am missing out on anything by not mixing with

81

them. I still do have friends who are not Muslims, at school, and also at where I work part time, but I suppose that makes them acquaintances, not really friends.

R.C. Is there anything else you would like to add ?

D. I would like everyone to know that I am very grateful that Allah (SWT) has shown me the right path at an early age. I feel very privileged to have learned about the true religion of Allah (SWT). I am grateful to my friend and his family who takes care of me. I pray to Allah(SWT) that He will take good care of them. Insha Allah.

****

82

In Islam, I have found food for the heart and food for reason at once!

Didier Ali Bourg is one of the 50,000 converts who entered the fold of Islam. He is French by origin, coming from Versailles, city of Louis XIV. He is quite young of 34 years who alongwith a small team set up in October 1993 the Islamic University, of which he is the head. He has been a journalist and editor and the founder of a monthly paper entitled 'Regards d' Islam' (Views of Islam).

After a comparative of study of religions including Islam, he was convinced by the reality and truth of Islam and without hesitation, he embraced Islam.

Didier Ali is lucky that he visited the Kingdom of Saudi Arabia, performed Umrah and Hajj.

He has devoted his life for the service of Islam. In the Islamic University of France, he teaches and propagates the teachings of Islam. - Editor [1]

At 33, has opened the first Islamic university in France, which, in itself, is a noticeable achievement. But even more noticeable, he is of French origin, from Versailles, city of Louis XIV. Excepting for his beard, he looks any other Frenchman, and he is not one of those lost people looking for an exotic spiritual philosophy. No, he has his feet firmly on the ground.

Didier Ali Bourg, alongwith a small team, set up in October 1993 the Islamic University of France, which he heads and where he teaches and learns. In an interview with Arab News, he explains how, through this institution, he hopes to benefit both the Islamic community and the French Society.

Regarding his conversion to Islam, Ali Bourg records that he first started militating at college for ecological, Third worldist, pacifist movement, and was a drummer in a group. In 1989, he studied comparative religions, including Islam.

---

[1] Islamic Future, July -August 1994, No. 39, page 8.

After two or three courses in Islam, Ali Bourg decided to convert . "In Islam, I have found, on the one hand, a logical result of Christianity, of revelation with common reference, like Mary or Maryam, who is mentioned in the Qur'an more often than in the Bible and , on the other hand, I have found strong rules and a strong interior feeling', he says adding; "some say Judaism was the religion of rules, Christianity was the religion of love, indulgence and wisdom, and Islam came to establish a balance between these two pillars that support religion. In Islam, I have found food for the heart and food for reason at once".

Not only did he pronounce al-Shahadah and convert to Islam, but he also strove to create an Islamic university. In France, two other institutions exist: one in Chateau-Chinnon, in the centre of France, with 70 students, and an institute of theology in the Paris Mosque, which opened four days before the Islamic University of France. But latter is the first university and boasts 300 students for the moment.

How did Didier Ali Bourg come to this capital step? "I was born militant", he answers. As I wanted to do something for the Islamic community, he noticed, first of all, that it didn't have any national newspaper. Having been a journalist for several years (another one of his numerous activities), he set up a monthly paper called **"Regards d'Islam"** (Views of Islam), with a double goal; spearing information within the community, making a link between Muslims, and developing dialogue between Muslims and other French people. Bourg wanted to trigger a debate on the situation, the role and importance of Islam in France. Unfortunately, with the opening of the Islamic University of France, the publication of this paper had to be suspended through lack of time and staff.

Another surprising phenomenon is what Ali Bourg calls the **"Islam of comradeship".** He noticed that when young Muslims go back to their religion after a period of instability, they drag with them their Christian friends, leading to a good number of conversions at the age of 16-20. Non-Muslims gain confidence and feel they are "entering a community", and this is the strength of

84

Islam. In all, Bourg says, there may be 50,000 converted people in France.

When asked what Islam he and his university preach, Ali Bourg answers : "There is only one Islam, the authentic one". It is not the Islam of fear, since Prophet Muhammad(peace be upon him) recommended not to provoke fear. The President of the university points out that in the early days of Islam, it was Muslim's behavior and morals that attracted other people and led them to conversion, rather than military conquest.

Didier Ali Bourg just went to Makkah for the first time in his life. What impression does Umrah leave? it is "a very strong experience" that is too personal to be explained, he says. "It is like describing the scent of a rose to someone who doesn't know what a rose is".

****

85

Prophet Muhammad (PBUH) has provided Muslims guidance dealing with anger!

These are the remarks made by a mother who wrote to a community worker who works with youth in Pleansantville, near Atlantic City, N.J., U.S.A. The man who touched the heart of this mother's son is Dwight Muhammad Abdul Qawi. He is a retired boxer, a former world lightweight and cruise-weight champion, 1981-1985, who is on the top of his new found fight to help American Youth final direction in their lives.

Brother Dwight Braxton, who is 42 years old, accepted the Religion of Allah ', i.e., Islam while serving a jail term from 1972-1975. After entering the fold of Islam, he took the Islamic name Muhammad Abdul Qawi.

Brother Qawi retired from the Championship three years ago. According to him, his fondest and sweet memories are of Durban, South Africa, where he participated in six fights. He recalls those memories by writing that:

"As soon as the word leaked out that he was Muslim, the entire Islamic Community in South Africa flocked around him in adulation and support."

According to sister Bonne Lovelace [1] brother Qawi has learned to channel his energy into a rewarding profession that he began by working with his brother. Brother Qawi says:

"Today's youth are full of anger and need to learn how to deal with it... By learning to control their anger, the youth learn to respect the boundaries of others as well as their own. Prophet Mohammed (PBUH) has provided Muslims guidance about dealing with anger".

Brother Qawi utilizes this wisdom in his endeavours with the youths within the secular realm of the public school system. He is endeavouring to mould and change the attitudes of the youths. 'Gangsta Rap' a form of rap music based on gangs, drugs defamation of women, foul languages and a general disregard for

---

[1] Islamic Horizon, March-April, 1995, page 40.

86

standard values and morals, send out negative messages that effect young developing minds.

According to Brother Mohammed Abdul Qawi, this influence on the youth is very powerful and affects their minds, attitudes and behavior, causing a general disregard for the life of others.

Muslim youth who have the treasure of the Qur'an are fortunate because it provides them with the right mental database, Islam, however, for non-Muslim youth such a database is missing or nonexistant, and they often seek to blame or even hurt others for their own negative action.

"Non-Muslims need change the way they think and become responsible for their own deeds, instead of assuming that someone else will bear their burden," says Qawi.

In working with inner city youth, Qawi, who has two sons, 10 and 11 years old, has experienced that Muslim youth often have a stable culture and family, but for the non-Muslims, it can be an ever shifting and constantly confusing family, culture and society, in general. However, in his work, Qawi talks to the youth and tries to help them resolve these inner-self conflicts.

"When the youth start thinking, not only do they regain their innocence but they also become independent," says Qawi.

Qawi who recently visited the ISNA headquarters after meeting with MikeTyson, who like him has embraced Islam while serving a prison term in Plainfield, IN, acknowledges that in dealing with the youth, he is, in a way, dealing with the youth in himself. He stresses to the youth that they need to grow and become adults. However, many non-Muslim youth are getting very little attention from their parents and are missing these opportunities of learning adult life skills and values. Because of these missed opportunities, Qawi claims, youth are becoming depressive and resorting to drugs, often not knowing that drugs are but a fleeting cure.

Qawi often points out to the youth that the 'high' in drugs is only followed by a 'low', that leads to more depression and an even greater drug dependency. In his work, Qawi attempts to combat this problem by working with groups of youth, where it is

87

easy for them to come forward with their inner feelings and enable them to build on these thoughts.

In this, his new career, Qawi, has dealt with about one hundred youths, and retains his enthusiasm to punch out evil and make way for good.

****

Why I embraced Islam ? Muslim by Choice!

We had the good fortune to read the 'Road to Islam' anecdote of brother Greg Noakes in the Islamic Future1 an organ of the World Assembly of Muslim Youth, and came to know that brother Greg Noakes is the Editor of 'Washington Report on Middle East Affairs'. Luckily, we got his postal address and sent a letter along with a 'questionnaire' to him on 30th April, 1995. We also told him that we had the chance of reading articles, i.e., Ramazan in America', 'American Muslim Organizations Rally for Chechnya', and 'American Muslims fear impact of anti-terrorist aid.'

We feel pleasure in saying that brother Greg Noakes very kindly responded to our request and favored us with the answers to our questions. So, for the general benefit of our Muslim and non-Muslim brothers, we present hereunder not only the answers to our questions but also brother Greg Noakes' Road to Islam ' story'. Moreover, brother Greg Noakes wrote an article on Ijtihad which was published in the Hamdard Islamicus2 under the title 'Ijtihad; a key to the renewal of critical Faith'. We also reproduce the 'gist' of the article mentioned above.-Editor.

Dear Br. Shahid,

Thank you for your letter of 30 April. It gives me great pleasure to know that you have found my article to be of interest. Please excuse my delay in responding to your requests for information, I am afraid I have been very busy writing for the magazine for which I work, the Washington Report on Middle East Affair, a copy of which I am enclosing for your perusal. I am also sending you a

---

[1] Islamic Future. Vol. 10, No. 46. page 7.
[2] Hamdard Islamicus. Vol. 18, No. 4 pages 113-21

photograph as you requested. I hope the informations below proves helpful:

1. I was born on 21 December, 1966 in Fort Worth, Texas.
2. I received a bachelor's degree in History from the University of Virginia in 1988, and a Master's degree in Middle Eastern studies from the University of Texas at Austin in 1990. Since that time I have been living in the Washington, Dc area and working for the Washington Report.
3. My mother passed away about seven years ago, but my father, my sister and my grandmother (my father's mother) all still live in Texas. We have no real family connection to the Muslim world; my ancestors came from Germany, France, England and Scotland, with the exception of a great -great grandmother who was an American Indian (Chickasaw tribe)
4. I was raised in a Protestant Christian household as member of the Disciples of Christ denomination. This church emphasizes good works and charity in its services and sermons rather than theology. It is considered to be much more liberal than the Roman Catholic Church or even most other Protestant denominations.
5. I became a Muslim because, as I read more about the faith, I realized that Islam was something in which I really believed. Even as a Christian , I had been taught to help others in need, to give to charity, to treat others with the same type of respect and kindness you wished for in return, etc. I found these same teachings in Islam, but expressed more clearly and in a more meaningful fashion. Islam, I found, was something that mattered every day, all the time where in my experience Christianity was generally confined to church on Sundays. Islam was truly a complete way of life. In addition, tawhid seemed much more sensible to me than the doctrine of the Trinity, and certainly the Qur'an and Hadith were more easily understood than the Bible, which I found difficult to comprehend due to some contradictions I saw. Interestingly enough, I knew very few Muslims before giving my shahadah; for me, Islam was

90

something I learned about from books, not something I observed first-hand.

6. I gave my shahadah at the Islamic Center in Washington, DC in August 1989, in front of Sheikh Fathi al-Mady, a gari at the mosque, and two witnesses, one a man from the Muslim world and the other an American convert to Islam.

7. I believe you will find my views on Islam Response No.5, but let me say in addition that Islam has touched every aspect of my life: how I see the world, how I relate to other people, the choice of a wife and now how I am raising my little girl who is 18 months old. The Qur'an is, off course, central to Islam. I find it to be of great beauty to read and listen to; al-hamdulillah I do know some Arabic and am able to understand much of the original language. There are now some very good translations of the Qur'an into English, and I enjoy just opening the book at random and beginning to read. It is a book held dear by a billion people, yet everyone feels that Allah is speaking directly to them and their situation through the Qur'an's words. That is truly miraculous. Muhammad (PBUH) is a model to be emulated, and just as I enjoy reading the Qur'an, I like to read various Hadith as well. I find the prophet(PBUH) to be a man of supreme abilities, yet very human. Again, every Muslim sees the Prophet (PBUH) as a friend and companion through his words and deeds.

8. I believe Islam will be the religion of the future, if for no other reason than it is the final risala from Allah (SWT), and thus nothing can stand up against its true expression. This is not to say that the Muslims do not face challenges; they have problems to overcome within and outside the ummah. Yet if Muslims hold fast to their Islam, making every attempt to educate themselves and to understand the true meaning of Islam, and then applying that understanding to the world around them, Islam has a beautiful future in every corner of the world, insha'Allah.

91

I grew up in Fort Worth, Texas, in a Christian Protestant family. As a child, our church was an important source of moral values-providing a scale to measure right from wrong and good from evil-but it was not a vital part of either my social or intellectual activity. Church simply was not engaging for me, and what was taught and discussed on Sunday mornings often appeared to have little relevance to the rest of the week-that is, to everyday life.

When it was time to go to college, I selected the University of Virginia. I have always had a love of history, and looking over the course listings I found an introductory class on the history of the Middle East. I thought this course would be beneficial for me since I had very limited knowledge of the region, I decided to pair it with a foreign language course in Arabic. I had studied French throughout and Arabic was about as big a change as I had been craving for.

As the years wore on, I started getting interested more in my Middle Eastern courses than in architecture. A year later, I switched over to the history department where I concentrated on the Arab world in my course work and research.

As New Editor of the Washington Report on Middle East affairs since my graduation from Texas nearly five years ago, I continue to follow events and trends in the Middle East. A few courses in college-and the professors who taught them-literally changed the trajectory of my life.

I was exposed to the teaching of Islam through my classes and assigned readings. The coursework assumed great importance. The more I read about Islam, the more it appealed to me, since I didn't know the faintest thing about Islam. I dug deeper, reading books by both Muslim and non-Muslim writers. What really caught my attention were writings by a handful of authors, especially European Muslim Charles Le Gai Eaton's masterful Islam and the Destiny of Man's, Fazlur Rahman's overview of the faith titled simply 'Islam' and non-Muslim Marshall Hodgson's three-volume history, 'The Venture of Islam'.

92

What I found was a religion whose moral teachings closely resembled the values I had been taught by my parents: belief in God, respect for others, truthfulness, courtesy, charity and honor. What was new was the clarity and vibrance of Islam, and the fact that all of these values were integrated into a complete and seamless system. Islamic teachings were sublime, subtle and easy to understand.

I told myself to wait one year, to make sure of my decision and to learn more about Islamic beliefs and practice where my level of knowledge was lacking. Giving Shahadah would be the single most important action of my life, and I wanted to be sure of my ability to live up to that commitment. After some three years of study, research and contemplation, I embraced Islam in the summer of 1989.

The question which always crops up in conversations with Muslims or non-Muslims is, "Why did you convert?" To reduce the beauty of Islam to a series of talking points is clearly absurd; there are a thousand reasons, small and large, why I became a Muslim. And yet three things stand out for me.

First, the Islamic belief in the day of judgment struck a chord deep inside my soul. every man and women will be held responsible for his or her actions-- and only his or her actions-- by a just but merciful Judge: Allah. I believe that justice tempered by mercy is the most important value in this world; how could it be any different in the hereafter? We have been provided with the means of discern right from wrong, and the ability to enjoy one while forbidding the other. Our actions and intentions have meaning (in the truest sense of the word), according to Islam.

Secondly, while I find a great deal of similarity between Christian and Islamic morals, Islams resolved a number of theological questions and issue of belief which I found Christianity could not satisfactorily address. Among these are the unity of Allah as opposed to the 'mystery' of the Christian's Trinity (which has yet to be explained to my satisfaction by Christian doctrine). the ability of each Muslim to stand before Allah without

93

the intercession of a priest or clergyman, and the whole issue of the language of the scripture.

The Qur'an has been preserved in its original form and the original Arabic since the time of the Prophet Muhammad (PBUH) while Isa (as) spoke Aramaic, the Gospel was first written in Greek, then translated into Latin and subsequently into English, French, Spanish, German, etc. Anyone who speaks tow languages and has ever translated from one into the other knows that something is lost in the process; subtle meanings of phrases and the connotations of words are inevitably sacrificed. How, then, can one refer to a passage in an English-language Bible and assert categorically that these were truly the words - and teachings - of Isa, Musa or Ibrahim (peace be upon them all)? Muslims have direct access to the Word of Allah (SWT), and are able to follow the Message of their Creator in its primordial form.

Since I became a Muslim, my depth of knowledge and understanding of the faith has increased, and has my recognition that I have still only skimmed the surface of the vast body of Islamic teaching, thought and scholarship. I also have grown to appreciate the diversity of Muslim community around the world and the variety of views and opinions that Muslims hold. This has been, in a sense, the opposite of my original task as a non-Muslim which was trying to reduce Islam to its essentials in order to understand it. Now I am reversing the process, trying to see how Islam unfolds in all its variety --- a faith which is applicable in all times and for all people is, by necessity, broad and diverse. From my perspective as "a Muslim by Choice", as those who embraced Islam are sometimes called, I find that these are exciting times for Islam, and that it is an exciting time to be a Muslim.

Greg Noakes

****

94

Ijtihad : a key to the renewal of critical Faith!

The word Ijtihad comes from the same Arabic root as Jihad, and both have the sense of "effort" or "struggle". Ijtihad is an intellectual effort defined by the Algerian Shaykh 'Abd al Hamid Ben Badis (1889-1940) as "the exercise of effort to define regulations using the guidance of Islamic law in conformity with basic principles". In order to perform Ijtihad, a Muslim should "be thoroughly familiar with the sciences of the book (the Holy Qur'an) and the Sunnah, comprehend the wider purposes of the Shari'ah and understand Arabic correctly".

Islamic jurisprudence is based on four sources, or roots of law (usul al fiqh), recognized by all four Sunni Muslim fiqhs, or schools of Law. The first is the Qur'an which Muslims believe is the "Word of God" as revealed to the Prophet Muhammad (PBUH) through the Angel Jibrail (Gabriel) and which serves as the ultimate source of authority in Islam. Some of the Qur'an verses are explicit commands, others are held to be broad guidelines, while still others are open to interpretation.

The second base of law is the Sunnah, or example of Prophet (PBUH) as preserved in the collections of hadith, or Traditions of the Prophet Muhammad's (PBUH) sayings and actions serve to illuminate the Qur'an and provide another source of guidance for proper belief and practice. While the Qur'an commands Muslims to establish regular prayer, for example, the proper ritual actions of the prayer are described in the hadith.

The third root of law is ijma', or consensus of either the community or of learned scholars. When the Prophet Muhammad(PBUH) was alive, any questions or disputes could be referred to him for his judgment and responses, many of which are preserved in the hadith. After Prophet Muhammad's (PBUH) death, questions of faith and practice were discussed among the companions of the Prophet (PBUH) until a consensus had been reached.

The consensus of the first four "rightly-guided" caliphs, or successors to the Prophet (PBUH) as temporal leader, is

95

considered by Sunni jurists to be the most authoritative. The ijma' of the Companions as a whole is the next strongest, and the ijma' of successive generations are judged to be progressively weaker. Seemingly the opposite of "Progress", this judgment is based instead on proximity to the revelatory event and the Prophet(PBUH) himself, those men and women who actually knew Prophet Muhammad(PBUH) had a deeper understanding of his teaching and practices than did later generations.

The Fourth basis of the Shari'ah is Qiyas, or analogy. If a jurist can find no rule of law in the Qur'an, Sunnah or consensus of scholars that applies to a given situation, he or she can reach a solution through analogy, applying the reasoning of an existing rule to a similar problem that is not covered by the letter of the law. The scholar is not creating a new law, but extending existing legislation to a new situation .

What the Muslims need, in the words of 'Abd al-Hamid Ben Badis," is the Islam of those who understand its principles, grasp its splendors through faith, its morals, its ethics, its values, its rituals and deepen -- as much as possible -- their knowledge of Qur'anic literature and the saying of the Prophet Muhammad (PBUH). Such men base all this on thought and deep examination, separating what Islam reveals through its beauty and proofs of its validity form what is accretion by reason of its ugliness and decrepitude. These men live their faith, their thoughts and their actions". Taqlid is a renunciation of "Critical faith", while 'ijtihad' is the key to "the Islam of those who understand".[1]
****

[1] Hamdard Islamicus. Vol. 18, No. 4 pages 113-114, 116-120.

The disciplined and orderly manner of prayers and concern and care for the poor and destitutes ordained by ISLAM are some of the most glaring attributes which have impressed me!

These are the tributes paid to Islam by brother Habib-ur-Rahman who accepted Islam due to the outstanding and glaring characteristics of this 'True Faith', i.e. Islam. Brother Habib-ur-Rahman hails from South India. Before entering the fold of Islam, he was rather upset, disgusted and confused with the conditions prevailing in his home town. Now he has found the Truth and he is fully aware of the fact that Islam provides the right way of life. Islam, in his opinion, is the religion of Truth and Rectitude and guides us to make a balanced progress of spiritual and material.

He is very much impressed by the mammoth gathering of pilgrims in the Sacred city of Makkah al Mukarramah currently being shown on television. This assembly inspires us to meditate that there is only One Allah, the Only Creator and our Nourisher.

With the courtesy of Riyadh Daily, we feel pleasure in presenting his 'Interview' : - Editor. [1]

The disciplined and orderly manner of prayers and concern and care for the poor and destitutes ordained by Islam are some of the most glaring attributes which have impressed a new Muslim immensely.

Habib ur Rahman, who hails from south India, said he decided to embrace Islam due to the outstanding characteristics of this Faith.

In an interview he said: "I am grateful to the Daw'a Cooperative Office for Islamic Research of the Ministry of Islamic

---

[1] Riyadh Daily. 19th April, 1996. page 9.

97

Affairs for guiding me to study about Islam and make up my mind on accepting this religion".

He said before accepting this religion, he was confused on the prevailing conditions in the area he comes from. He said: "Now I recognize that Islam provides the right way of life. It is the religion of truth and rectitude and guides us to make a balanced progress of spirit and material."

He said he was highly impressed by the mammoth gathering of pilgrims in Makkah currently being shown on television. This assembly inspires us to meditate that there is only One Allah, the only Creator and our Nourisher. All have to ask for His help and guidance, he added.

He said he is currently studying about the Hajj rituals and is being guided by other brothers in the Daw'a office and hoped to proceed to Hajj this year.

Habib ur Rahman said he is fortunate to have found the truth of this religion and is now determined to carry on this message to others, mainly his relatives and friends.

He said this religion explains the best lessons of disciplines, respect to others including elders, and love and affection for youngsters.

We are taught to give care to the needy, destitutes and handicapped. "Any one of us may suffer from these disabilities, therefore, it is our duty to care for those who are less fortunate amongst us," he added.

*****

98

How did Dr. Hassan Nakata embrace Islam?

by Muhammad Haneef Shahid

Dr. Hassan ko Nakata is one of the famous Japanese Muslim scholars who has devoted his life for the service of Islam and Muslims. He is a diplomat, writer, educationalist and scholar. He was born on the 22nd July, 1960. He got his early education from Japan. Later on, he enroled his name in the University of Cairo and got his Ph.D. degree from the same University, his thesis being 'The Political Theory of Ibn Taimiyya'. This thesis has been published in the form of a book by Dar-Ul-Akhla, Dammam and is available in Riyadh at Markaz al Darasat wal Aalam. The first edition was published in 1994. At present Dr. Hassan is serving University of Yamaguchi, Japan, as Head of the Department of Education, after completing his tenure at the Japanese Embassy in Riyadh.

Upon our request, Sister Khaula Hassan, wife of Dr. Hassan, answered our questionnaire. Regarding the family background of Dr. Hassan, sister khaula said that 'his mother became Muslim in 1988, his father is not Muslim yet but very sympathetic to Islam. He said he would become Muslim in future, Inshaallah.

Dr. Hassan got married in 1991 in Egypt at the end of his 6 years' student life in Cairo. His wife, Khaula, born in 1961, embraced Islam in 1990 in France before she met Dr. Hassan. It is worth mentioning that one of her sisters embraced Islam in 1991 and got married in 1993 with a close Muslim friend of Dr. Hassan.

Talking about the previous religion of Dr. Hassan, sister Khaula, wrote: There was no particular religion, but very close to Christianity. He has believed in God since childhood. As he had the belief in God since his childhood, he often went to the church. At University, he belonged to a Bible study club. At the second year of the University, when he had to choose the majoring subject for the next year, the Islamic Study Department was newly created, so he chose Islam as his subject. And it is quite surprising, after one year's study, he embraced Islam in 1983.

99

Answering the question yes. Dr. Hassan's views about Islam, Qur'an, and the Holy Prophet Muhammad (P.B.U.H.), sister Khaula said: 'Islam is the most integral and all-encompassing religion. All the human beings must learn the Holy Qur'an, for it reveals its deep meanings according to one's intellectual and spiritual ability. The Holy Prophet Muhammad (PBUH) is the greatest Messenger only through whom we can learn about Islam to get to Paradise.

Regarding future of Islam in Japan, she told that the encounter with Islam started very recently in Japan with the increase of the Muslim workers from the Third World. Most of the Japanese Muslims are wives of these born Muslims from Pakistan or Iran. Because of the poor Islamic materials in Japanese, new converts feel often at a less not knowing how to distinguish the regional custom and Islamic customs, whose saying to follow.

The recent increase of Japanese Muslims is remarkable. Moreover, the eagerness for the acquirement of Islamic knowledge and for the obedience to the Divine Order is characteristic of today's Japanese Muslims, very different from the previous generation. One proof: They are very concerned with the Islamic education of their children. We have to work hard for the preparation of better circumstances for our young Muslims. The Da'wah activities in Japan have depended too much on the foreign aid. Now is the time for us to start the Da'wah by our hands.!

Lord Headley Al-Haj El-Farooq's Conversion to Islam

by Muhammad Haneef Shahid

The Right Honourable Lord Headley Al-Haj El-Farooq Sir Rowland George Allanson-Winn, Baron Shaikh Saifurrahman Rahmatullah, B.A., M.I.C.E.I., M.S.I.C. (France), F.S.E., F.S.P., was born in London in January 1855. He was educated at Westminster School, London, and Trinity College, Cambridge, where he took tripos in Mathematics. At Cambridge, he was a noted amateur boxer. He won the heavy and middle weight boxing championships of the University(1). After leaving the college, he engaged himself in educational work and later became the Editor of Salisbury and Winchester Journal, Winchester, which position he filled for two years, and then served as secretary to Sir Frederick Seager Hunt, M.P., for the next seven years. He became peer in 1877. He served in the army as a Captain and later on as Lt. colonel in the 4th Battalion of North Minister Fusiliers. Ultimately in 1892, he took up Civil Engineering as a profession. (2)As a Civil Engineer he supervised many important public works in India, and in recognized authority on coast erosion and foreshore protection.(3) He completed the Baramula-Srinagar road in Kashmir in 1896.(4) He has many publications on engineering subjects to his credit, as well as others on boxing. Lord Headley was twice awarded the Bessemer premium of the Society of Engineers, London, the silver medal of the Royal Society of Arts, and the silver medal of the Institution of Civil Engineers of Ireland. He was elected President of the Society of Engineers London.(5).

He succeeded his cousin in 1913 and was the fifth Baron and the 11th holder of the Baronetcy of Nostell, Yokrshire (created in 1660). Although an engineer by profession he had wide literary tastes. He was the author of several books on Islam. After entering the fold of Islam, in 1913,(6) he formed a Trust for the Encouragement of Muslim Literature of which he was the Chairman, and M/s. K. Kamal-ud-din, Sir Abbas Ali Baig,

101

K.C.I.E., C.S.I., and K.N.Ahmed, Barrister-at-Law, as its trustees(7), His writings on Islam include:

The Three Great Prophets: Moses, Jesus and Muhammad with a brief sketch of the life of the Holy Prophet. A beautiful comparison from four points of view; their respective moral influence on their followers; how they found and left the world; how the world fared after them ;Islam and the hereafter.(116pages.) (8)

The Affinity Between the Original Church of Jesus Christ and Islam ; The book seeks primarily to find some effectual means of establishing an understanding between Original Christianity and Islam . It deals with Islam's opportunity in the West, and one feature which has specially commended itself to us is its laying bare, in dispassionate terms, the ignominious methods pursued by the Christian missionary in conducting his malicious propaganda in the West against Islam and its great Arabian Teacher. The book comprises 156 pages.(9) and Western Awakening to Islam and Thoughts of the Future.

Brought up as a Protestant he also studied Roman Catholicism and was struck by what he called their "believe this or be damned" attitude. It is, he said on one occasion, the intolerance of those professing the Christian religion, which more than anything else is responsible for my secession. I was reared in the strict and narrow forms of the Low Church party. Later, I lived in many Roman Catholic countries including Ireland. The intolerance of one sect of Christians towards other sects holding some different form of the same faith of which I witnessed many instances, disgusted me."(10)

As stated earlier, Lord Headley embraced Islam in 1913 and adopted the Muslim name of Shaikh Saifurrahman Rahmat-Ullah El-Farooq. His devotion to the cause of Islam was unique in many respects. He rendered valuable services for the Muslims and Islam as President of the British Muslims Society, London for a number of years. He delivered speeches and gave lectures on the auspicious occassions of Eid-ul-Fitr, Eid-ul-Azha and the Holy

102

Prophet Muhammad's Birthday during the years of his Presidentship.

His acceptance of Islam was not only welcome in Europe, America and England, but also in the Middle East and Indo-Pak. Subcontinent. Under the guidance of Maulana Abul Kalam Azad, a resolution was passed in a meeting by the Muslims of Calcutta in which Lord Headley was congratulated. It was also resolved to send a regular monetary help to the Muslim Mission. (11)

Lord Headley had been twice married, and had four sons. His second marriage, in 1921, was the outcome of a meeting in Hyde Park, when both he and his wife were speakers at a public gathering.(12)

Before the marriage they had known each other for many years. Both possessed literary gifts. Lady Headley, Mrs. Barbara Bayton, was the authoress of several books dealing with Australian life, and also a stirring three-act play, 'The Surrender.' She was the personal friend of Mr. Hughes, the Australian Premier and was reputed to be very wealthy. (13)

Lord Headley performed the Haj in 1923, and 1927. On Friday, the 22nd of June, 1923, Lord Headley, set out on his journey to Mecca. It was a long-contemplated pilgrimage. Soon after his declaration of Islam in 1913, his thoughts were set on a visit to Mecca and Madina. He had booked his passage by the P. and O. steamer Persia in 1914. The First World War broke out, and under the circumstances, his duty was to stay at home with his children, who were then of tender age. He at once cancelled his passage, and in that he did what a true Muslim should have done. In fact, with great dismay he had to give up the idea so dear to his heart. Lord Headley's pilgrimage had a peculiarity of its own. He was the 'First Muslim' of England and the First Pilgrim of that country too. In Egypt, he was given unprecedented reception and was treated as a 'State Guest'. In Arabia also, he was received with open arms and a splendid reception was accorded in his honour. During his stay in Arabia, he was the guest of King Hussain. Lord Headley was the 'state guest' in Arabia. The King

103

sent his motor-car to Jeddah to take him to Mecca, and convey him back to the seaport when the pilgrimage had been completed. The King's private doctor was deputed to drive the car, doubtless as a double precaution first, against accidents; and, secondly, if misfortune should be encountered, to ensure that medical aid should be immediately at hand. King Hussain displayed the utmost solicitude for the pilgrims comfort. On one occasion, when the pilgrims were encamped in the desert, the King learned that Lord Headley had no bed. He immediately sent his own camp-bed, himself sleeping on the ground. Lord Headley was awarded the Order of Nadha of Arabia by King Hussain, besides he was given two pieces of the Kiswa (the Holy Carpet).(14)

Describing his experiences, Lord Headley, in a letter dated July 21, 1923 from Mecca, wrote :

"I have seen it stated that the Mecca pilgrimage is made use of by political propagandists to further their own ends. Nothing is further from truth, and were politicians of any kind to air their views in Mecca, they would find themselves in about the most un-congenial atmosphere possible.

The first thing that struck me on arriving here from Jeddah was the complete elevation of the mind above earthly matters. All the pilgrims ... are so much bent on serving God that they have no room in their minds for other considerations.

The most impressive sight of all is the service at the big courtyard surrounding the Kaaba ... It must be remembered that this huge congregation consists of representatives from all parts of the world... Everywhere the intense desire to thank God for His goodness and implore His direction in the right path is so strongly manifested that there is no room for worldly considerations."(15)

Lord Headley spared any pains nor money in the service of Islam. At the old age of 70, he undertook long journeys to Egypt, South Africa(16) and India for the cause of Islam. It was his earnest desire and it was decided by the Trust to build a mosque in London, and towards the end of 1927, he went to India for the purpose of collecting sufficient funds for the building of a really

104

find edifice somewhere not too far from the centre of the Metropolis. He hoped to have a site free, but it was not possible. Lord Headley stayed with the Nizam for nearly two months and the Nizam contributed the magnificient sum of 60.000 Pounds towards the cost. It was the first gigantic mosque to be built in London for the Muslim community at large and to be named after the name of the Nizam of Hyderabad. (17)

Lord Headley, on the invitation of the Organizers of the All-India Tabligh Conference, presided over the annual session of the conference which was held on the 25th December, 1927 at Delhi. It was for the first time in the history of Islam in India that a western Muslim was honoured by his brother Muslims to the extent of being invited to join them in the furtherance of a common cause, on which his views as to the ways and means of the propagation of Islam in the western countries were eagerly awaited. It was the brotherhood of Islam which united the Muslims of the East and West.

Khan Bahadur Pirzada Muhammad Hussain, M.A., C.I.E., President of the Reception Committee in his address paid glowing tributes to Lord Headley by saying :

"This occasion is unique in the history of Islam, more so, because we have in the person of our President-elect one whose name is well known in the Islamic world. His presence here shows that in Islam there are no divisions of race or colour, and that every Muslim, whatsoever his nationality or position, has the desire to share the blessings of the faith inherited by him, with the rest of mankind. I refer to our Nobel guest, Al-Hajj Lord Headley El-Farooq, who is to guide our deliberations and his conference. The Nobel Lord, as you are all aware, is one of the earliest British Muslims, and we are proud to think that his faith has given him the strength to face the spears of a prejudiced and intolerant Christian population and to hold a loft the banner of Islam inspite of his busy public and private life. His position as a peer of England and Ireland, coupled with his untiring zeal and devotion as well as his

105

conspicuous ability, enables him to serve the cause of Islam with unique success in the British Isles.

We know how firmly His Lordship is devoted to Islam and its propagation in the world. His participation in the deliberations of this Conference is sure to give a strong impetus to the cause of Tabligh".

Lord Headley delivered a thought-provoking, heart-rending and informative address which is an epitome of the moral philosophical aspects of the teachings of Islam.

A few extracts for the general information of our brother-Muslims are reproduced.

"Since I declared my faith in Islam, It has long been my desire to see my brethren and make personnel acquaintance with them.

It is not because I believe in Islam that I wish to see my beliefs shared by my fellow-beings, but because I consciously believe that real human progress and true fellow-feelings for all the human race can only be achieved through the spread of Islamic Principles.

Islam presents a religion most simple, comprehensive and practical. Duty to God and duty to our fellow-men is its essence. Its theology, therefore, is neither a dogma nor a collection of some metaphysical and mysterious conun-drums. It brings theology out of the labyrinth of myths and riddles and places it on a practical basis.

The world, and especially the Western world, would jump at it, if Islam be preached to them in its "PURE FORM" and if its tenets and doctrines were explained to them in reasonable way. I come from the west, I know my people. They are mostly tired of the religion current in their midst. They want a religion of the type of Islam. Their angle of view in many things is already that of Islam. When you come across a thoughtful person in the West and talk to him of Islamic verities, he will see eye to eye with you on all that you say to him of Islam and will declare that he thought of religion in the same way... They showed that the religion taught by Jesus was Islam, and not the formal Christianity. Thus within a very short time remarkable success has attended their efforts by

106

spreading Islamic literature either free or charged or at a nominal price. We should therefore concentrate on bringing out more literature on Islam on these lines. Even in this country you will, I think, find more English readers than others. We need the publication of a series of Islamic books --- say some twenty-five in number, of shilling edition, dealing with various aspects of Islam; every booklet a self-contained exposition on some of the aspects of Islam, touching culture, progress, love, tolerance and so on. Again, we need a handbook of the life of our Holy Prophet in addition to various books dealing with the many aspects of his Holy life. The day has come when the world should know more of Muhammad. No one would fail to love that great character in the world if one is supplied with his true picture. The Holy prophet is laboring under gross mis-representation. His character, pure and chaste as it is, has been presented in hideous colours by vilifying agencies. Depict Muhammad in his real colour to the world, and that itself is sufficient to win millions for Islam.

What I have said about "Tabligh" in the West is more or less applicable everywhere. You can preach Islam in Europe, in South, East and West Africa, on the same lines.(18)

Lord Headley died in London on 22nd June, 1935. His death has left a gap which time alone can fill. His death was mourned not only in the Muslim Ummah but also in England, U.S.A. and Europe. He was charming, gentle, kind, lovable - a loving son , a loving father, a loving husband and a loving but, above all, a sincere friend. His was an extremely charitable nature, and God had gifted him with virtues of the highest order.

He was a God-fearing man, a true son of Islam. He has left behind a fine tradition of selfless service, spotless character and reputation, which the present generation and that to come, are not easily to forget.(19)

The Hon'ble M.H. Kidwai, while paying tributes to Lord Headley, wrote :

"By the death of Lord Headley I have lost a dear personal friend. He was very courteous, very obliging, very sociable. He

107

had a good and loving heart. He was straightforward and unostentatious. He mixed freely with all and never 'took airs'. With innumerable personal qualities he was destined to get openly converted to Islam. He was a Muslim in his heart even before he was converted to Islam. Lord Headley was made a Christian by his parents, but because he was intelligent, he had the courage of his conviction and because he came in touch with Muslims and thereby came to learn a good deal of Islam. He declared himself boldly and unequivocally to be a Muslim. His belief in Islam was a matter of very strong and very intelligent conviction. He had studied Christianity very thoroughly and when he gave it up and preferred Islam to it, was no matter of sentiment but as a result of very thorough investigation and deep study. He gave up the Christianity of Church - the Christianity of Paul and accepted the Christianity of Jesus Christ - one of the greatest Prophets that came on this earth. When Lord Headley accepted Islam, he accepted that Christianity which had been truly reformed more than thirteen centuries ago by the greatest of all Reformers of whom Christ himself had foretold - the Great Comforter - The Mercy for the worlds - the last and the final Guide and Prophet for all Humanity, for all times and for every country". (20)

One special characteristic of Lord Headley which is not known to the general public at large is that he was a very good poet. He contributed a number of poems to the Islamic Review and other literary journals. The well-known British poet, Rudyard Kipling (1865-1936) in his famous 'Ballad of East and West' said:

> Oh! East is East
> And West is West,
> And Never the Twain
> Shall meet! (21)

But Lord Headley, after his acceptance of Islam, wrote a poem entitled "The Brothers in Islam" and refuted Rudyard Kipling's notion by saying:

> 'East meets West in the University of Islam'.

It had been said we could not meet
Or join in prayers for further grace -
Together reach Thy mercy seat -
Or mingle praise in the same place.
O Heavenly Father, Thou hast shown
To us, Thy loving faithful sons,
How Brotherhood has quickly grown
Insep'rable while time still runs.
In all the ages of the past,
In all the future years to come,
Thy Name alone can bind us fast,
Whilst we can say, "Thy Will be done".
Great Allah, Lord, our God our King,
Who knowest what for us is best,
We praise Thy Name and loudly sing
The fusion of the East and West, (22)

After this brief introduction, we would like to give some extracts from Lord Headley's own writings which help us in understanding the reasons of his acceptance of Islam. Lord Headley says:

"It is possible some of my friends may imagine that I have been influenced by Muhammadans; but this is not the cause, for my present convictions are solely the outcome of many years of thought. My actual conversations with educated Muslims on the subject of religion only commenced a few weeks ago, and need I say that I am overjoyed to find all my theories and conclusions are entirely in accord with Islam.

Conversion, according to the Koran, should come out of free choice and spontaneous judgment., and never be attained by means of compulsion. Jesus meant the same thing when he said to his disciples: "And whosoever shall not receive you nor hear you, when ye depart there... (St. Mark, vi,2) (23)

As a child I always resented the idea of the "Eternal Father, strong to save," requiring any assistance from any quarter whatever being in need of a sort of propitiatory bribe or "sop to

109

Carberus", and as particular way as set forth in a highly complicated rigmarole evidently composed to bewilder and frighten the ignorant and superstitious? The final and clinching recital in this enigmatic guide to Heaven reads terribly: "This is the Catholic Faith: which except a man believe faithfully, he cannot be saved." for it leaves no loophole for escape: the miserable sinner who either cannot or will not accept is doomed to everlasting damnation or to a punishment worse than any that could be inflicted by the harshest human tyrant in his harshest mood". (24)

I have known very many instances of zealous Protestants who have thought it their duty to visit Roman Catholic homes in order to mark 'converts of the inmates. Such irritating and unneighbourly conduct is, of course, very obnoxious, and has invariably led to much ill-feeling - stirring up strife and tending to bring religion into contempt. I am sorry to think that Christian missionaries have also tried these methods with their Muslim brethren; though, I am at a loss to conceive, why should they try to convert those who are already better Christians than they are themselves? (25)

I need not tell you that I am a Muslim by conviction; the grandeur, simplicity, absence of sacerdotalism and freedom from dogmas would alone have been sufficient to draw me to the Faith, but there are other weightier and more compelling reasons - connected with repeated manifestations which have made me a humble and, as yet, unworthy follower of the Holy Prophet (God's blessings on his memory!) and have given me happiness in misery and strength when the forces of evil seemed about to overwhelm me. I speak also as one who has never believed in the baptisms and creeds of the Christian religion being necessary to salvation; so that I cannot be said to have deserted a faith I never had any faith in. (26)

A few years ago I wrote the following in a little booklet entitled "Thoughts of the Future":-

"After over forty years of thought and prayerful effort to arrive at a correct view, the dominant idea in my mind is that the whole

110

fabric of so-called religion is of man and not of God. But I must also confess that visits to the East have filled me with very deep respect for the simple Faith of the Muhammadans, who really do worship God all the time and not only on Sunday. Their beautiful trust in their Almighty and Merciful Creator, Who is never absent from them for a moment of the day or night, awakens feelings of the keenest sympathy in my heart. I love to join in the devout praise of the earnest Mussulman because I know he is genuine; there is no pretense about him when he takes off the little bit of carpet from his horse's back and prostrates himself before his Maker. This happens several times everyday from sunrise to sunset, and in his devout and happy mind he is present with God Himself. There has been no need of priestly aid; he has found the Mercy Seat alone and without any help from outside source whatever". (27)

When I openly avowed the Muslim Faith in 1913, members of my family came to me with expressions of the gravest concern because I had deserted the religion of my fathers, and they assured me most positively that salvation was impossible for me now that I had taken the terrible step. I pointed out that, though I was willing to admit that I might deserve to be damned for the sins which I had committed, I would never believe that the God of mercy and Justice to whom I had prayed all my life would be so unjust as to pass such a terrible sentence as " everlasting damnation" on me for being an honest man, and telling the truth about my beliefs to Him" to whom all hearts be open," all desires known, and from whom no secrets are hid." (28)

Over two years ago, when I openly confessed the Muslim Faith, some of my relations wrote assuring me that if I did not believe in the Divinity of Christ I could not be saved. In reply I pointed out that, so far as I could see, the Divinity of Christ was not so important as that other question: "Did Christ give God's messages to mankind?" We believe that he was the divinely inspired Prophet, and that he did give the messages which were followed up, later on, by the revelations to the equally inspired Prophet Muhammad,

111

who also delivered what he was told to mankind. Looking at the question of belief, I cannot imagine that the All-Merciful One would punish me with everlasting damnation for my inability to accept the teaching of certain religious sect -- to wit the Christians; but I can quite believe that He can and will punish me for all my misdeeds... Islam does not deny salvation to those who do their duty to God and their neighbours, whatever they may think on other subjects; but Christianity positively affirms that salvation is impossible without the atonement, a belief in the Divinity of Christ, sacraments, and the Trinity, and here is where the dogmas of Christianity stand out in such marked contrast to the simple and charitable tenets of the Muslim Faith".(29)

Almost the first letter I received after becoming a Muslim was one in which the writer put it quite plainly: "if you do not believe in the Divinity of Christ you cannot be saved." Only think of it: the unfairness: the downright cruelty! Here am I, a poor little mortal, created and placed in this world by a BEING so great, so wise, so merciful, and so mighty that I am unable to form even and estimate of my own idea of His Majesty, suddenly informed that it was very wicked of me to be born in sin and to be a child of wrath, and that so awfully wicked am I that nothing but the slaughter of an entirely innocent person can possibly save me. I am then told that my sins are of such an awful nature that my Maker (who presumably knows most about my construction and sin-capacity) has decided that He ought to be propitiated, and that in order that the sacrifice may be sufficiently important to satisfy Him and appease His anger, He has decided to put him to a somewhat cruel death by crucifixion." (30)

I am personally acquainted with several Bishops and many of the clergy of the English and Roman Catholic Churches. They are friends, and I am perfectly certain that they do not really, in their inmost hearts, believe that I am doomed to everlasting damnation because I do not believe in any single one of the Christian dogmas as being necessary to salvation and yet, as ordained priests, I imagine that they are compelled to look upon me as a lost soul.

112

Here we may well repeat the well-known question: "What do they believe?" I some times fear that they deceive themselves and that the "truth is not in them". (31)

Only a few years ago, I myself was not quite free from vindictive remarks --- I had "deserted the religion of my fathers," "I was apostate." "I could not be saved," etc. So I pointed out that I could hardly have deserted a faith which had never meant anything to me, but which I openly professed in order to obey my parents and please them. (32)

There are thousands of men -- and women, too I believe -- who are at heart Muslims, but convention, fear and adverse comments, and desire to avoid any worry or change, conspire to keep them from openly admitting the fact. I have taken the step, though I am quite aware that many friends and relatives now look upon me as a lost soul and past praying for. And yet I am just the same in my beliefs as I was twenty years ago; it is the outspoken utterance which has lost me their good opinion.

Having briefly given some of the reasons for adopting the teachings of Islam, and having explained that I consider myself by that very act a far better Christian than I was before, I can only hope that others will follow the example - which I honestly believe is a good one- which will bring happiness to any one looking upon the step as one in advance rather one any way hostile to true Christianity. (33)

Failure of Christianity:

Modern Christianity has failed to keep the churches filled because education and enlightenment have advanced by leaps and bounds during the past century. More inventions useful to mankind have come to the front within that small span of a hundred years than in all the previous ages since the first appearance of man upon the earth. (34)

The time has come for the clergy of all denominations to freely admit the unpleasant fact that half of the foundation of that Christianity, which was set rolling some three or four hundreds of

113

years after Christ, was merely the fabrication of monks and holy fathers who were bidding for the temporal power. (35)

"Believe or be damned" is the slogan of certain Church parties, but not of Christ's teaching. The Crusaders showed the aggressive sword policy and millions of human beings perished through this insane and cruel method of enforcing religious views. (36)

But Christianity further tells me that He (God) had an only Son, and that, being dissatisfied with the doings of human race -- the weaknesses of which H, as the Maker, was fully aware of -- determined to propitiate Himself by killing that only Son, who was also Himself and the Holy Spirit: the ruthlessness of the action being fully in accord with the old heathenish idea of sacrifice to propitiate an angry Deity - all of which is not in accord with ISLAM. (37)

I was brought up as a Christian, and had a Christian training until my early manhood, when, by a diligent study of Biblical critics, I discovered that the story of the alleged fall of man in the Garden of Eden was a myth, and I asked myself this question: "If man did not fall in the Garden of Eden, what need was there for Jesus to come down on earth and die, that by His death H might blot out the sins of humanity?" The result of my inquiry led me to conclude that 'if the first Adam did not fall there was no need for the Atonement by the second Adam, and the whole raison d'etre of the Christian scheme of salvation was gone for ever. I gave up belief in the anthropomorphic conception of God as revealed in the pages of the Bible and ultimately discovered by a study of the evolution of the God idea that all ideas of God were man-made, and that all the 'Gods' were but figments of the imagination. (38)

Anti-Islam Propaganda : -

I feel sure that if the people of England fully grasped what Islam really is, common sense, and the natural desire we all have to use our reasoning faculties as well as our emotions, would do much to remove the misunderstandings which exist. It is, I think, much to the discredit of certain persons that they have wilfully spread abroad incorrect accounts of Muhammad's work and

114

teaching, and have generally misrepresented Islam to Western nations. To show that Islam stands on a firm foundation and is a religion appealing strongly to the intellect as well as to the natural sentiments engrafted in human nature, should now be our closest duty. (39)

No one will deny that a certain class of Christian Missionary has brought discredit on Christianity by persistently vilifying the Muslim Faith and pouring contempt on our Holy Prophet Muhammad, who is constantly misrepresented and alluded to as 'the false prophet'. These ardent but unscrupulous folk do not hesitate to spread false reports, well knowing them to be false, in order to advance their own views. I suppose they are quite well aware that their parrot-like cry about our worshipping Muhammad, having to have four wives, women having no souls and not being allowed inside the Mosque, are all figments of their own brains, and yet they go on in the cheerful belief that the Muslims, being a long-suffering and peaceful lot, will stand any amount of abuse without even a murmur of remonstrance. Possibly they twist the old "saw", "All's fair in love and war," into "Any lies are fair in hate and religion." (40)

Islam:

What we want now is a living religion to comfort the souls of those who might slide from Christianity into idolatry or atheism. Followers of Islam do not attempt to force their opinion on others, and anything like compulsion is entirely forbidden by the Qur'an. The absolute fairness of Islam is what has struck most of the people to whom I have explained various points. It cannot be right to be without any religion - though what are called religious people are often so disagreeable and uncharitable - but do let us choose that faith which is least hampered by improbabilities or absurdities.

The spirit of Islam is exactly the same to-day as it was thirteen hundred years ago; the charity and love inculcated differs not from those sweet attributes as applied by the Holy Prophet when He freely forgave all his deadly enemies. (41)

115

I believe in what religion which is freest from gross improbabilities and, above all, one leading me to absolute belief and trust in the goodness, justice and mercy of God Almighty and one leading me to never-ceasing efforts to be of use to my fellow-creature. This, of course, is Islam. (42)

There is nothing in Islam which is in any way revolting to our reason or our scientific discoveries, and I have been surprised and pleased in recent years to find so many people in all classes in England who have entirely abandoned a belief in any necessity for the dogmas. I have, for example, frequently described our simple Faith, and I have been gratified by the remark: "Why, that is my belief. Is that really Islam? If so, then I must be a Muslim." My reply has been : "You certainly are one, though you may not like to openely avow it just at present, out of fear of adverse criticism." I have then usually repeated the unfavourable Christian animadversions which were passed on me at the time of my conversion to Islam. (43)

In Islam there is complete freedom of the soul. There are no priests, or saints or virgins to invoke. No tolls to pay on the road to Heaven. No need of candles or masses. Each human being has an equal right to the Keys of Heaven, which can be used by any man, woman or child without external aid of any kind from prophet , priest or king, (44)

Islam ; the Religion of the Future :

Islam stands on a solid foundation, and is a religion appealing strongly to the intellect, as well as to the natural sentiments engrafted in human nature, we should, I think, give most careful attention to the very difficult and delicate task of showing that a UNIVERSAL adoption of the Faith by Western nations is POSSIBLE without seriously interfering with the manners and customs of the West or the spirit of the teachings we find in the Qur'an. There is so much adaptability in Islam that we may hope to surmount any difficulties which may arise.

Most of the conditions of life in the East and West are very different, and the habits and customs of thirteen hundred years ago

116

were not the present-day's habits and customs either in the East or West, but the grand and fundamental principles laid down over and over again by the Holy Prophet are as correct and applicable today as they were in his day. (45)

The strongest and most convincing argument we can bring forward to support our claims and win Western sympathy is that no idea of atheism or idolatry can possibly exist in the mind of true believer, and this fact should go far to mark ISLAM as the great Religion of the Future. We observe in Christianity a lack of cohesion and uniformity, but in Islam we find all that should satisfy the created in this desire to be at one with and to return to the Creator, the ever-present and omnipotent Protector of all creatures. (46)

The religion which runs entirely with Christ's teaching is not far from us; it appeals to all, which is nearly always self-interested, and it does not condemn those who think differently to everlasting flames.

This religion is one of pure Faith in God alone and in good works. ISLAM is that religion, and we should all pray that it may soon become the universal and rational religion of the whole world. (47)

The Qur'an abounds in such passages divinely inspired and suited for the guidance of mankind for all time, and it is to be hoped that those who study the Bible will also read the sacred books of Arabia. We want the spirit of Islam in the West. The Holy Prophet was ever chivalrous, fair, and tolerant, and we could not do better than emulate the example He set us. ... with my dear brothers in the Faith I pray most earnestly that the pure and simple faith of Islam may be so presented in all the Western countries, that ultimately the whole world may become Muslims.

We have seen that Christianity - a religion from the East - has in past centuries spread over the Western world, and there appears to be no reason whatever why Islam also a religion from the East, unhampered by dogmas and ceremonials, should not take its place in the countries where there is a tendency to abandon religion

117

altogether, or insulted its intelligence. Islam is not handicapped by priestcraft and heavy calls on the credulity, and it should find favour amongst the learned and scientific as well as with the untutored and simple-minded. (48)

I have always looked upon Islam as fitted for the whole of the human race and for all time, and I have thought that the spirit of the great Faith which we profess with so much delight and happiness soars far above pretty conventionalities. Moses and Jesus were for the Jews, but Islam is for Humanity without any distinction, as to race, or climate, and it this which, in my humble opinion, will make the reasonable teachings of Muhammad prevail in the end.

In all the beautiful religions of the world there are the evidence of that strong desire of the created to return to and be at one with the Creator, and a compassionate regard for the welfare and happiness of others is a characteristic feature of the Buddhist, Christian and Islamic Faiths, and the last named, being the simplest and most free from dogmatic encumbrances, is most likely to be the universal religion of the world. (49)

Imagine for the moment if every one in the British Empire became a true Muhammadan in heart and spirit.

Government would be much easier, because men would be actuated by the true religion, and there would be no Church parties to consider, no dissenters to conciliate, and no heavy bills to pay the tolls on the path to heaven. (50)

What we should aim at is a true representation of the essentials of Islam - belief in the one and only God and beneficence to all our fellow creatures - a following of the Divine precepts as given by the Almighty to the Divinely inspired Prophets down to the Holy Prophet Muhammad who furnished the world with a religion suitable not only to one section of the human race but to the whole of mankind. (51)

REFERENCES AND NOTES
1.   Islamic Review; 14:5, May 1926, page 173
2.   Islamic Review; 23:9, September 1935, page 324

118

3. Islamic Review; 14:5, May 1926, page 173
4. Islamic Review; 14:6, June 1926, page 211
5. Islamic Review; 14:5, May 1926 page 172
6. Islamic Review; 16:11, November 1928, page 388
7. Islamic Review; 16:2, February 1928, page 80
8. Islamic Review; 15:3, March 1927, page 81-82
9. Islamic Review; 15:3, March 1927, page 82
10. Islamic Review; 23:8, August 1935, page 323
11. Islamic Review; 22:4, April 1934, page 118
12. Islamic Review; 14:5, May 1926, page 173
13. Islamic Review; 9:2, February 1921, page 45
14. Islamic Review, 14:5, May 1926, page 172; June-July, 11:6-7 page 206; August 1923: 11:8, pages 269-70; September 1923:11:9, page 301; October 1923;11:10 page 343; November 1923; 11:11, page 388; December 1923; 11:12, pages 443-444
15. Islamic Review; 11:11, November 1923, page 417-18
16. For more details see Islamic Review, 14:5, May 1926, pages 163-172 and 14:6, June 1926, pages 206-213.
17. Islamic Review; 17:7, June 1929; pages 205-207. In this connection a Trust was formed and the Trustees were His Highness the Aga Khan, Sir Abbas Ali Baig, the Hon. Sir Nizamat Jung Bahadur, Khawaja Kamaluddin and Lord Headley being the Chairman of the Trust. The site ultimately chosen by Lord Headley and His Highness the Aga Khan and Sir Abbas Ali Baig was particularly well situated within a few minutes 'walk of West Kensington Station on the District Railway, close to a capital taxi rank and admirably served by the 28 Service of omnibuses. The area of this site was a little under 50,000 square feet. (Islamic Review; 17:9, September 1929, pages 340-41). It was decided that London Nizamiah Mosque was to run on strictly non-sectarian lines, and that the Imams and others would not be members of any special sect. They would be Hanifi. According to the

119

agreement the buildings, and especially the Mosque and Minaret, would be of a handsome and imposing type and the building would be a fitting monument to Islam. (Islamic Review; 18:12; December 1930, page 427). For more details see Islamic Review; 16:4-5; April-May 1928, pages 121-22 and Islamic Review; 16:9; September 1928, pages 326-28.

18. Islamic Review;15:12; December 1927, pages 435-36; March 1928;16:3, pages 82,86 and 88-89, 110,114-116.

19. Islamic Review; 23:9; September 1935, page 325

20. Islamic Review; 23:9; September 1935, page 327

21. Familiar Quotations by J. Bartlett. London, Macmillan Press, 1968. page 872; During the pilgrimage, Lord Headley was accorded as a splendid reception by the Muslims of Egypt, a reception said to be without precedent in the case of an Englishman - drawing there from a happy augury as to the ultimate stultification of the oft-quoted lines of Kipling touching East and West. We like to think those lines to be false; and false, by the mercy of All. (Islamic Review; 11:9, September 1923, page 329-30); Maulvi Bashir Pickard commenting 'East is East' said :
"Kipling's 'never' has oft been refuted :-
    God made the East, God made the West;
    Behold! they blend at His behest.
(Islamic Review; 11:11 November 1923, page 387)

22. Lord Headley's other famous poems are : Muslim Equality (Islamic Review; 2:1; January 1914, page 5); Hymn of Praise (Islamic Review; 2:2; February 1914, page 80); After the Battle of Life (Islamic Review; 2:3; March 1914, page 81); The Sacrificial Vista (Islamic Review; 6:7; July 1918, page 294); In the Name of the Most Merciful Allah (Islamic Review; 8:12; December 1920, pages 428-29) and Prayer (Islamic Review; 9:5; May 1921, page 65.)

23. It is noteworthy that the compiler of Islam; the First and Final Religion (Published by Aisha Bawani Trust, Karachi, 1978, page 106) has written that Lord Headley embraced

Islam on 16th November, 1918. This statement is not correct because it is refuted by a number of Lord Headley's own writings. Same is the case with the book namely, 'Why We Embraced Islam? (Urdu) by Mr. Abdul Ghani Farooq. It seems that the author did not bother to give the reference and thought it sufficient just to copy the information from the previous book. With the result, the authenticity of the book becomes doubtful.

24. Lord Headley: What do We Believe? Islamic Review; 15:3; March 1927, pages 91-92

25. Islam; the First and Final Religion, by Aisha Bawani Trust, Karachi, 1978, page 107.

26. Lord Headley; Presidential Address. Islamic Review 3:1; January 1915, page 9.

27. Lord Headley; Islam and Modern Religious Thought. Islamic Review; 17:6; June 1929, pages 192-93.

28. Lord Headley: The Strength of Islam. Islamic Review: 15:7; July 1927, page 237.

29. Lord Headley: What Is Dogma? Islamic Review: 4:4; April 1916, pages 148-149.

30. Lord Headley: Simplicity of Islam. Islamic Review: 6:6; June 1918, page 241.

31. Lord Headley: What do We Believe? Islamic Review: 15:3; March 1927, page 99.

32. Lord Headley: Islam In the West. Islamic Review: 11:2; February 1923, page 49.

33 Islam : The First And The Final Religion, by Aisha Bawani Trust, Karachi, 1978. page 108.

34. Lord Headley: What Do We Believe? Islamic Review: 15:3; March 1927, page 92-93.

35 Lord Headley: A Conversazione. Islamic Review: 10:1; January 1922; page 13-14.

36. Lord Headley: The Strength of Islam. Islamic Review: 15:7 July 1927, page 235.

37. Lord Headley: What Is Dogma? Islamic Review: 4:4; April 1916, page 147.

38. Lord Headley: What Do We Believe? Islamic Review: 15:3; March 1927, pages 95-96.

39. Lord Headley: Islam In The West. Islamic Review: 11:2; February 1923, page 48.

40. Lord Headley: The Strength of Islam. Islamic Review: 15:-7; July 1927, page 235.

41. Lord Headley: Islam In The West. Islamic Review: 11:2; February 1923, pages 48-49.

42. Lord Headley: What Do We Believe? Islamic Review: 15:3; July 1927, pages 236-237.

43. Lord Headley: The Strength Of Islam. Islamic Review: 15:7; July 1927, pages 236-237.

44. Lord Headley : Islam in The West. Islamic Review: 11:2; February 1923, pages 50-51.

45. Lord Headley: Presidential Address delivered at the meeting of the British Muslim Society. Islamic Review: 3:1; January 1915, pages 10-11.

46. Lord Headley Islam in the West. Islamic Review: 11:2; February 1923, page 51 and Presidential Address. 3:1; January 1915, page 11.

47. Lord Headley: The Simplicity of Faith. Islamic Review: 6:6; June 1918, page 241.

48. Lord Headley: A Few Thoughts on Inspired Writings. Islamic Review : 8:1 January 1920, page 23.

49. Lord Headley: The Strength of Islam. Islamic Review: 15:7; July 1927, pages 237,245.

50. Lord Headley: Presidential Address delivered at the meeting of the British Muslim Society. Islamic Review:3:1 January 1915, page 15.

51. Lord Headley: The Faith and The Fanatic. Islamic Review: 15:9; September 1927, pages 313-14.

Why I embraced Islam!

Sir Jalal ud din Lauder Brunton, Barrister at Law, M.A., M.Sc., F.R.G.S., F.R.S., was a well-known British Baronet who was reared under the influence of Christian parents, at an early age he became interested in Theology and Ethics and followed up Christian teachings very minutely. He was not prepared to accept the commonly understood doctrines as God's Revelation of Himself for Man, and he turned his attention to the Church's teachings only to find all very un-satisfactory[1].

He was not satisfied with the socalled Christian dogmas. He found the creeds of Christianity conflicting. But after a careful study of the Bible, he felt that there was something wanting. Talking about the 'Failure of Christianity', he wrote:

We are to speak of the 'Failure of Christianity', It can be in this sense: that it has failed to become a living principle in the hearts and wills of men; that it has, so far, remained out of touch with the existing aims and emergencies of life : that it has been an ideal -beautiful indeed, but nevertheless impracticable and beyond the reach of mankind. Men, we have been informed, have broken away from the religion: it is no longer a factor in their lives, and its consequences can only anticipate a state of affairs that must go from bad to worse.

It is certainly a failure. Not only has it failed to avert the most appalling calamity which has befallen the world, it has failed to convince man of the need of co-operating with a new to making its avowed objects and principles prevail in the course of human affairs.

If Christianity is to survive --- which is more than doubtful - the Christian religious leaders have shocked the world with the attitude they had assumed as to the significance of that terrible conflict.

Christianity must go the way of all things, and hence-forth perish utterly and for ever to make room for the True religion

---

[1] Islamic Review. Vol. 26., No. 26, July 1938. Page 242.

of God to mankind, and that is ISLAM, which is Truth, Sincerety, Toleration, looking to the interests of man and pointing to the Right Way. Islam alone can satisfy the needs of every member of the human family, and Muslims are the only people among whom can be found the True Bond of Brotherhood in reality and not mere 'make-belief' as in Christianity.[1]

To find and reach the Truth, he devoted himself to the study of Islam. It was Islam which appealed to him. He toured the Sub-Continent, stayed at Ichhra, Lahore now capital of Punjab, Pakistan and held meetings and discussions with the religious scholars. As a result of all this, he entered the fold of Islam. During his stay at Lahore, he entered the "World Brotherhood of Mankind". Talking about his 'Reversion to Islam', Sir Jalal ud din writes :

"This Brotherhood is not merely an ideal; it is an accomplished fact, and I have the honour to testify that I have personally experienced the electric force, as it were on the occasion that I embraced Islam in the Badshahi Mosque in Lahore on the 17th November, 1931, where over sixty thousands of Muslims had assembled to witness the great event, and everyone of these sixty-thousand "Brothers-in-Islam" were anxious to embrace me and welcome me as their Brother"![2]

I am deeply grateful for this opportunity of saying a few words as to why I embraced Islam. I was reared under the influence of Christian parents. At an early age I became interested in theology. I associated myself with the Church of England, and took an interest in Mission work without an actual active part in it. Some years ago, I gave my attention to the doctrine of "Eternal Torment" of all mankind except a few elect. It became so abhorrent to that I almost became a skeptic. I reasoned that a God that would use His power to create

---

[1] Islamic Review. July 1938: Vol 26, no. 7. pages 244,245, 247 and 250.
[2] Islamic Review : May 1936, Vol. 24, No. 5, page 179.

human beings whom he fore knew and predestinated should be Eternally Tormented, could be neither wise just for loving His standard would be lower than that of many men. I continued, however, to believe in the existence of God, but was not willing to accept the commonly understood teachings of God's revelation of Himself to men. I then turned my attention to the investigation of other religions, only to feel myself baffled.

An earnest desire to worship and serve the True God grew in me. The creeds of Christianity claim to be founded on the Bible, but I found these to be conflicting. Is it possible that Bible and the teaching of Jesus Christ had been misrepresented? So I turned my attention again to the Bible and determined to make a careful study, and I felt that there was something wanting.

I determined to strike out for myself ignoring the creeds of men. I began to teach that men possessed a "Soul", and an "Unseen Force" which was immortal, that sins were punished both in this world and in the next, that God in His Goodness and Mercy was ever ready to forgive our sins if we only were truly repentant.

Realising the necessity of living up to the Truth and digging, deep, so that I may find the "pearl of great price," I again devoted my time to the study of Islam. There was something in Islam which appealed to me at this time. In an obscure and almost unknown corner of the village of Ichhra (Lahore) I was devoting my time and service to God's glory amongst the lowest classes of society with the earnest desire to uplift them to the knowledge of the True and only God, and to instil a feeling of brotherhood and cleanliness.

It is not my intention to tell you as of how I laboured amongst these people, nor what were the sacrifices I had undertaken nor the extreme hardships I had undergone. I was simply going on with the singleness of purpose to benefit these classes both physically and morally.

125

I eventually took up the study of the life of Prophet Muhammad. I knew very little of what he did, but I knew and felt that the Christians with one voice condemned the celebrated Prophet of Arabia. I was now determined to look into the matter without the spectacles of bigotry and malice. After a little time I found that it was impossible to doubt the earnestness of his search after Truth and God.

I felt that it was wrong, in the extreme, to condemn this Holy Man after reading his great achievements for humanity. People who were wild idol-worshippers, living in crime, filth and nakedness, he taught them how to dress, filth was replaced by cleanliness, and they acquired personal dignity and self-respect, hospitality became a religious duty, their idols were destroyed and they worship the True and only one God. Islam became the most powerful Total Abstinence Association in the world. And many other good works were accomplished which are too numerous to be mentioned. In the face of all this and his own purity of mind, how sad to think that such a Holy Messenger of God should be run down by the Christians. I became deeply thoughtful, and during my moments of meditation, an Indian gentleman named Mian Amiruddin came on a visit, and strangely enough it was he who fanned the fire of my life into a flame. I pondered over the matter a great deal; brought one arguement after the other bearing upon the Christian's present - day religion and I concluded in favour of Islam felling convinced of its truth, simplicity, toleration, sincerity and brotherhood.

I have now but a little time to live upon this earth and I mean to devote my all to Islam.[1]

Talking about Islam and its importance in the modern world Sir Jalal ud din says :

---

[1] Islam, the First and Final Religion, pages 115-117.

"Islam is a religion of everyday life and is very practicable. This is what a man of understanding requires from the world and this is what the Holy Qur'an offers to the world. Allah is the Fountain of Islam. Islam teaches us to be ever-constant to the All-Prevading Allah. Islam takes its followers higher and higher, day by day, spiritually, socially, and politically. No other religion is so inspiring and at the same time so natural and so simple that a man of small understanding, having faith in God, can attain salvation." [1]

"Islam is a Living Religion, it gives a tone to human character and civilization, just as our scientific research adds to the prosperity and happiness of mankind. There is perfect harmony between a true religion and science; and it must be so, because both are based upon truth. The only difference is that the domain of religion is the moral and spiritual side of human character, while science is the physical and material side.

In Islam alone can one find the Unity of God. Every human being acknowledges the existence of One God, it is only the fool who says that there is no God ---that person is sadly lacking in sense and reason. There are some who lose Him in His attributes. They are not able to get into touch with the All-Mighty Creator." [2]

"Islam has played the most important part in making the world more desirous of worshipping and adoring the One and Only God than in the past, and the Religion of God which was revealed to the Great Prophet of Arabia is undoubtedly destined to make still greater contributions to the progress of humanity. The ideal state of society which is the goal of Islam, has not yet been reached: but as the past shows, it will surely reach through Islam alone".

"The Kingdom of Heaven has come to man in the shape of Islam. Now it is for us to realize it in practice. There is no

---

[1] Islamic Review. May 1936, Vol. 24, No. 5 page 182.
[2] Islamic Review. June 1936, Vol. 24, No. 6. pages 212 & 214.

127

phase of life in which Islam has not given us a lead : there is no situation in the world for which Islam has not made adequate provision. In fact, Islam has come into the world with the words of the Holy Qur'an: "to lead us into light from Darkness".[1] And it has done so in the promotion of knowledge and science, in the cultivation of higher morals, in bringing mankind to the very borders of Divinity, in the reformation and uplift of humanity, in inculcating the spirit of true nationalism and in expounding the creed of a Cosmopolitan Deity, and thus establishing a real Brotherhood of man.

Islam has done all the above and many other unique services to humanity. It has elevated mankind to a nobler, purer, and holier plan of life, made men and women better than they had ever been. Without religion is like being without God! And Islam surely is the only force which can transform the most wicked, for it is the Mighty Voice of God. It is beyond my understanding why men neglect so great salvation as given by God through Islam! To a true Muslim, Islam is his all. His very life depends upon its teachings; with him no progress is possible without religion. Islam stands for progress and civilization. Plain living and high thinking is the motto of every Muslim. Islam, as we have seen, wants us to live with Divine morals. It wants us to subjugate everything in the universe and to use them to our benefit.[2]

Commenting on the relationship between 'Islam and Science', Sir Jalal ud din writes:

"We stand much in need of knowledge and experience for our material progress; we stand in need of knowledge for the uplift of the spiritual life of our nature. We make progress in civilization through our scientific knowledge, i.e., by reading the Will of God in His Book of Nature. Similarly, we soar higher and higher in the regions of morality and spirituality

[1] Quran Surah Al-Ahzab 33: 43. Editor
[2] Islamic Review. July 1936. Vol. 24, No. 7. pages 261-262.

through the knowledge which we acquire from the "World of God'. Through science, we study the character of the Creator from His works, and through religion, we study the character and Will of the Creator from His Word, the Holy Qur'an. Both are seeking after knowledge--- the Will of God manifested in the world. But the channels are difficult, i.e., one reads of the works of the Great Creator, the other of His Word and Commandments, and the ultimate goal is one and the same. Science and religion can be called the 'Twin Sister'. [1]

"Science is the hand-maiden of Islam, and true religion and research go hand in hand; but in former days in Christian lands men who tried to probe the 'Secrets of Nature' were burnt at the Stake, or forced to recant by the Church. We must not forget that Allah, in His Beneficence, created all things necessary for man, but man has to utilize all the faculties with which he is endowed to come into his proper Kingdom. Science points out to us that everything is governed by an Immutable Law; all Nature works in accordance with a grand scheme, and behind this is an 'Intelligence'. [2]

Sir Jalal ud din is of the view that the solution of problems and difficulties of mankind lies in the teachings of Islam and Islam alone. Mankind can achieve happiness and progress through Islam, and to be very frank, Europe today is the greatest hindrance in the way of man's ethical advancement. Addressing the European nations, Sir Jalal ud din says:

"Islam occupies an unique position among the prominent religions of this world. While Christianity and Hinduism deny its continuity, Islam upholds the continuity of Divine Revelation... No wonder the Jews did not accept Christ as their promised Messiah. We acknowledge Christ as a Holy Prophet but not the son of God.

---

[1] Islamic Review. June 1936. Vol. 24, No. 6. page 212.
[2] A few gems of Truth from Islam. Islamic Review. May 1939. Vol. 27, No. 5. page 170.

This is the Age of Skepticism. The conduct of the Europeans and Americans clearly shows that they have very little faith in Christian doctrines." [1]

Humanity needs three things today--- a spiritual interpretation of the universe and spiritual emancipation of the individual, and basic principles of a universal import directing the evolution of human society on a spiritual basis. Modern Europe has, no doubt, built idealistic systems on these lines, but experience shows that truth revealed through reason alone is incapable of bringing that fire of living conviction which personal revelation alone can bring. Believe me, Europe today is the greatest hindrance in the way of man's ethical advancement. It has devastated the peace of the world and deteriorated its ethical mentality for its own interests. It has become, at the present day, the 'Cancer of Human Society'. [2]

"The Day of Islamic Culture is here today renewed and restored and will again lead the nations to harmony and peace. God is the cherisher of the human family, whether on this planet or on another, and it is our duty to bring happiness, peace, unity, civilization and progress to all mankind" [3]

****

---

[1] Islam; The Voice of Allah'. Islamic Review. June 1939. Vol. 24 No. 6. pages 213, 216.
[2] Our Present Situation in the world and Islam. Islamic Review. July 1936. Vol. 24, No. 7. page 260.
[3] A few gems of Truth from Islam. Islamic Review. May 1939. Vol. 27, No. 5. pages 171-72.

How did Dr. Kamal H. Ali embrace Islam ?

We had the good fortune to read an inspiring article entitled 'American Muslims: A growing force' in the Yaqeen International.[1] While going through this article, we came to know about Dr.Kamal H. Ali, Director of Minority Affairs and a lecturer at Westfield State College in Westfield (Mass.) introducing Dr. Ali the magazine wrote:

"Dr. Kamal Ali said that black started to convert to Islam in large numbers in the late 1960s and early 1970s when the expression 'black is beautiful' represented a return to roots. Mr. Ali said the current movement among some blacks to call themselves African-Americans has also renewed interest in Islam. 'There were more African Muslims in the bowels of those slave ships than we have acknowledged', he said.

But having an African background, he added quickly, is not sufficient reason to become a Muslim. "I would not go through all the rigours of the religion just because my great grand-uncle did, said Mr. Ali, who was brought up as a Christian. It is a lot deeper than that it has to do with my relationship with the Creator and my belief system".

Having come to know about Dr. Ali, we wrote a detailed letter along with a 'questionnaire' on 14th October, 1995, and requested him to supply us the answers to our questions. We also congratulated him for the 'sacred service' which Dr. Ali has rendered for the cause of Islam and Muslims. Dr. Ali very kindly sent us the reply. He also supplied us with his 'Curriculum Vitae'.

Dr. Ali was born on September 3, 1943 in Springfield, Mass. of Christian parents. He got his Master of Education (M.Ed.) from University of Massachusetts, in 1977 and Doctor of Education (Ed.D.) from the same University in 1981. He has very long but bright career. He served as Director of Minority and Biligual Vocational Teacher from 1979-1981 and Director of Minority Affairs from 1981 to 1993. Presently he is associate Dean

---

[1] Yaqeen International. 22nd July 1989. page 68.

131

Academic Affairs office of Multicultural Development. He also served as Vice-President and Founding member of Islamic Society of Western Massachusetts, from 1986 to 1990, Member, Board of Directors, Dunbar Community Center, from 1983 to present; Founder Advisor, Westfield State College Urban Education Alumni Association, Springfield, M.A. from 1991 to present; and Member Board of Directors, Islamic Society of W. Mass. from 1993 to present: Member of Muslim Social Scientists, Plainfield, In.; Member Center for Research in Islamic Education, Mecca al Mukarramah, K.S.A. and Member Council of Minority Educators in Mass. He worked as Acting Imam, Masjid al Tauhid, MA from 1976 to 1979 and Editor, Al Jihad al Akbar, Dar ul Islam Community, Brooklyn, NY. from 1971 to 1973. He got a number of awards for his outstanding and marvelous services, for example, President's Distinguished service Award, Westfield State College, May 15, 1991; Career Service Award, Third World Organization, Westfield State College, May 19, 199` and Governor's Pride of performance Award, for the outstanding accomplishments of the Urban Education Programme, Westfield State College, 1984. Dr. Ali is a Sunni Muslim who performed Hajj in 1990/1410 A.H. Regarding Islam, the following are his activities and creative products:

****

In reply to our 'Questionnaire' Dr. Ali wrote:

My Dear Brother in Islam,

It is my sincere hope that this rather brief letter will find you in the very best of health and spirits. And may Allah, Bless you and your family and keep you all well, and may Allah,T'ala, shower you with His infinite mercy and accept your prayers and may He protect us all from the evil of created things.

My Brother Shahid. I was most pleased to hear from you and to learn of your past studies and accomplishments in service to Allah and His ummat. I am currently the Associate Dean of Academic Affairs at Westfield State College, Which is a rather provincial, liberal arts college in the New England Berkshire mountains and,

132

concurrently, I am adjunct professor at Springfield College where I am teaching a course in their newly restructured Humanities department. The course is entitled "Introduction to Islam" and is the very first course offered at the college that deals with the religion of Islam from the perspective of a practicing Muslim with teaching credentials. By Allah's leave, I have had the pleasure of teaching similar courses here at Westfield State, but it is especially gratifying to teach at a host institution in my native Springfield MA. I am grateful to Allah, subhana wata'la, for the unique opportunity to attempt to communicate some fundamental historical and theological issues in Islam to these basically all-white students(there are 20 of them) and, to date, I am rather pleased with the results. Enough of that.

I read your letter with great interest. I had nearly forgotten about that NY TIMES piece, it was written around the same time that the apostate Salman Rushdie published his demonic tome slandering our beloved Prophet Mohammed (PBUH) and, typical of the opportunistic nature of the western press, the TIMES sought out credible Muslims for their "spin" on events and issues in the various Muslim communities around the country. My name was given to them by a long-time brother and friend, Imam Al Amin Latif, from the Dar ul-Islam movement in Brookly, New York (a 1960s and 1970s orthodox Muslim movement of central importance to the expansion of Islam in this country). I was Associate Editor of a magazine the movement put out in the early 1970s called "al Jihad ul-Akbar," which was funded by Rabeta'Alam al Islami, and which stands to this very day as the definitive example of authentic Islamic journalism typical of the times. Perhaps, in future--Allah willing--you and I may have the opportunity to elaborate on this theme, a crucially important one indeed as far as one's gaining an accurate understanding of the development of contemporary Islam in America is concerned. Interestingly enough, I am preparing to take a sabbatical as soon as possible in order to begin to research and write about the Dar ul-Islam movement (from an insider's perspective) and I am in

133

the process of lining up a series of interviews with extant former members of that community. I hope you will pray for me regarding the hoped-for success of this singular venture.

Regarding the questions that you posed in your letter, let me try to respond to them in turn via the following narrative:

I was born on September 3, 1943 in Springfield, Massachusetts of Christian parents. Significantly, my maternal great grandfather is a Moroccan who immigrated to the US in the early 1900s; his religious bent, which was Islam, never figured into the lives of his children who were raised, as were most African-Americans, as Christians. Incidentally, a colleague of mine, Prof. Allan Austin has written the definitive study of narratives of the lives of slaves who came to this country before the American Civil war (1860-65) and it is entitled <u>Antebellum Muslims in America : A Source Book.</u> I recommend it highly to you. To continue, I was educated in Springfield schools, attending Classical High school! then Hunter College and New York University in New York City. Even though I had not completed the Baccalaureate degrees in International and Multicultural Education by 1981. My doctoral dissertation was entitled "Muslim Schools in America : An Analysis of Issues, Problems and Possible Solutions."

I am the father of three children, Hassan, 27, Sana'a, 22 and Ibrahim, 21. All are married, al hamdu lil-lahi. Hassan and his wife are expecting a child (a son, so says the Ultrasound) in February, in Sha'Allah; Sana'a is a first-year law student at the University of Southern California, her husband, an engineer who recently graduated from Harvard, is a computer analyst and a good, struggling Muslim, Ibrahim is a sophomore at my alma mater, the University of Massachusetts and is himself the father of three boys, Saddiq, nineteen months, and twin boys, Sa'id and Na'im, two months. All are in good health and spirits, al hamdu lil'lahi. May Allah Bless them all and have Mercy on them, and may He make Islam most pleasing to them and guide them on the <u>Sirat ul-Mustaqeem.</u> They are third generation Muslims in America; the future of Islam will be in their charge. I am trying to leave large

134

enough footprints to enable them to know that during my lifetime, I was attempting, above all else, to emulate the example of Muhammad Mustapha al-Amin (PBUH), the Prophet of Allah and the leader of a universal brotherhood, and that real success can only come by their continuing the tradition of trodding steadfastly on this self-same path. Again, I pray that this might be my family's (and that of our Muslim brethren everywhere) collective destiny.

I hope this will suffice as a sort of introductory account of how we are faring in the very bowels of one of the most truculent market economy cultures on the face of the earth. There is much more to tell about the burgeoning Muslim communities that are emerging all over America! for example, our own local community, a hodge-podge of Pakistani, Indian, Arab, African-American, African and Euro-Americans has recently completed work on a $1.2 million Islamic Center and we are currently involved in establishing a full-time, alternative school and a plethora of programs for both children and adults aimed at under-girding Islamic teachings and values in the society. No small task; but one that is critical and, in real terms, inevitable. May Allah, T'ala grant us His perfect Guidance and Blessings in this work.

And so, my Brother Shahid, I must close. I apologize for the length of this epistle but I have only scratched the surface of these matters. There is much to be discussed and I look forward to hearing from you at your earliest convenience.

You may reach me by telephone at my place of employment at (413)572-5388 during most days. My home telephone number is (413)783-1590. Also, you may FAX information or materials to me at Kamal Ali, Westfield State College, Fax # (413) 562-3613. Please know that I will be eager to pick up this communication with you, Insha'Allah. I can feel, after reading your letter, your obvious sincerity and tawfiq in dealing with the Religion of Allah and I will always be willing to take the time out of my schedule, as I am doing right now, to speak with you over whatever medium is available.

Until then, be well, my Brother, and be in Peace.

135

The Adhan (call to prayer) as I remember hearing it, I can only describe it as a stunning but beautiful sound that just made me stop dead in my tracks and filled me with something I cannot describe!

This is the 'Journey to Islam' of brother Jamal Ali William. He hails from Canada and was brought up in the Christian faith. In the beginning, he had no idea about Islam. He tried to live like a true Christian but he always found something missing. He read and did a lot of soul-searching in this regard but his quest for Truth was not satisfied. After long years journey, he decided to study Islam. He visited the Mosques in Abadan, Basra, Kuwait and Karachi during his tour abroad. He was over-whelmed by the Adhan (call to prayer) in such a way which cannot be described in words. After consultation and discussion with different persons, he embraced Islam and it was the most important day in his life when he made the " Declaration of Faith".

The attitude of his family after his acceptance of Islam and the suffering and hardships which he faced are heart-rending. We can only share his feelings after going through his 'soul-inspiring' story. So, let us spare some out of our precious time and share the feelings of brother Jamal Ali who needs our solace and guidance. With the courtesy of the Saudi Gazette, we feel grateful in presenting it for our esteemed readers. - Editor 1

"My first encounter with Islam came as I was employed as a seafarer. Shipping took me many places and, of course, the Middle East was no exception. I had no idea what Islam was all about, but just a title bestowed upon people from what part of the World. But right away it did spark my interest. In my own naive way I know that there was something in this to seriously look into. I was brought up in the Christian faith and tried to live like one but there

---

1 Saudi Gazette, 22nd March, 1996, page 7.

136

was always something missing. I didn't exactly shop around for religion, but I did read and done a lot of soul searching and could never come up with a satisfying answer. This went on for years until I finally decided to look into Islam. I realized that there was something in it for me. Many times I wished to go to the mosques but I could never go. Not afraid but reluctant as I didn't know anything about it. My first visit to the mosque was in Abadan. After that in Basra, Kuwait and Karachi. The adhan (call to prayer) as I remember hearing it, I can only describe it as a stunning but beautiful sound that just made me stop dead in my tracks and fill me with something. I cannot describe. Now that I am a Muslim and can understand it, it still has that effect on me. As a matter of fact, when I perform my salah at home I have it on tape and use it.

I came nearer to Islam by association with Muslim brothers in Detroit. However, this was just more or less talking with them. I've used Vancouver as a shipping out post for over 20 years and finally returned to retire out here in 1982. This is when I decided to work in a sincere way to find out the answer to my long quest. I was given a phone number and invited to speak with the Imam in Richmond Masjid a rather busy brother who in turn introduced me to brother Firoze, also a revert but born Muslim. This was about a year ago. It was and still is the most important day of my life, especially making the "declaration of faith". At first it seems to be a struggle learning the basic belief and teachings of Islam. The proper procedures and prayers in Arabic but with a lot of help from various brothers and faith in Allah I have come a long way but still have much to learn.

Suffering and hardships have not been too hard on me. As for friends and relatives? Yes, I have lost a few friends but I have gained more in the universal Islamic Fraternity. My relatives who are few (one sister and two aunts) are rather cool towards me, especially when I changed my name. Infact, they refused to use my Muslim name, but this does not bother me. What does bother me is they have closed mind towards Islam. I still retained my sur

137

name -William - besides my new name Jamal Ali. The reason for the same surname is for business purposes only. However, I have informed those who called me by the former to refer me by the latter, that I wouldn't react otherwise.

The Muslim community have been both very helpful before and after my reversion.

There are a few things that came to mind as regards future ambitions. The first, however, would be to perform the Hajj, Insha Allah. I remain fairly healthy and able to do this. Some of the brothers went just a while back.

My faith is strong. Native Canadians (but of Indian origin), of which I am a half breed, would like to think and ponder over Islamic beliefs and teachings and I shall explain what Islam is all about to them. They are a very spiritual people. When the first Christian came to North America, they forced Christianity upon them and almost stripped them of their peaceful way of life. They even went so far as to forbid them to speak in their own language. And still even today there are Catholic and Anglican Churches on every Indian reservations across North America. But many natives are going back to the "old ways". There are a few West Coast natives here I know and in particular a couple of friends of mine, I speak to them of Islam. One lady lives in the same building I do and she has indicated some interest. She realizes that I am Muslim and the first time mentioned it was or seemed quite surprised. I pray to Allah that they may discover what is so beautiful about Islam.

****

138

Why Dr. H. B. Khalid Sheldrake Adopted Islam?

Muhammad Haneef Shahid

Dr. H.B. Khalid Sheldrake is one of the pioneers who embraced Islam in July 1903. Before we give the details of the circumstances under which Dr. khalid Sheldrake embraced Islam, we would like to say a few words about the pioneers of Islam in England. When we go back into the history of Islam in England, we find the names of Lady Hester Stanphope and lady Ellenborough, both of whom accepted Islam and died as Muslims. (1)

Sir Francis Drake and the late Lord Stanley of Alderley are prominent figures in this respect. Lord Stanley accepted Islam in Constantinople in the year 1875 taking the name of Abdur Rahman and when he died in 1903, was buried with full Muslim rites by the Imam of the Ottoman Embassy in England.

The credit for commencing the introduction of Islam in England upon an organized basis goes to the late Mr. W.H. Quillam of Liverpool, who became a Muslim in 1886, when in Morocco, and started the Liverpool Mosque and Institute and edited two papers, "The Crescent", and "The Islamic World". He died in 1932, and had converted during his period no less than 500 English people to Islam. In London, we must never forget the name of late Sir Abdullah Suhrawardy who founded "The Pan-Islamic Society" in 1905 of which he was the President. He ran a monthly Journal "The Light of the World", issued the Pan-Islamic Series" of pamphlets, and carried on an active propaganda. Among those who joined the fold of Islam at his hands was the late Major-General J.B.Dickson of the British Army. (2)

Dr. Khalid Sheldrake was brought up by his parents in strict conformity to Church of England principles, and for seven years was a chorister. During his boyhood days religion troubled him very little, and his service was rather that of an automation. Later on he came into contact with a new environment, but he felt attracted to one sect. only, and that was the Unitarian Church. He was in favour of the Trintarian Church and thought that

139

Christianity was the only true religion, and that all others were not of Divine origin, and retained bias against other creeds. (3)

What were the circumstances, he forsake Christianity, we come to know through his address which he presented at the White City, London, in which he says:

"At last I decided that the religion I had evolved in my own heart was far from the teachings of the Churches of Christendom. First of all I found that they taught me I was "conceived in sin", thus insulting the ones nearest and dearest to me - my parents. I read that they had committed a sin in bringing me into this world. Then I found that I was born with a sinful nature, that I really could not help sinning, and therefore, to my mind, I should be glorifying as great a sinner as I could, as He had given me sin as a part of creation. I also found that, being sinful, I was already destined for Hell, that if I were not baptized and should die there was no hope for me, even as an infant; my soul would perish. What a constrast to what I later learned of Islam on this point: "All children are born with a disposition to the natural religion, its parents make of it a Christian, a Jew, or a Magian", thus by the saying of the Holy Prophet this pernicious doctrine is given the lie. I also found that God, as represented by different phases of the Bible, was in reality not a kind Creator but an inhuman monster, who wished for the destruction of all humanity in order to gratify the national desires of one petty people. it wished me to believe that God, after creating mankind, found that He had so bungled the work that He wished to destroy all nations but the Jewish. Then I found that although He sent scores of Prophets, mankind were as stiff-necked as ever, and that he made up his mind to utterly condemn all to and Everlasting Hell. I found that whilst Christianity was triumphant, everyone who dared to think for himself was burned alive, or imprisoned and tortured, that the rule of the Church was steeped in Blood. (4)

In fact, Christianity, though we hear that it was persecuted by the Roman Emperors, has never been the religion of toleration. No sooner did Constantine declare his allegiance to it, than we find the

140

Arians, who believed in Jesus as a Prophet, were persecuted with the utmost ferocity by the Trinitarians. Always when in the ascendant Christianity has persecuted anyone who dared to differ from it, and Protestants burnt Catholics as merrily as Catholics performed the same operation upon Protestants in England. Christianity is wrong as it stands by presenting an unknown book as the evidence of the mission of Jesus".(5)

Now we would like to shed some light on the circumstances under which Dr. Khalid Sheldrake came to Islam. He came into contact with the great writer W. Stewart Ross, who so admired that great champion of Islam that he adopted as his pen name 'Saladin'. It was through him that Dr. Khalid began to study Buddhism, but he found it rather a philosophy than a religion. He needed a practical faith, not a faith to dream away one's life, to disassociate oneself from others, but a creed that would be helpful to him each hour in his conduct to others and himself. He studied the other 'systems' (as he uses) as they are styled by many people who have never taken the trouble to try to understand them, and found that the thoughts within himself which have crystallised into a kind of creed met their counter-part in 'ISLAM'. He had noticed the continual attacks made upon Islam by Christian writers, and He used to ask himself these questions: "Why are they so afraid of Islam"?, "What does Islam teach that renders it such a formidable enemy to the Church?" He studied every book which he was able to obtain, but these were only by Christian critics. After studying these books, he came to the truth and realized that he was a Muslim. The first Muslim he ever came into contact with was that noble example of self-abnegation Dr. Abdullah al Mamun Suhrawardy. Dr. Khalid had discussions with him, even inquired very critically the Christian bias, and at last, he had all his doubts removed and declared himself Muslim. (6).

Dr. Khalid was a man of talents, a staunch Muslim and a famous journalist. He served the British Army for a few years. Afterwards he devoted his whole life for propagation of Islam. He worked as Assistant Secretary afterwards Hon: Vice-President of

141

"The Pan-Islamic Society. He was the founder of the "Western Islamic Association" and its Life President. Its branches were spread over Great Britain and over 30,000 Muslims were its members. He was also a member of the "Lafratenite Musulman de Paris" which was also founded by Islamic warrior, Mahmoud Bey Salem in 1907 in Paris. Dr. Khalid worked as Hon. Secretary of "The British Muslim Society" for a number of years. (7)

It is noteworthy that Dr. Khalid presided over the remarkable function of November 29, 1917 held under the auspices of the British Muslim Society when Mr. Muhammad Marmaduke Pickthall openly declared his acceptance of the faith of Islam and delivered an address namely 'Islam and Modernism'. Dr. Khalid congratulated Mr. Pickthall on behalf of the British Muslims, who, he added, looked upon him as a 'Tower of Strength'.

As mentioned earlier Dr. Khalid was a well known journalist. He contributed numerous articles in the Islamic journals, i.e. Islamic Review in particular and other Islamic journals in general. He himself edited a monthly journal which continued for many years. Dr. Khalid toured Far East, Middle East and India for the propagation of Islam. During his stay in India, he had the pleasure of meeting many of our old Muslim warriors, such as Allama Dr.Muhammad Iqbal, Sir Sultan Ahmad, Prof. Abdur Rahman, and Mr. A.H. Khudad Khan who did good services in England. (9)

Now we will give Dr. Khalid's views on Christianity, the religion which he left for good and embraced Islam, the True Religion. Writing on "Christianity or Christ", he says:

"Looking back upon the different religions of the world and their development, it is most interesting to notice how the pure teachings of the Prophets have been corrupted, and the Prophets themselves have been raised to a position of Deity and worshipped as such. In this way Christians, instead of looking up to God and following the teachings of Jesus, began to worship Him as the actual Deity. Most remarkable is it that no record of the teachings of Jesus was written in his day, but by reading the ancient authorities we can trace the dates of the compilation of books on his teachings about 200-400 A.D. The higher critics admit there is a doubt as to the dates and authorship of those books collected into one volume by the Christian Church and called to-day the "New Testament". (10)

In another article entitled "Islam and the Unity of Mankind", Dr. Khalid writes on the same subject as under :

"Ancient Rome and the Grecian Age contributed to the world of religion a vast amount of what to-day is termed-not 'theology' but 'mythology', but it is as well to bear in mind that at the period of these cults in 'theology'. Christianity came into being in the midst of these "gods" and "goodness", who reigned supreme in the minds of the people, and as it was impossible for the Roman mind to conceive the purity of revelation brought by Jesus of the "One God", it is hardly surprising that they paid more attention to the man himself than the Message he brought. (11)

Commenting on the mission and teachings of Jesus, Dr. Khalid in his article "The Message to Mankind", writes:

"In studying the question of the mission of Jesus, we are compelled, if we rely upon the Bible, to come to the following conclusions :-

1. His mission was that of a teacher sent to the Jews alone,
2. That as a Jew he regarded all non-Jews as "dogs", and thus deliberately instructs his disciples to preach only to the Jews.
3. That they were even forbidden to enter the cities of the Samaritans, who worshipped God as the Jews did, but differed in certain details, thus showing that Jesus was an orthodox Jew by faith.
4. That he had no conception of God as the Cherisher of the human family.
5. He realized that, far from uniting even the Jews, he would bring only bloodshed upon earth. (12)

In "Our Duty To-day" writing on the Christendom, he says: "We find that Christendom to-day is divided into two classes - those who believe and those who are indifferent. The believers are in the minority, and are divided between the Catholic Church, the

143

Orthodox Greek Church, and the 490 odd different sects of Protestantism. Of these Churches the Catholic Church has lost but few adherents, the Orthodox Church is mainly the basis of certain nationalities, whilst the different sects of Protestantism are to-day fighting for a bare existence." (13)

Reminding the teachings of the Holy Qur'an to the "People of the Book;" Dr. Khalid says:

"How sublime it is to be thus guided by Allah in the pages of the Holy Qur'an in our dealings with others, how much richer we are than others who possess no guidance. The People of the Book (the Jews and Christians) are called to the imperishable Truth, and if they persist in refusing this great gift then they are indeed the losers, and we must leave them in the hands of Allah. The Holy Qur'an holds out a promise to the Jews and Christians in the following verse : "But if the People of the Book"* , believe and have the fear of God, we will surely put away their sins from them, and will bring them into gardens of delight; and if they observe the Law and the Evangel, and what hath been sent down to them from their Lord, they shall surely have their fill of good things from above them and beneath their feet". (14)

Commenting on the failure of Christianity in providing peace and brotherhood to Europe, Dr. Khalid, in his article 'The Religion of Peace', writes :

Christianity has had nearly 2000 years of trial in which to turn Europe into a 'Paradise' upon earth, to so thoroughly dominate nations and rulers that they must obey its teachings in every hour. Let us not forget that Christianity has been all-powerful; no one dared lift a voice against her, and she ordered things as she chose. Christianity has lamentably failed. She is supposed to posses the hearts of these peoples; nominally, they are followers of the teachings but in reality they follow their own selfish ways". (15)

Christianity teaches us that "There are one and one is three". That if we accept the dogma of a crucified God-man we are

---

* Holy Qur'an : Surah Al-Maidah 5:65-66. Editor.

144

saved". It teaches that the only door to heaven is by believing in this dogma.

Christianity has failed utterly to uplift humanity, to give a logical answer to the great questions of human happiness. Christianity is divided into over 490 sects - a pitiable picture to the observer, a jangling, quarreling crowd of misguided fanatics, who would even now - if they dared - burn men at the stake of opinions. It has been given the chance for 2,000 years to beautify the earth, to civilize mankind, to bring happiness and peace, and it has failed miserably and utterly. Jesus, who was a true Prophet of Allah, foretold this in the parable, and prophesied that the help would come from people whom the priest and Levite, the Jew and the Christian regarded as outside the pale." (16)

In another article namely, "Is Christianity destined to be the Universal Religion?", Dr. Khalid makes the future of Christianity very clear by saying:

"Sometimes we are told that Christianity is destined to become the religion of the world, but its champions always omit to inform us which of the four hundred varities of that system is to be the one universal creed?

Christianity is fast losing its ground. It is scoffed at by many, and the essential doctrines are not now accepted by even those who call themselves Christian.

Dr. Clifford also makes the following admission, which surely must open the eye of professing Christian: "But it is confessed that the Churches of our day are reciting, and in some cases demanding assent to creeds in which nobody really believes". I will make a few quotations from the letter of J.P. Donovan in the Daily Telegraph. Writing on the subject, "Is it a new world"? he says: "There is a consensus of opinion among the most intelligent of the laity that the creeds of the Church are out of date". Again: "It is now generally admitted that Jesus Christ formulated no creeds, prescribed no ritual and formed no ecclesiastical organisation. Why people should be bound by creeds which were drawn up in the fourth century by men who were neither as enlightened nor as divinely inspired as those of the twentieth century is incomprehensible".

The whole structure of Christianity has been erected upon a foundation of sand and has given way. Some persons remain nominal Christian owing to lack of knowledge of other creeds." (17).

Dr. Khalid, before accepting Islam, had a thorough comparative study of religion. Now we would like to give his views on this subject, i.e. Islam versus Christianity. In "Islam and the Occident", he says :

"Let us examine why Englishmen and others become Muslims. First of all, we require a creed that is simple, logical and essentially practical, for we pride ourselves upon being practical people; one suited to the condition, custom, and time of all people; a creed Divine and true, where the Creator and man stand face to face without any intermediary, and one that shall enable us to be at one with each other as brethren throughtout the world.

Let us see if ISLAM fulfills these requirements. The Kalima of Islam is, "There is no deity but God, and Muhammad is His Prophet". Here are two simple truths to which anyone may consent - Unitarian, Theist, or any believer in One God, We ask no blind credence; we have no mysteries such as the trinity of the Christians. We appeal to you, firstly, to seek these things out for yourself, and if you do not see eye to eye with us, unlike Christianity, we do not condemn you, for Islam gives perfect liberty of thought, which you must admit is eminently logical. We deduce arguments for our beliefs, we do not ask you to accept them in a blind manner and condemn you to a hell if you find them too nauseous to digest. Islam is 'quite suitable' to European civilization. Islam teaches man, nobility, makes a better citizens; and owing to its reverence for constituted authority anarchy is unknown to Islam. It teaches respect to all, and dignifies labour by the teachings of our Holy Prophet, who was a worker, and even attended to his own domestic needs - cobbling his own shoes. It mitigates the great curses of the lands where Christianity is

146

impotent. Islam has abolished drink and gambling. Can Christianity claim one victory such as this?

All in Islam are brethren, are equal socially, and this unifies all people who accept Islam, whereas Christianity - so divided itself - still further completes the confusion of the races. A man is Catholic or Protestant before he is Christian. Islam has no invidious colour or class prejudice, but all men-black, yellow, red or white, prince and peasant - meet together as brethren. The Sublime teachings of Islam recognize the truth of all Prophets - Buddha, Krishna, Zaiathustra, Moses, Jesus, and Muhammad, all are messengers of God to mankind - and thus one can be Muslim and yet retain belief in one's own individual prophet. On the other hand, Christianity requires that faith in Prophets other than Biblical must be given up, thus being narrow in its conception of revelation. The broader view of Islam certainly commends itself to the observer as more logical, and a more worthy conception of a merciful and beneficent Creator". (18)

In "Christianity or Christ", he says:

"We Muslims love and revere Jesus as one of our prophets; therefore, why should we quarrel? Are we not bound by this strong link, our mutual belief in Jesus? Look back upon the conditions in Europe under Christianity and the dogmas of the churches to-day then read the saying of Jesus and compare them. Take the doctrine taught by Muhammad, that great Arabian, and examine his teachings side by side with those of Jesus; are they not the same? Was not the message of God given to mankind by both of these teachers? Study Islam and by so doing you will realize that you have slumbered, that it is actions which count and not beliefs, and you will be the better Christian for so doing." (19)

Dr. Khalid delivered a lecture on April 12, 1914 under the title, "The True Catholic Faith", in which he said :

"Islam believes in the ascent of man, to the divine state, Christianity teaches the descent of man... The triumph of Islam is that it makes such an appeal to our reason, our logic, argument succeeding argument in proper sequence. It does not ask us to

147

believe blindly because certain things are mysteries, but asks us first of all to convince our selves that these things are so. Our God is He who reveals Himself to all mankind, He is not a mysterious power whom we must fear and tremble when we see the terrible pictures of punishment prepared to frighten the imaginative and sensitive by Christian orthodoxy. We Muslim believe in one God and we strive for the Unity of Mankind - that true Brotherhood.

The very conception of a ruling Trinity - Three in One - destroys all unity of belief, of thought, of worship - yes, of life itself. What does Islam posses that renders it the only religion which can gather all men to God as workers? If a person becomes Muslim, he becomes at once broadminded; instead of refusing to believe any but his own particular revelation he believes in all God's prophets and in all Divine revelations. Christianity denies any revelation not made to the Jewish race by a Hebrew prophet; not so Islam.

Turn to the Holy Qur'an, still taking Christian testimony: even Sir W. Muir, the greatest opponent of Islam, has to admit that "the Qur'an I hold is that which is translated from the very revelation of God given to us over 1,300 years ago by our Holy Prophet, and has remained unchanged and uncorrupted- this is, indeed, the greatest miracle". (20)

Christianity was the official religion of Europe, not the Christianity of Christ, but the Christianity of the Church, which is a widely different thing. Jesus taught brotherhood and self-sacrifice - the Church teaches discord and pomp. If Jesus were on earth to-day, he would fail to recognize his followers in Christendom, but would find more Christ-like men outside; his own teachings are so corrupted and changed that we would repudiate them. Islam was the creed taught by Jesus and all the prophets and to-day we invite all thinkers to study Islam with an open mind, to argue with Muslims, to read books on Islam, to exercise the same sane judgement in religious matters that they do in business dealings and we do not fear the result. The Prophet of Allah, Muhammad Rasool Allah said, "The best among you is he from whom accrueth

148

most good to humanity," and "No man is a true believer unless he desireth for his brother that which he desireth for himself." Islam is the beacon of progress - it taught the world when the Christian Church dragged it into the darkness of superstition; it gives hope to all men irrespective of colour or race." (21)

Now we would refer to another subject, i.e. Dr. Khalid's message to the West. After Christianity's complete failure, he invites the West to study Islam and its teachings in order to get peace and tranquillity.

In "Islam and the Occident", he says: "Europe and the whole Christianity has had nearly two thousand years in which to convert Europe and to make a perfect civilization, and owing to her own incompleteness has signally failed. Today Christians cling to orthodoxy as mariners in their despair to the drowning craft. The various divisions of Christians are at loggerheads and the unity of Christendom is a chimera. Let all who are really sincere and hope for deliverance study the truth of Islam". (22)

Talking about the Brotherhood of Islam, Dr. Khalid, in one of his articles namely, "Islam - a Perfect Brotherhood", writes: "The Brotherhood of Islam is the common property of the world. A white man is no better for having a pale skin, neither is a black man nobler for the presence of this pigment; a yellow man is just as much a creature of God as any other... A man in Europe is no better for having been born outside Asia, and vice versa, therefore among Muslims there is perfect connexion and freedom whether the man is African, European, Asiatic or Polynesian, whether his skin be fair or tawny. These wretched distinctions of caste, colour, and race have stood in the way of a united world, have hindered the complete understanding of the peoples, and have prevented the realization of the 'Kingdom of God' on earth". (23)

Addressing to the West in 'Islam and the West', Dr. Khalid says: "I appeal to all those who are dabbling in the New Thought, those who have travelled beyond the narrow limits of orthodox in doubt, to study ISLAM without bias, to read and study the whole intelligence. I appeal to Muslims generally to give every attention to the spread of Islam in the West. Remember that our fathers in the Faith carried the Flag of Islam far and wide, enduring great hardship and trial, and if we are to be worthy of them, we must not shirk our responsibilities. The seeds of Islam are being sown, and we confidently leave the harvest in the hands of Allah". (24)

Reminding the Muslims of their duty to preach and propagate Islam, he says: "O Muslims! cannot you understand that it is your duty to spread over the whole earth the knowledge of Islam? The fight in the west is carried on by a handful of pioneers, will you stand aloof? England is no longer Christian, but it is our duty to present to the people the pure teachings revealed through the lips of our Holy Prophet. .. Here is your opportunity; it must be firmly taken hold of, and we can bring to Islam all those who to-day have forsaken Christianity and seek truth. In Islam we have no 'dead dogmas', but vital truths which will bring mankind into the one great Universal Brotherhood. Christianity is dead, and with the help of Allah we will give to the West honest belief and real religion, built not on sand of uncertainty and doubt, but upon the solid rock of Divine Revelation." (25)

Let us remember that the world is not yet Muslim, that we must all do our share to hasten the great day when the 'azan' will ring out from every city in the world with its call to all men to commune with Allah! We must not sit idle, but work for the triumph of truth. There is no need of navies or armies, but the weapon is in our hands always, it is the precious gift of Truth: the Opener of Hearts has vouchsafed us this illumination, our weapon is the Holy Qur'an, the Book of Books, the guide, the blessing, the arguement. With this we can conquer the hearts and minds of men, and make the sun of Islam shine in the darkest depths, uplifting, purifying and uniting mankind. Awake, ye Muslims! Help to convert the West into a 'Dar-ul-Islam' in reality and truth." (26)

Reminding the 'People of the Book' of the clear instructions from Allah, Dr. Khalid calls upon them to study seriously and with an open mind the teachings of the Holy Qur'an by saying: "May I ask all non-Muslims to study seriously and with an open mind the

150

pages of the Holy Qur'an and to dispute with Muslims 'in kindly sort' upon the teachings of Islam. And to all Muslims I say, "Help us in the West, strive for the advancement of Islam as your fathers did, and as the first gleams are piercing the clouds of darkness here, so hasten the day when in all its glory the 'sun or Islam' shall illuminate every country of the world and bring reconciliation, peace, brotherhood and divine harmony to the human family". (27)

"Let all those who to-day are struggling to free themselves from the shackles of false dogma and doubt study the teachings of the Holy Qur'an and investigate fearlessly. The Final Revelation from Allah clears away all the mists of theological mysticism, and gives to the world the healing Message of Brotherhood and Peace, (28) Dr. Khalid is of the opinion that the future religion of the world would be Islam. In one of his articles entitled 'The New Era in the West', he prophesies by saying : "The Holy Qur'an has given us the key to the present situation when it bids us turn our enemy into a friend, and it is thus that we shall triumph. Every person who has the courage to openly admit belief in Islam is influencing enemies from the religious point of view and making them study to that they will awake, and one day "Islam will be the religion of the whole world". The New Era in· the West is beginning, and we must all do our share of the work. Remember that it means making enmity to cease, to drive away discord and bring peace, to give to mankind the real spirit or brotherhood springing from the awakening of the heart and intelligence by the Message of Allah".(29)

References :

----

1. The Pioneers of Islam in England, France, Germany & America (by Dr. Khalid Sheldrake, written in the mid of 1930) Yaqeen International. May 22, 1985. p. 23
2. -ibid-

151

3. Why I adopted Islam? (Dr. Khalid Sheldrake). Islamic Review. September 1914. Vol 2, no. 8. p.373
4. - ibid - p. 374
5. - ibid - p. 375
6. Yaqeen International. May 22, 1985. p. 23
7. The Religion of Peace (by Dr. Khalid Sheldrake) Islamic Review. January 1915. Vol 3. No. 1. p. 26
8. Islamic Review. January 1918. vol 6. no. 1. p. 4
9. Yaqeen International. May 22, 1985. p. 23
10. Christianity or Christ. (by Dr. Khalid Sheldrake). Islamic Review. April 1914. Vol 2, no 4. p. 147
11. Islam and the unity of Mankind (by Dr. Khalid Sheldrake) Islmaic Review. October 1921. Vol 9, No. 10. p 373
12. Message to Mankind (by Dr. Khalid Sheldrake) Islamic Review. January 1921. Vol 9, No. 1. p. 22.
13. Our Duty Today (by Dr. Khalid Sheldrake). Islamic Review February 1921. Vol. 9, No. 2. p. 72.
14. People of the Book (by Dr. Khalid Sheldrake). Islamic Review July 1921. Vol. 1921. Vol. 9, No. 7, p. 255.
15. The Religion of Peace (by Dr. Khalid Sheldrake) Islamic Review. January 1915. Vol. 3, No. 1. p. 26.
16. The Good Samaritan (by Dr. Khalid Sheldrake) Islamic Review. July 1917, Vol 5, No. 7. p. 274-75.
17. Is Christianity Destined to be the Universal Religion (by Dr. Khalid Sheldrake) Islamic Review. December 1920. Vol 8, No. 12, p. 446-48
18. Islam and the Occident (by Dr. Khalid Sheldrake) Islamic Review. Vol 2, No. 2, p. 66-67.
19. Christianity or Christ (by Dr. Khalid Sheldrake) Islamic Review. April 1914, vol. 2 No. 4 , p. 149
20. The True Catholic Faith (by Dr. Khalid Sheldrake) Islamic Review. June 1914. Vol. 2, No. 5. p 240-241
21. The Good Samaritan (by Dr. Khalid Sheldrake) Islamic Review. July 1917. Vol. 5, No. 7, p. 276.

22. Islam and the Occident. (by Dr. Khalid Sheldrake) Islamic Review. Vol. 2 No. 2 p. 66.
23. Islam : A Perfect Brotherhood (by Dr. Khalid Sheldrake) Islamic Review. November 1914. Vol. 2, No. 10 p. 489-90
24. Islam and the West. (by Dr. Khalid Sheldrake) Islamic Review. August+ September 1920. Vol 8, No. 8+9. p. 308-309
25. Is Christianity destined to be the Universal Religion? (by Dr. Khalid Sheldrake) Islamic Review. December 1920. Vol. 8, No. 12. P. 449.
26. Our Duty Today. (by Dr. Khalid Sheldrake) Islamic Review. February 1921. Vol. 9, No. 2. p 74.
27. People of the Book. (by Dr. Khalid Sheldrake) Islamic Review. July 1921. Vol. 9, No 7, p 255.
28. The New Era in the West. (by Dr. Khalid Sheldrake) Islamic Review. September 1921. Vol. 9, no. 9. p 322.
29. - ibid - pp. 325-326.

The experience of Haj, has helped me to integrate Islam into my heart and my vocabulary. Haj took care of my heart."

Prof. Michael Abdul Majeed Wolfe was fortunate to perform Haj in 1990. While expressing his views about Haj and other rituals of Islam, he said that Hajj took care of his heart. Prof. Michael Abul Majeed is an American Scholar and a prolific writer. He also delivered a lecture namely 'Islam and the West' at the 11th National Heritage and culture Festival sponsored by the National Guard.

Prof. Abdul Majeed is a poet, author and a publisher of modern literature. He hails from the Northern California. He entered the fold of Islam at the age of 40 years in 1986. But, according to him there was no eventful or extra-ordinary happening to convince him to embrace Islam. Moreover, no one persuaded or forced him to accept Islam. On the contrary, he entered the fold of Islam after 20 years of continued study of Islam and deep thinking it over. He came to the 'Religion of Abraham' after traveling in the North and West Africa, after occasionally publishing translations of Arabic fiction, after writing numerous books on poetry, fiction and travel. He has a number of literary and Islamic books to his credit. His literary and Islamic books are available in the King Faisal Foundation Library, Riyadh.

He read the English translation of well-known Muslim scholar Allama Abdullah Yusuf Ali and loved his commentary. He had the chance to study the foot notes on the translation of the Holy Qur'an by Dr. Muhammad Asad, an eminent Australian Muslim scholar, who after embracing Islam, contributed a very valuable Islamic literature which is a great asset for the Muslim Ummah.

154

Brother Furqan Ahmad interviewed Prof. Abdul Majeed which was published in the Riyadh Daily. With the courtesy of the newspaper, we feel obliged to reproduce this interview for our esteemed brothers and sisters and hope that they will find it useful.

It is noteworthy that Allah, the All-Mighty, bestowed His favours and bounties upon Prof. Abdul Majeed and gave him health and strength to perform the fifth pillar of Islam in 1990. - Editor.

An American intellectual and a prolific writer embraced Islam just by meeting the people of the Faith and exchanging views and talking with them on various subjects of Islam.

Prof. Michael Abdul Majeed Wolfe, who recently attended the conference on "Islam and the West", in the sideline of the 11th National heritage and cultural festival sponsored by the National Guard, said, "There was no eventful or extra-ordinary happening to convince me to embrace Islam. The people I met with, convinced me that they follow the right path based on a true religion of Islam which I should accept and practice during the rest of my life".

Talking to Riyadh Daily here recently, the scholar said that no one persuaded him or forced him to accept this religion. It was his own thinking, understanding and knowledge about the religion that he accepted it in real earnestness, he noted.

But, he continued, it took him over 20 years to read study and research about Islam.

This study and research, Prof. Wolfe added, entailed him a lot of traveling to Africa and particularly, North Africa, including Morocco, with the aim of meeting people and talking with them and listening to their lectures and sermons on Islam.

"I liked the people. By this I mean the people who were truthful, kept their promises and sympthathized with others. They were committed Muslims and practiced the religion in real earnestness", Prof. Wolfe, a prominent poet and an author, added.

155

He said his literary and Islamic books are available in the King Faisal Foundation Library in Riyadh. "Probably through these books the sponsor of the National heritage festival invited me to attend the conference. They gave me a chance to speak in one of its sessions. I am very grateful to them", the scholar added.

In reply to a question, he said, he read the English translation of eminent scholar, Abdullah Yusuf Ali and loved his commentary.

But, he added, he appreciated most footnotes on the translation of the Holy Qur'an by Muhammad Asad, an Australian Muslim who made a great contribution to Islamic literature and books. May his soul rest in peace and eternity, the scholar said about late Mohammad Asad.

As Prof. Wolfe did not understand Arabic language very well, he said, he read the translations of many authorities and tried to imbibe the meaning and the message of Holy Qur'an.

This is the book of great guidance to mankind, he noted and said, "I have been learning Arabic language as well in my free time". On the spread of Islam in the West, the scholar said : "In America, mosques are playing an important role in teaching the people about Islam and imparting them Islamic education. Especially, these mosques which have been set up in prisons by the American Muslims, are doing a remarkable service to criminals to change their ways of life and become good citizens".

About 50 percent of those who complete their terms of imprisonment are becoming Muslims in the United States, the scholar noted.

"In my country, the United States, we now have more Muslim citizens than Episcopalians or possibly even Jews. Islam is expanding in the West," he said.

Narrating an account of his life, Prof. Wolfe said: "I am an author and a publisher of modern literature. I live and work and write everyday in Northern California. In 1986 at the age of 40, I embraced Islam after 20 years of thinking it over. I came to Islam after travelling in North and West Africa, after occasionally publishing translations of Arabic, fiction, after writing numerous

156

books of poetry, fiction, and travel." In 1990, the author added, he performed Hajj to Mecca and, as for many other 'new' Muslims, "the experience has helped to integrate Islam into my heart and my vocabulary." "Hajj took care of my heart", he said.

"The book I wrote about my experience helped me to build a working vocabulary as an American Muslim. I arrived at Islam in middle Life. I was not seeking a new culture or a new country. Rather, Islam has helped to renew the taste of life's lost sweetness, and it has driven a deep well into the spiritual reservoir that feeds all the world's faiths," the author observed.

****

157

Why Islam appealed to me?

Muhammad Hanif Shahid

Muhammad Alexander Russell Webb was the 'First Muslim American' Journalist. He also published a book on 'Islam in America, the first book on the subject. We feel much obliged and grateful to the Editorial Board of the 'Minaret' who have started publishing the same book which is out of print and rare. It, will, undoubtedly, help understanding and propagating Islam and Islamic teachings in Europe and America, Insha Allah! It is heartening to note that two installments have appeared in the 'Minaret'.

Muhammad Alexander Russell Webb was born on November 18, 1846, in the city of Hudson, Columbia Country, New York State. He was educated at the public schools of Hudson, and at private schools in the states of Massachusetts ("Home School" of Glendale) and New York (Claverack, near Hudson). At an early age he showed a liking for literature and wrote numerous essays and short stories. Journalism soon became his specific interest.

In 1873, at the age of 27, he bought and managed his own newspaper. At the end of three years he sold it and established successive connections with the staffs of other newspapers, as The St. Joseph Day Gazette, The St. Louis Morning Journal, The Post Dispatch and The Globe-Democrat of St. Louis. He eventually became the night editor of the Missouri Republican. It was while serving in this position that in 1887 President Grover Cleveland appointed him American Counsul at Manilla, Phillippine Islands.

In 1872, being of a rationalistic turn of mind, Muhammad Alexander Russell Webb disclaimed his belief in Christianity and for a time became a spiritual vagabond.

In 1881, in his search for a satisfying faith to replace Christianity, he was let to inquire into the nature of Eastern religions and philosophies. He started first with the study of Buddhism. At the end of a six years' investigations of compatible with his official duties, because of the necessary time and solitude

158

it would afford him, to delve more deeply into these Oriental studies.

At Manilla he came into contact with a number of works by Muslim authors which dealt honestly, comprehensively and interestingly with the subjects of Islam and Islamic Philosophy. These works immediately engaged his most earnest attention. At last, he had found what he wanted.

In 1888, Muhammad Alexander Russell Webb declared Islam to be for him the only acceptable Faith. He expressed his newly formed conviction thus :

"Islam is founded upon that eternal truth which has been handed down to man from age to age by the chosen prophets of God, from Moses to Muhammad. It is the only system known to man which is strictly in harmony with reason and science. it is elevating and refining in its tendencies, and develops the higher, nobler elements of humanity when it is faithfully, wisely and intelligently followed."

While living at Manilla Muhammad Webb met a certain Parsee gentleman from Bombay, India. While discussing with this person the subject which had come to lie closest to his heart, he was promised an introduction by letter to an intelligent and influential Indian Muhammeden, named Budruddin Abdullah Kur of Bombay. This Indian Muhammedan would be pleased to answer for him any unsettled questions which might occupy his mind. The introduction was duly effected and an eventful correspondence between Webb and Kur followed. In turn, Budriddin Abdullah Kur introduced Muhammad Webb by letter to one of his dear , especially devout Muhammedan friend a wealthy Indian, Hajj Abdullah Arab by name, who had established branches of his business at both Jeddah and Madinah, Arabia. Webb and Arab now entered into a long and gratifying correspondence. Hajji Arab was so impressed by Webb's sincerity and interest, that he at once travelled to Manilla to visit him.

Hajji Abdullah Arab in due time was instrumental in introducing Muhammad Webb to many other devout and influential Indian

159

Muhammedans of Calcutta, Bombay, Hyderabad, and Rangoon, Burma. These gentlemen, after most seriously and carefully considering the matter, at last, suggested to Webb that he may return to America, under their joint sponsorship, to serve as a Muhammedan missionary to his own countrymen. Webb was elated by this assignment.

In June, 1892 , Mohammed Webb resigned his consular office and set sail for the United States, via India, where he delivered lectures en route, at Madras, Hyderabad, Deccan, and Bombay. His lectures were three in number, and were entitled "The Better Way," "Islam," and "Philosophic Islam." Incorporated in a small booklet, they were published (1892) at Madras, India, by an Indian Muhammedan Missionary, Maulvi Hassan Ali, who, in an introduction to this booklet, pays his touching tribute to Webb:

"We could not find a better man. He came to the East as the representative of a great nation, but he is now returning home as the representative of a great faith of the Prophet of Islam. He carries with him to the New World the prayers and good wishes of the whole Moslem World.

Mohammed Webb arrived home on February 16, 1893. Inspired by a consuming enthusiasm for his assignment he commenced immediately to organize his propaganda work for Islam. He established himself in an office on upper Broadway (1122), New York, under the designation of the Oriental Publishing Company. Here was born the first issue of "The MoslemWorld" ("Devoted to the Interests of the American Islamic Propaganda"; "To Spread the Light of Islam in America"). It was published on February, May 12, 1893, a monthly paper, tabloid size, sixteen page in length. So far as it has been possible to determine the matter, The Moslem World ran through seven issues, from May, 1893, to November, 1893, after which there is no further evidence of its publication. Coincident with the launching of the Moslem World, Muhammad Webb wrote and published one booklet of 70 pages entitled "Islam in America." "Islam in America" contains eight chapters : I. Why I became a Mussalman; II. An Outline of the

160

Mohammedan Faith; III. The Five Pillars of Practice; IV. Islam in Its Philosophic Aspect; V. Polygamy and the Purdah; VI. Popular Errors Refuted; VII. The Moslem Wars Defensive; VIII. The American Islamic Propaganda." Webb also established an American Moslem headquarters at 458 West 20th Street, New York (described in Volume I, Number 7, of The Moslem World), where public lectures where delivered by him about Islam.

On September 20th and 21st, 1983, at the Chicago World's Fair, Muhammad Alexander Russell Webb appeared on the program of the First World's Congress of Religions, and delivered two lectures - "The Spirit of Islam" and "The Influence of Islam on Social conditions." These lectures are published in the 2nd Volume of the massive two volume work, which contains the entire proceedings of , and which is entitled, "The First World's Parliament of Religions" (1893)

Muhammad Alexander Webb's public efforts on behalf of the cause of his beloved Islam seems to have ended with the year 1893. The reason for their termination is not known. To attribute it to an indifferent public response, or to inadequate or unsustained financial support from India, would be to deal in speculation. In any case, while he did carry on, it was with an unmistakable fervor and persistence which could have been inspired only by a sure conviction.

As a seeming reward for, and an appropriate climax to his tireless endeavors, at the turn of the century, the Sultan of Turkey, Abdul Hamid II, appointed Muhammad Alexander Russell Webb as the Honarary Turkish consul of New York. He complimented Webb upon the plans he had revealed, to build a mosque in America, and to obtain the grounds for a Moslem cemetery.

From 1898 to the time of his demise on Sunday Morning, October, 1st, 1916, Muhammad Alexander Russell Webb resided in the city of Rutherford, New Jersey. He died at 70 years of age, a devout Moslem to the end. his earthly remains, alongside those of his devouted wife, Ella G. Webb, who survived him by four

161

years, rest in an ivy-covered grave on the out-skirts of Rutherford, in the beautiful hillside Cemetery.

It is noteworthy that the father of brother Muhammad Alexander Russell Webb remained editor and proprietor of Hudson Daily Star for about twenty five years and his brother Edward E. Webb, M.D., is a prominent physician in San Francisco. [1]

On September 20, 1893, the first World's Congress of Religions was scheduled to be held but due to certain reasons, it was postponed and took place on the 27th September, 1893 Mr. Emory H. Tunison, Secretary of the New Year Islamic Centre covered the proceedings of the Congress. Nearly four thousand people were present to witness the deliberations of the congress. Talking about Brother Muhammad Alexander Russell Webb, Mr. Emory writes: "He is a dark, sturdy man of medium height, and about forty-seven years old. Dressed in turban and robe, he rises from his seat and confidently talks forward to a conspicuous place on the platform. He is the first American citizen to have embraced the Muhammedan Religion -- correctly known as ISLAM. The programme announces him as Muhammad Alexander Russell Webb; and subject is "The Spirit of Islam".

"I wish I could express to you the gratification I feel at being able to appear you today, and that I could impress upon your minds the feelings of millions of Mussalmans in India, Turkey and Egypt, who are looking to this Parliament of Religions with the deepest, the fondest hope. There is not a Mussalman on earth who does not believe that ultimately 'ISLAM WILL BE THE UNIVERSAL FAITH'.

I am an American of the Americans. I carried with me for years the same errors that thousands of American carry with them today. Those errors have grown into history; false history has influenced your opinion of Islam. It influenced my opinion of Islam and when

---

[1] The Minaret, November 1995, page 30.

162

I began, ten years ago, to study the oriental religions, I threw Islam aside altogether as too corrupt for consideration.

But when I came to go beneath the surface, to know what Islam really is, to know who and what the Prophet of Arabia was, I changed my belief very materially, and I am proud to say that I am now a Mussalman.

I have faith in the American intellect, in the American intelligence, and in the American love of fair play, and will defy any intelligent man to understand Islam and not to love it.

I have read every history of Muhammad and Islam published in English, and I say to you, there is not a single one of them, except the work of Ameer Ali of Calcutta ("The Spirit of Islam" : a standard work even today, 1945), which reflects at all in any sense the Spirit of Islam.

Now, let us see what the word Islam means. It is the most expressive word in existence for a religion. It means simply and literary resignation to the will of God. I means aspiration to God. The Muslim system is designed to cultivate all that is purest and noblest and grandest in the human character. Some people say that Muslim is impossible in a high state of civilization. This is the result of ignorance. Look at Spain in the eighth century, when it was the centre of all that was worth knowing --- languages, arts, all the new discoveries were to be found in Muslim Spain and in Muslim Spain alone. There was no civilization in the world as high as that of Muslim Spain.

When this Spirit of resignation to the will of God is inculcated the idea of individual responsibility, that every man is responsible not to this man, or the other man, but responsible to God for every thought and act of his life. He must pay for every act that he commits; he is rewarded for every thought that he thinks. There is no mediator; there is no priesthood; there is no ministry.

In closing I want to say this : that there is no system that has been so willfully and persistently misrepresented as Islam, both by writers of so-called history and by the newspaper press. There is no character in the whole range of history so little, so imperfectly,

163

understood as Muhammad. I feel that Americans, as a rule, are disposed to go to the bottom facts, and to ascertain really what Muhammad was and what he did, and why they have done so, I feel we shall have a universal system which will elevate our social system where it belongs."[1]

Giving the reasons of entering the fold of Islam, brother Muhammad Alexander Russell Webb writes in his book, namely "Islam in America":

I have been frequently asked why I, an American, born in a country which is nominally Christian, and reared 'under the drippings' of an orthodox Presbyterian pulpit, came to adopt the faith of Islam as my guide in life... I am the only American in this vast and progress country capable of comprehending the system taught by the inspired prophet of Arabs, and of appreciating its beauty and perfection. Nor do I believe that I am so deficient mentally as to accept, as truth, a religion which no one else in this country would be foolish enough to accept. But whether those who do accept it are wise or foolish in the estimation of their fellow men, I feel quite confident that at least a few may be benefited by my experience.

I was not born, as some boys seem to be, with a fervently religious strain in my character. I was emotional in later years, but not mawkisghly sentimental, and always demanded a reason for everything. I attended the Presbyterian Sunday School of my native town-when I could not avoid it and listened with weariness and impatience to the long abstruse discourage of the minister, while longed to get out into the glad sunshine, and hear the more satisfying sermons preached by God Himself, through the murmuring brooks, the gorgeous flowers and joyous birds. I listened incredulously to the story of the Immaculate conceptions, and the dramatic tale of the vicarious atonement failed to arouse in me a thrill of tearful emotion, because I doubted the truth of both dogmas. Of course, the narrow minded church Christian will

---

[1] The Arab World, Vol. 1, No. 3, 1945. pages 14-15.

say at once, that the scriptural bogeyman, Satan, had me in his clutches as soon as I was born.

When I reached the age of twenty, and became, practically, my own master, I was so worried of the restraint and dullness of the church that I wandered away from it, and never returned to it. Fortunately, I was of an inquiring turn of mind, I wanted a reasonable foundation for everything, and I found that neither laymen nor clergy could give me any rational explanation of their faith; that when I asked them about God and the Trinity, and life and death, they told me either that such things were mysteries, or were beyond the comprehension of ordinary mortals.

After trying in vain to find something in the Christian system to satisfy the longings of my soul and meet the demands of reason, I drifted into Materialism; and, for several years, had no religion at all except the golden rule, which I followed about as closely as the average Christian follows it.

About eleven years ago I became interested in the study of the Oriental religions, beginning with Buddhism, as students of the Eastern system usually do, and finding much to interest me in the Theosophical literature, which was not easy to be obtained in this country at that time. So intensely absorbed did I become in my studies and experiments, that I devoted four and five hours a day to them.

I saw Mill and Locke, and Kant and Hegel, and Fichte and Huxley, and many other more or less learned writers, discoursing with a great show of wisdom, concerning protoplasm, and protogyny and monads, and yet not one of them could tell me what the soul was, or what becomes of it after death.

I have spoken thus much of myself in order to show the reader that my adoption of Islam was not the result of misguided sentiment, blind credulity or sudden emotional impulse, but that it followed an earnest, honest, persistent, unprejudiced study and investigation, and an intense desire to know the truth.

After I had fully satisfied myself of the immortality of the soul, and that the conditions of the life beyond the grave were regulated

165

by the thoughts, deeds and acts of the earth life; that man was, in a sense, his own savior and redeemer, and that the intercession of anyone between him and his God could be of no benefit to him, I began to compare the various religions, in order to ascertain which was the best and most efficacious as a means of securing happiness in the next life. To do this it is necessary to apply to each system, not only the tests or reason, but certain truths which I had learned during my long course of study and experiment outside the lines of orthodoxy, and in the fields which priest and preacher usually avoid.

And now let us see what Islam really is, and I think the reader will readily understand why I accepted it". [1]

[1] The Minaret, January 1996, page 30. Written in 1893, the ideas are still relevant and help us understand the apathy among fellow Americans about Islam.

*Lust was not behind my conversion to Islam
M.K. Ghazi

*I have found solace and dignity in Islam !
Hina Ghazi

Brother Muhammad Karim Ghazi, formerly Gian Chand Ghosh was born and brought up in Bangalore, India, in a Hindu family. He graduated from Indian Institute of Management (IIM) and got a degree in Management from Huxley College, London. Presently, he is running a firm which deals with construction equipments. An atheist by birth, Mr. Ghosh felt closer to Islam since his childhood, because he was surrounded by Muslim friends. He had a strong urge and feeling to find the Truth. During his stay in London, he studied Islam and held discussions with a number of scholars. His first marriage took place in 1984, and his spouse was influential business-woman, but it remained un-consumated in the hope that the other partner too would join to adopt the new faith, i.e., Islam. In 1987, Mr. Ghosh accepted Islam and changed his name from Gian Chand Ghosh to Muhammad Abdul Karim but bad luck had fell on him, when Susmitha Ghosh started a vengeful campaign. With the result, he was driven to the court through the Crime Against Women Cell (CAWC) of Delhi police. He was tried for bigamy. His counsel Mr. RK Jain and Meenakshi filed a review petition saying that the court's judgment was violative of article 20(1)21,22, and 25 of the Constitution. It was last May 1995 when the Supreme Court advised the Central Government to formulate a Uniform Civil Code.

A staff writer of Islamic Voice (Bangalore) had an interview with Brother Muhammad Karim Ghazi and

167

his wife Hina Begum at their Delhi residence. With the courtesy of Islamic Voice[1] we reproduce their interview. Editor.

A staff writer of Islamic Voice talked to Muhammad Karim Ghazi and Hina Ghazi Begum at their Delhi residence to inquire about their views on Islam, their conversion, and the Supreme Court judgment. Here is the account of their narration.

Media images could be unreal, often farcical. Last May when the Supreme Court advised the Central Government to formulate a Uniform Civil Code, more concerned amongst us muttered curses over those who desert their religion for no other reason than marriage. The case had revolved round four male converts who had taken new Muslim spouses after joining the fold of Islam. Media had painted them in dark colours dubbing their conversion to be a shield for opportunists providing the easy escape route out of responsible matrimonial life. And for the communalists, the rather "liberal provisions" constituted a constant incentive for conversions. The communal politician had discovered a godsend in the verdict. The intellectual Muslim was simply fearful of the communal fallout. The Media had lapped it all, choosing to keep the entire background of the case concealed from the public knowledge and thus helping the communalists rope the verdict into the service of its partisan electoral strategy.

But tear the veil and there pop out numerous victims of a matrimony gone sour. They found no way but to come out of their ancestral faith to dissolve an estranged marriage and to relive the life. One among such couples is Muhammad Karim Ghazi, formerly Gian Chand Ghosh and his wife Hina Ghazi. Hina was Vanitha Gupta till 1987.

The press and the other media had targeted them as spouse deserters, unscrupulous individuals who feel no qualms in renouncing the faith for the sake of taking a new spouse. Far from being apologetic, Ghazi has sought a revision of the Supreme

---

[1] Islamic Voice. September 1995, page 5.

168

Court judgment asserting that the retrospective application of the law would have grave implications.

Born and brought up in Bangalore, Karim Ghazi is a suave professional running a firm dealing in construction equipments. Engineering (UVCE) in Bangalore in 1976 and later graduated from the Indian Institute of Management (IIM) in the same city. To cap them all he took a management degree from Huxley College, London. An atheist by birth Ghosh had felt culturally closer to Islam amid his Muslim friends in Bangalore since his childhood. The element of scientific enquiry in him kindled an urge to find the truth behind the religion. It was during his studies at London that he studied Islam and interacted with numerous scholars. however conversion came much later at Delhi after his first marriage in 1984 to an influential businesswoman. According to him the marriage remained unconsummated in the hope that the other partner too would join him, to adopt the new faith, Islam. It was in 1987 that Karim embraced Islam. All hell broke loose and Sushmitha Ghosh unleashed a vengeful campaign. He was taken to the Court through the Crime Against Women Cell (CAWC) of the Delhi Police.

"Lust was not behind my conversion to Islam"

I do not hold a brief for other three converts. But for myself it is plain and well known that the first marriage (with Sushmita) had remained unconsummated only because of incompatibility of our religious beliefs. In such a situation no aspersion need be cast on my conversion. I married Hina Begum, her self a convert and deserted wife on an irresponsible Hindu husband, in 1992. Could this be attributed to lust? If at all lust was involved, why should I marry a mother of two children? Moreover the Supreme Court judgment is flawed in directing me to be tried for bigamy, an act which was not an offense when it was done. My Counsel R.K. Jain and Meenakshi Arora had filed a review petition saying that the court's judgment was violative of Article 20 (1), 21,22, and 25 of the Constitution. The religion and nothing else could curb his right.

169

"I have found Dignity for Women in Islam"

I was born in a bania family of Agra. My father was an IAS officer. I studied at a convent school and went upto M.A. degree. We had a lot of Muslim friends. I was first married in 1982 and was deserted by the Hindu husband merely for the crime of bearing him two daughters. Besides I was constantly harassed for dowry. It was not a happy marriage and my parents too were struck with grief. My husband disappeared and his whereabouts could not be known. I was completely broken as there was none to support the family. It is next to impossible to extract maintenance under the Hindu law. We tried to find the whereabouts of my husband but there was no response to notices in newspapers. This led to legal dissolution of my marriage. Meanwhile the Muslim families in our contact helped us tide over the crisis. I was impressed by the way the girls were tended in Muslim families. I embraced Islam in 1987. It was through them that my marriage with Mr. Karim Ghazi was arranged. I have found solace and dignity in Islam. I have a son from Ghazi. He is also looking after my two daughters from the earlier marriage. My family is happy with my current status. My mother-in-law has also embraced Islam.

I have studied Islam and observed Muslims from close quarters. Muslims are lively people and they enjoy at high degree of social communion. We receive threatening calls from fanatic elements but we have the faith that the Almighty Allah is the greatest protector.

****

170

"The Qur'an is the only Divine Scripture that is now available in its original form"!

Just like Dr. Zakir Naik, brother Muhammad Sharif is a well-known Islamic propagator and preacher who hails from Sri Lanka. He was born to a Catholic family, like brother Abu Bakr of Tanzania, his father was a Protestant Priest but his mother a Roman Catholic. His parents wanted him to become a priest and propagate Christianity.

During his study and preaching, he found a number of contradictions in the Bible. In this regard, he made correspondence with the Pope, but to his utter disappointment, he did not get any reply. After six years, he said good-bye to the Roman Catholic belief and joined Protestant Group. He continued to be an active missionary worker and tried to preach Christianity amongst the Arabs after getting job in Dahran, KSA. During his meetings with the Arabs, he came to know that all the Muslims believed in Jesus Christ as a Messenger of Allah, not as a 'Son of God'. Jesus Christ is mentioned in the Holy Qur'an 25 times while Prophet Muhammad(PBUH) is only 4 times. This was an eye-opener for brother Sharif, though he had studied more than 16 religions and theologies of the world. He had also studied the Holy Prophet (PBUH) but from a quite different point of view. During his stay in Majmaa, he happened to meet a Pakistani, who donated him a translation of the Holy Qur'an. When he studied the Holy Qur'an, he found a lot of similarity between the first Surah-Al-Fatiha and the Biblical verses. The more he studied, his questions and queries were answered. He discovered that our Noble Prophet Muhammad (PBUH) did not come with a 'NEW RELIGION', on the contrary, his teachings

171

were a continuation of the Message brought by the earlier Prophets.

Brother Muhammad Sharif declared his 'Shahadah', i.e. reverted to Islam at the Shariah Court in Majmaa on his birthday (Which he thinks is the happiest day of his life) in 1984. He has devoted his life for the propagation and preaching of Islam which he is doing for the last 10 years with the collaboration of Dawah and Irshad Centre and the WAMY, World Assembly of Muslim Youth.

Brother Sharif knows and speaks many languages, i.e., English, Spanish, Portuguese, German, Greek, Hebrew, Urdu, Hindi, Tamil, Sinhalese etc. He is an active Daee and has planned a 100day tour to South America to preach Islam and Islamic teachings among the people of this region. He has performed valuable services of Dawah during the liberation of Kuwait.

Dr. Ahmad Saifuddin interviewed brother Sharif which was published in the Arab News.1 With the courtesy of this esteemed newspaper we reproduce it for the benefit of our Muslim and non-Muslim brothers and sisters. May be some one comes to the Right Path after going through this informative, thought-provoking and soul-inspiring 'Reversion to Islam' story -Editor.

Muhammad Sharif is a well-known Islamic preacher from Sri Lanka. He was born and brought up in a Catholic family. His father was a Protestant priest. His mother, a Roman Catholic, wanted him to become Roman Catholic priest. A Scholar of Christianity, he used to give religious lectures in Colombo before embracing Islam.

While studying and preaching Christianity in his early years, he had found a lot of contradictions in the Bible. He had been writing

---

[1] Arab News, 30th August, 1995, page 12.

172

to the Pope since 1970 to get answers for his doubts but received no reply. After six years, he left Roman Catholic church and joined Protestant group. "Ultimately my aim was to unite the Protestants but I failed. The reason was that each and every faction has got its own Biblical version and claimed to be their holy scripture", he said.

However, he continued to be an active missionary worker. He did not stop his missionary work even after getting a job in Dhahran, Saudi Arabia. He tried to propagate Christianity among the Arabs. "While introducing Jesus Christ to the Muslim Arabs, they told me, 'look, we have already accepted Jesus.' Then I learned that Muslims believed in Jesus as a Messenger of God, not as a son of God. I also understand that Jesus Christ is mentioned in the Qur'an 25 times while Muhammad only four or five times".

This was an eye-opener to Sharif, though he had studied more than 16 religions and theologies in the world. "I thought that Muslims were worshippers of crescent as I found them putting the replica of crescent on the minaret and beginning Ramadan fasting after sighting the new moon. So I believed that my Jesus Christ was much better than the crescent," he told Arab News.

Sharif had earlier studied the Qur'an to find out the 'mistakes and contradictions' in the book and invite Muslims to Christianity. In the meantime he was appointed to a new job in Majmaa, 200 kms from Riyadh city. He took over the job from a Pakistani Muslim Engineer. "The Pakistani invited me for a dinner. In his reading room, I accidentally found an English translation of the Qur'an. When I took the translation and started going through the book, the Pakistani told me : 'You can take it as a gift from me."

Sharif found a lot of similarities between the first chapter of the Qur'an - Al-Fatiha and the Biblical verses. "This encouraged me to read the second chapter in which I found the answers to my questions," he said. Sharif learned from the first two chapters of Qur'an that Prophet Muhammad(PBUH) had not brought any new

173

religion, as his teachings were a continuation of the message brought by Jesus and prophets before him.

Sharif reverted to Islam in 1984. At that time he did not know how to perform the five-time prayers or make ablution. He used to take a bath before each prayer until he learned ablution. He used to perform salah secretly at his office room. "One day a Saudi came to my office while I was praying. He was surprised to see me pray and asked me 'Are you a Muslim?' and told me it was better to pray at the mosque.'

"The imam of the mosque was very happy to know that I had become a Muslim. He announced my conversion. It was a remarkable day in my life," Sharif recalled. He declared the Shahada (There is no God but Allah and Muhammad is the Messenger of Allah) at the Shariah Court in Majmaa on his birthday.

After coming to the fold of Islam, Sharif regretted his past efforts to spread Christianity in different countries. So he intensified his efforts to propagate Islam among expatriates living in residential and industrial areas. He purchased Islamic books in English from North American Trust Publication and the Islamic Foundation in England. Sheikh Ibrahim Al-Turki, director of the Scholarly institute in Majmaa gave him a box full of Islamic books in English. Many people have accepted Islam as a result of his dawah work.

Sharif, who has about 10 years experience in dawah, now carries out his dawah activities in association with the Riyadh-based Dawah and Irshad Center and the World Assembly of Muslim Youth. He has also started a dawah training program.

"There is no specialized people for dawah in Islam. Each and every Muslim is a preacher or should be a preacher of Islam." he said and referred to Prophet Muhammad's (PBUH) directive to Muslim while delivering a speech at his farewell pilgrimage. The Prophet had urged Muslims to convey the message of Islam to those who have not received it. "So if we are Muslims, it is our

174

duty to take this message to others," he added. He is going to write a book on Prophet Muhammad's teachings.

Sharif speaks several languages including Sinhalese, Tamil, Urdu, Hindi, Spanish, Portuguese, German, Greek and Hebrew. "We have not ignored the Latin American countries. There are 150 million people in Brazil alone. Their language is Portuguese. In Argentina and other Latin American countries many people speak Spanish," he said. Sharif has planned a 100-day trip to South America to preach Islam among people of the region.

Sharif succeeded in convincing his parents that Islam is true religion. By the Grace of Allah, his father accepted Islam as his way of life, and thanks to the efforts of his father his mother and two brothers became Muslims.

Sharif says the Roman Catholic Bible has 73 versions while Orthodox Bible has 80 versions. But in the case of Qur'an there is only one version. He says he can prove the Oneness of God (Tawheed) as well as the prophethood of Muhammad (PBUH) on the basis of Christian, Hindu, and Bhuddist scriptures. Prophet Muhammad's name is mentioned in the Old Testament written in Hebrew, he said. "According to my research, Bhudda's teachings were based on Islam," he said. "Christians believe that Jesus is the saviour of the whole mankind. "My question is : who was the saviour of humanity before the arrival of Jesus," he said.

"I have read in the Bible that Jesus Christ had predicted the arrival of a person, who will bring complete knowledge from God, but we were programmed to believe that that person was holy ghost. The holy ghost came but received nothing from him," he said.

Sharif had a chance to discuss Islam with the Western troops participated in the liberation of Kuwait. He convinced them that the scriptures contained a lot of misconceptions including the faith in Trinity.

He urged the followers of all religions to seek the eternal truth. He said the Qur'an is the only divine scripture that is now available in its original form. "The Qur'an presents us complete way of life.

175

Its teachings cover the economic, political and social aspects of life," he said and urged Muslims to work hard to propagate the message of Islam.

****

Islam was and is the True Religion of Allah!

We sent a letter alongwith a 'Questionnaire' to brother Nur-ud-din Abdullah Muhammad, formerly Norman Bryant. He not only replied our letter on 21.2.1996, sent answers to our 'Questionnaire' but also forwarded our questions to other brothers in Islam. For which we are very thankful to him and pray to Al-Mighty Allah to reward him.!

Brother Nur was born on November 30,1969 in a Christian family. After reading Islamic literature, he realized that Christianity was 'false' and that Islam is the 'Haqq' from Allah who blessed him and guided him to the Right Path.

Brother Nur is studying at Masjid at Tawhid, Dallas, Pa, USA but facing some difficulty in getting the following books: Tafsir Ibn Kathir; Tafsir at Tabri, Tafsir Al-Qurtabi, Fath ul Bari, The Sisilah as Sahihah of Albanee, Sharh an Nawawi, Sahih Muslim, Shahih al Jami, etc.

Brother Nur is following the teachings of Islam and Traditions of our Noble Prophet Muhammad (PBUH) very strictly as is clear from the opening paragraph of his letter which he wrote to us. It is an eye-opener for us all! After this brief introduction, we reproduce brother Nur's answers which are :-

Below you will find the answers to the questionnaire you sent and asked if I would be kind enough to assist you by providing information for your book. Just as Brother Jihad (Jeffery Ford) explained we don't take pictures so that too is the only thing. I am unable to provide you with is an autographed photograph of myself. due to my fear of Allah, and my love and obedient observation of the authentic sunnah of the Prophet Muhammad (Salallahualayhe wa salaam) to not participate in any type of image creation or recreations.

I have provided you with the answers to the rest of your request :

1) Please let me know about your date of birth?
November, 30,1969
2) Please shed some light on your educational qualifications ?

177

As far as general education, I have my G.E.D. (General Equivalency Diploma and have not attended college. As for my Islamic education, I study here at Masjid at-Tawhid at the institution here in U.S.A. I have been studying various topics and science in the deen such Sira and Aqida Classes (sub topics such as Tawhid, Shirk, Kufr, Nifaq), Intro. to Tafsir, Intro to Fiqh, Intro. to Hadith Science, Arabic 1 and 2. Classes all taken at Masjid at-Tawhid. And I am continuing at the present as the student of the language.

3) Kindly give some details of your family?

My family consists of my Mother, older brother and younger sister. My parents separated when I was a child. I'm the only Muslim in my immediate family members.

4) Please give me a few details of your previous religion?

I was born into the Christian Faith before Entering the Islamic Faith.

5) Please let me know the reasons of leaving your previous religion?

Allah had blessed me to recognize that Christianity was false and that Islam is the Haqq from Him (S.W.T.)

6) What were the circumstances which led you to embrace Islam?

I came into contact with some Islamic Literature and read them and came to realize and accept that Islam was and is the true religion of Allah Ta' ala. So from then on, Allah has guided me upon the siratul mustaqim. Al-Hamdulillah!

7) What are your views about :

(a) **Islam :** It is the true way of life that Allah has laid out for mankind to live by.

(b) **The Glorious Qur'an :** Are the words of Allah revealed to mankind such as those who believe.

(c) **The Holy Prophet Muhammad (SAW)** : Prophet Muhammad (SAW) is the Arab Prophet whom Allah revealed the Qur'an to, and through him Allah perfected His Deen and

178

favour upon us and chose Islam to be our religion. He is also the Seal of all the Prophets of Allah (AS).

(d) Salat : it is obligatory for the Muslim to perform the five daily salats and we also have the option to perform the nafl salat.

(e) Saum: It is obligatory for the Muslim to observe the fast of Ramadan each year if he/she is able to. We also have the option to observe the nafi fast through the rest of the year.

(f) Hajj.: It is obligatory for the Muslim to make the pilgrimmage to the Ka'ba in Mecca atleast once in once lifetime if he/she is able to afford it. Hajj is a duty and right that the Muslim owes to Allah.

(8) Is Islam going to be the Religion of the Future? Yes!

Also as Brother Jihad Abdullah stated we are in circumstances of financial difficulties and we would ask your aid in furthering our studies and the brothers of our Jamat. We are all students of the Arabic Grammar and could use copies of Ameena Bilal Philips. Easy Grammar and other Grammar material we would like to obtain any of the following if you can help us Insha-Allah, Ibn Kathir, Tafsir, AT-Tabari Tafsir, Al-Qurtubi Tafsir, Fath ul-Bari, the Sisilah As-Sahihah of Albanee, Sharh an -Nawawi 'ala Sahih Muslim Sahih Al-Jami' As-Saghir and other source literature that may be in your ability to aid us in your pursuit of the ilm which is needed here. Insha-Allah you will receive this and other questionnaires for we have sought to do as you asked and passed these around to a few others who are seeking to follow the Haqq.

****

How brother Qasim S. Nohara accepted Islam?

In a meeting brother Tariq Alvi disclosed that brother Qasim S. Nohara who hails from Japan and who is currently their chief entered the fold of Islam a few years ago. Brother Tariq Alvi, on our request, supplied us the postal address of brother Qasim. So, without wasting any time, we sent a letter plus some questions and requested brother Qasim to spare some of his precious time and favour us with the answers. Unluckily, brother Qasim was admitted to the hospital in connection with some kidney problem, the time our letter reached his office. Brother Qasim was operated upon and was advised rest for about two months.

As soon as brother Qasim felt a bit better, he sent us the following reply covering our questions. We are grateful to brother Qasim for this special favour and pray to Allah, Most Gracious, Most Merciful, to grant him complete health and bestow upon him His favours and bounties, Ameen!.

At the outset, please accept my apology not sending the reply so long.

I had small operation for the Kidney stone and due to this I had to slow down all my work during last 2 months.

Here, you have my reply to your questionnaires.

(1) Date of Birth : October 11, 1948

(2) Education Background : Graduated from Rikkyo University (St.Paul Univ.) in Japan in 1971, majored in Economics.

(3) I'm a bachelor. My mother lives in Tokyo. I have two brothers, one of them is living in Los Angeles, the other lives in Tokyo, but not with my mother.

(4) I was Anglican.

(5) Reason of embracing Islam is the conflict idea of Trinity. Knowledge of Arabic.

(6) View of Islam (a) through (f) I cannot figure our the background of your questions. I don't think you expect Clich's explanation, so I refrain from commenting.

180

(7) Future of Islam - Allah only knows. My personal feeling is that unless those non-Mutallim so called Daies shall be wiped out from Japan, It will never spread in Japan.

In the meantime, please let me give some comments on your letter.

1) Dr. Nakata was not Ambassador, he was a researcher at Japanese Embassy.

2) I embraced Islam in 1970. So I'm not categorized in the Lucky Figures you mentioned in your book.

3) I don't know anyone who became Moslem recently.

May Allah guide us all to the Right Path.

****

181

How Rene Guenon; Sheikh Abdul Yahya discovered Islam?

Rene Guenon; Sheikh Abdul Wahid Yahya was a well-known French Scholar, writer, philosopher and mystic. He was born on the 15th November, 1886 to a well off Catholic family of France. His father was an engineer of repute. So, Rene Guenon was born with a silver spoon in his mouth. He got his early education from Blois. From his childhood, he was an extra-ordinary intelligent and made distinction amongst his classmates. He got his Bachelor's degree with distinction and joined the University of Paris where he studied mathematics for about two years.

During his study, he did not restrict his activities to formal education only but started searching for the 'Ultimate Truth', because he was not satisfied with his ancestral religion; Christianity. He did not accept the so called Christian dogmas and rituals. Consequently, he had not only a thorough and deep comparative study of religions, but also he held discussions and had meetings with thinkers and philosophers of fame. Even then, his thrist for Truth was not quenched. Due to this spiritual journey and mental chaos, he left the university even though his education was incomplete. This states of affairs lasted upto 1909. In the meantime, he met two 'Reverts to Islam' who were not only well acquainted with Islam, but also competent in sociology. The first of these two scholars was Sheikh Abdul Haq formerly Schamrino of French origin. He was a scholar of repute and edited a magazine namely 'Al-Tareeq'. The second scholar was Abdul Hadi who hailed from Finland. His Christian name was Iavon Gustav. After his reversion to Islam, he learned Arabic and had full command over it. He used to contribute articles to 'Ansari' magazine which was being published from Egypt.

In 1909, Rene Guenon started a magazine entitled "Al-Maarifat" (Knowledge of God) with the collaboration of these scholars. Discussions, discources and critical articles relating to comparative study of different religions were published in this journal, which covered Hinduism, Judaism, Christianity and Islam.

182

This journal remained active for about four years and ceased publication in 1912, the year in which Rene Guenon entered the fold of Islam. He took the Islamic name Abdul Wahid Yahya. His 'Reversion to Islam' was the result of his own continuous search for Truth coupled with the cooperation and guidance of Sheikh Abdul Haq and Sheikh Abdul Hadi. But, in reality, he was impressed and inspired by Sheikh Abdur Rahman Elish El-Kebir El-Alim El-Malki El-Maghribi and accepted Islam. Sheikh Abdur Rahman was "Grand Mufti" of Malki School of Thought in Egypt, a mystic and competent in Islamic Jurisprudence. As a token of respect, Rene Guenon dedicated his book : "Symbolism of the Cross" to the venerated memory of Sheikh Abdur Rahman who gave him first idea of the book. Abdul Hadi had direct and close relations with Sheikh Abdur Rahman and it was Abdul Hadi who introduced Abdul Wahid (Rene Guenon) to the Sheikh.

Afterwards, a well established publishing House of Paris offered its services to Rene Guenon to visit Cairo, study mysticism, translate the important writings of famous sufis and prepare them for printing.

In February 1930, Rene Guenon went to Cairo and settled there permanently. Before his departure to Cairo, his father, mother and wife died, so left for Cairo with a heavy heart. In 1937, Rene Guenon married Karima Bint Abdur Rahman, which proved a sort of solace and comfort for him. He dedicated the rest of his life for the cause of Islam and Muslims. It is note-worthy that through his writings and personnel contacts a large number of European scholars embraced Islam. Among his disciples who entered the fold of Islam is Sheikh Isa Nuruddin, formerly Frithjof Schuon. (born 1907). He is a well known Professor of philosophy and is regarded an authority on 'comparative study of Religions'. He has written a number of books. The following books have won fame for him: -

Islam and the perennial philosophy; Understanding Islam; Dimensions of Islam; In the Tracks of Buddhism; Spiritual Perspectives of the Self; Genosis; Divine Wisdom; Stations of Wisdom; In the Face of Absolute; Survey of Metaphysics and Esoterism; To have a Center; Christianity : Islam.

Then comes the name of a great mystic Abu Bakr Sirajuddin formerly Martin Lings who has full command over English and Arabic and is considered as 'specialist' on mysticism. He is not only a religious scholar but also a poet and translator of repute. His writings include : Muhammad: his life based on the earliest sources; The Qur'an; Catalogue of an exhibition of Qur'an manuscripts at the British Library; The Qur'anic Art of Calligraphy and Illuminations; What is Sufism? A Sufi Saint of the Twentieth Century; The Secret of Shakespeare. Commenting on the life of Prophet Muhammad, Prof. Hamid Dabashi of Temple University writes :-

"In Reading Lings & Muhammad; we detect an alchemical effect in his narration and composition which so evenly combines scholarly accuracy with poetic passion. Lings is a scholar-poet. His life of the Prophet is a biographical 'qasida; it is a historical ghazal; a spiritual triumph; it is a majestic display of impassioned scholarship". This book was awarded the first prize of $5,000/- by General Muhammad Zia ul Haq, the President of Pakistan at the two-day 8th International Seerat Conference, held in Islamabad... This book was adjudged as the best work in English in the biography of the Prophet Muhammad(PBUH) published in 1983.[1]

Titus Burchhardt is another scholar who embraced Islam after being inspired and impressed by Rene Guenon. He has made a thorough research on Ancient Civilization and written a marvellous book on mysticism. His book on 'Chemistry' is regarded the best one on this subject. He is a multi-linguist and has full power over German, English, French, Swiss, Arabic and Persian Languages. His books include : Marokko; An Introduction to Sufi Doctrine; Sacred Art in East and West; Moorish Culture in Spain; Art of Islam; 'Abd Al-Karim Al-Jili's De l' Homme Universal; extraits du livre al-Insan al Kamil.

---

[1] Hamdard Islamicus. Vol. 7, no. 1. pages 105-106.

In addition to the above-mentioned scholars, there are a lot of other personalities who entered the fold of Islam under the persuasion and guidance of Rene Guenon and are busy in the propagation and preaching of Islam in Europe and America.

Rene Guenon breathed his last on 7th January, 1951 at the age of 65 years. His death was mourned throughout the world. He had devoted his life for the cause of Islam. He wrote countless articles and numerous books. East and West; Reign of Quantity; The Crisis of the Modern World; Symbolism of the Cross and The Multiple States of Being are his best writings.[1] May his soul rest in peace!.

****

---

[1] Translated (from the Urdu book namely 'Why we embraced Islam) revised and adapted by the editor.

How I embraced Islam?

Brother Yusuf Ntsane Motloung entered the fold of Islam in 1989. He, as he says himself, was desperately looking for a source of information through which he could come to know more about Religion in general. Luckily, he found a booklet namely, 'Is the Bible God's World'? through I.P.C.I. Durban.

When at school, he studied Biblical Studies and Religious education but to his disappointment both of them failed to answer his burning questions. he did not ask these questions to his teacher because critical thinking was discouraged and even the textbooks were useless. He was mentally disturbed on the warning of his Minister when he said to him that 'Islam is a polytheistic Religion, they (Muslims) worship the idol called Allah and His Prophet known as Muhammad (PBUH)'.

Brother Yusuf had long correspondence with I.P.C.I. in Durban. Moreover, he received religious guidance from Islamic Da'wah Movement and Da'wah Centres around Durban from 1989 to 1992. We feel pleasure in producing brother Yusuf's 'Reversion to Islam' narration in his own words with the courtesy of Yaqeen International and Al-Jamait, Editor.[1]

I embraced Islam in the year 1989 during autumn season. I came to know about this DEEN through a Booklet from I.P.C.I. which I had picked up from the pile of reading material that was deserted in a dumping area. It looked like somebody had received this booklet (IS THE BIBLE GOD'S WORD) through correspondence with the I.P.C.I office or some other means. The booklet fell into my hands when I was desperately looking for a

---

[1] Yaqeen International, February 22, 1995, page 145.

source of information through which I could come to know more about RELIGION in general.

Among the subjects that I was studying at the school were BIBLICAL STUDIES and RELIGIOUS EDUCATION, both of which failed to answer some of the burning questions that I used to entertain in my mind. I could not think of asking my teachers those questions since critical thinking was openly discouraged by both our teachers and by the textbooks themselves.

Even though most of the pages from the booklet were no more there, I managed to have access to two things; The Durban address of the I.P.C.I. and some loose pieces of information which inspired me to ask for some more. I must point out at this moment that my enthusiasm was made to be even more intense when my Minister happened to see the booklet (pieces) - this was when I was still teaching RELIGIOUS EDUCATION as one of the eight subjects that I was responsible for in a government school - and the (Minister) was very much cross with me for being in possession of something that was a "threat" to the fundamentals beliefs of Christianity.

I ignored his warning that Islam "is a polytheistic religion... they worship the idol of Allah and his prophet known as Muhammad", he said in a convincing manner after his anger had cooled down. I kept on corresponding with the I.P.C.I. office for more booklets; the action of which caused me my two most important positions in our church (Lutheran Church): that of interpreting and Teaching in our Sunday School.

The decision to embrace Islam came after I had been advised by a certain Muslim who happened to give me a lift in his car when I was on a trip to one of our teacher's in-service training sessions in the year 1986. I did not do it immediately since there was no Muslims in our town (Harrismith) to go for further information in connection with being a practical Muslim. I could only entertain the idea of being a Muslim for the whole period of three years (1986-1989). From 1989 to 1992, I was given the necessary Islamic education by the Islamic Dawah Movement through its

187

D'awah Centres around Durban. In the year 1992, I was sent to Ladysmith for a teaching post in the township called EKUVUKENI, I request the duas of my fellow Muslims.

****

I realized that being a preacher is more important than being a doctor. I got more pleasure when I treated patients who were spiritually ill than when I treated those who were physically ill."

This is the viewpoint of brother Dr. Zakir Abdul Kareem Naik, Secretary General of the Bombay based Islamic Research Foundation, India. He received his MBBS degree from the Topiwala National Medical College, Bombay. He is one of the most promising young Islamic scholars and preachers in the Muslim World. He has won name and fame in a very short span of time. He has delivered a number of lectures on different aspects of Islam. Dr. Zakir has command over different religions as he has gone deeply and studied these religions comparatively which include, Islam, Buddhism, Judaism, Hinduism, Sikhims, etc. His lectures supported by quotations (verses) from the Holy Qur'an, Traditions of the Noble Prophet Muhammad (PBUH) and scientific findings have impressed and encouraged many fortunates to enter the fold of Islam.

Dr. Zakir established the Islamic Research Foundation in 1990 to spread the True Message of Islam. He was impressed by the renewed scholar brother Ahmad Deedat who helped remove his misconceptions and mis-understandings about Islam. It was in 1987, that brother Ahmad Deedat went to Bombay and was guest for Dr. Zakir's family. He was lucky enough to meet brother Ahmad Deedat who inspired him and guided him to the Right Path. Nay, in fact, it was not brother Ahmad Deedat but Allah, the All-Mighty, who guided him to the Straight Path:

" For God guides whom He will to a Path that is Straight". (Holy Qur'an, Surah Al-Baqarah 2:213)

189

We can call Dr. Zakir, 'Deedat the Younger' because brother Ahmad Deedat proudly considers him as his successor and is hopeful that Dr. Zakir would bring more credit to Islam.

During the last four years, Dr. Zakir has delivered more than one hundred lectures in different cities of India, USA, UK., France, Germany, South Africa, the United Arab Emirates, etc. On his visit to the Kingdom of Saudi Arabia to perform Umrah Dr. Zakir delivered the following lectures: The Qur'an and Modern Science; Education in Islam and Al-Qur'an: Should it be read with understanding? More than fifty of his lectures are now available on video cassettes. Dr. Zakir's video cassettes are being distributed by the Islamic Research Foundation, which has one of the largest and most broad-based collection of video cassettes on Islam and comparative religions in the world.

It is worth mentioning that an average of one person a week embraces Islam as a result of his da'wah, preaching and propagation. During Dr. Zakir's stay in Saudi Arabia, brother PK Abdul Ghafour, Fozail Aqdas Ghazali and Shahid Ali Khan interviewed him which were published in the Saudi Gazette. With the courtesy of Saudi Gazette,1 we feel much pleasure to present Dr. Zakir's views about Islam, Holy Qur'an, Noble Prophet Muhammad (PBUH) and comparative study of religions - Editor.

Dr. Zakir Naik, who is just 30 years old, is one of the promising young Islamic preachers in the Muslim world. His impressive lectures supported by verses from the Holy Qur'an, sayings of Prophet Muahmmad(PBUH) and scientific findings have encouraged many people to embrace Islam. A young Deedat with

---

[1] Saudi Gazette, 14th January, 17th January and 26th January, 6th May, 1996.

190

a difference, Dr. Zakir has been an inspiration for Muslim youth as he enthused them to be proud of Islam, giving convincing answers to the doubts raised about their religion.

Born in Bombay on Oct. 18, 1965, Dr. Zakir received his MBBS degree from the Topiwala National Medical College in this western Indian business city. He is the Secretary General of the Bombay based Islamic Research Foundation, which was established in 1990 to spread the true message of Islam. Dr. Zakir devotes most of his time to research and dawah activities. "I realized that being a preacher is more important than being a doctor. I got more pleasure when I treated patients who were spiritually ill than when I treated those who were physically ill" he says.

Zakir switched on to dawah being inspired by the well-known Islamic preacher Ahmad Deedat, a successful debater who entered into dialogue with prominent Christian religious leaders like Jimmy Swaggart and tried to remove the misconceptions about Islam. "In 1987" Mr. Deedat came to Bombay. He was the guest of my family. He was the person who inspired me. I would not have been inspired by Deedat. I would have been doing now some operations in Bombay." said Dr. Zakir, who came to the Kingdom to perform Umrah and deliver lectures on various Islamic topics.

Deedat is proud of his successor and hopes that Zakir could bring more credit and acclaim to Islam. "I consider him a committed and exceptional preacher of Islam as well as a dynamic analyst and speaker of international standing for Islam and Muslims. With his strong scientific and logical base associated with keen Islamic and comparative religious studies, he can be a Deedat-Plus," says the South African preacher about Dr. Zakir.

During the last four years, Zakir has delivered more than 100 lectures in various cities in India, the United States, Britain, France, Germany, South Africa, the United Arab Emirates and other countries. More than 50 of his lectures are now available on video cassettes. "There is very good scope for dawah if we do it properly," Zakir says. An average of one person a week embraces

191

Islam as a result of his work. The converts included Hindus, Christians, Bhuddists, Sikhs and Chinese, with the majority being educated people such as engineers and doctors.

Dr. Zakir has been successful in presenting Islam in the right perspective and giving convincing answers to questions like : Is the Qur'an the word of God? Why do Islam allow polygamy? Why does Islam require two women witnesses in the place of one man? Is there any conflict between the Qur'an and modern science? Is religious fundamentalism a stumbling block to the freedom of expression? Islam & secularism: which is more tolerant?

Muslims and non-Muslims alike have been impressed by Zakir's lectures as he presented his ideas and points with the support of proof - verses from the Qur'an, Hadith, Bible, Hindu scriptures, science and press reports. "When I say something I produce the proof. This makes the answer more convincing. When I quote the Bible and Vedas, giving graphic details of the quotation like the number of the page, chapter and verse, even the opponents sound convinced and accept the fact."

Dr. Zakir has been following a different style in dawa. "We in the Islamic Research Foundation ask non-Muslims what do they find wrong with Islam and provide answers to them. First we try to remove the misconceptions before telling the features of Islam. our research found that there is hardly 15 to 20 common questions directed against Islam. If we answer these questions all the misconceptions about Islam can be removed.

Logic, reason and science are the main weapons Zakir used to fight the opponents like Taslima Nasreen, Salman Rushdee and Arun Shurie. "I have taken the help of science to prove that Qur'an is the word of God. I know science is not the ultimate truth. Since non-Muslims and atheists take it as an ultimate truth, I use their yardstick to prove the truthfulness of Islam. People say Islam is outdated. I ask them to point out which teaching of Islam is outdated? Which law of Islam is wrong? You have to prove it scientifically.

192

Dr. Zakir is of the opinion that Muslims who were supposed to be the best nation, became backward because they kept away from Islam. "Unfortunately, Muslims do not read the Qur'an with understanding. Hardly 20 percent of Muslims know Arabic as a language and understand the Qur'an directly. If they cant understand the Qur'an how can they implement its teachings. The first instruction of the Qur'an was: Read. But we Muslims are most illiterate. We should bring our Muslim brethren closer to Islam and the Qur'an. I am sure that they will then outshine in all walks of life." He pointed out that Muslims were in the peak of their glory when the Westerners were lagging behind during the Dark Ages.

Dr. Zakir urges Muslims in India to concentrate their efforts on dawah. "So far we have not faced any trouble from the BJP-SS Government in Maharashtra. We are also in good terms with non-Muslims. Residents of more than 850,000 houses (90 percent of them Hindus) in Bombay watch our cassettes at least for two to three hours daily. "There are about sixty private video channels in Bombay. We supply our cassettes to all the cable operators. Initially, we paid for getting our programs aired. Now the cable operators have started relaying free of charge. Now they are ready to pay us. But we don't want money. We are bargaining to increase the hours of relaying our cassettes."

According to Zakir, the future of Indian Muslims is bright. "As long as we do dawa perfectly, I don't think there will be any trouble. So far the BJP-SS government has not harassed us. We are in their good record. This does not mean we go and butter them. We should stick to dawa and then these politicians will come to our lectures," he said.

Dr. Zakir argues that Islam is more tolerant than secularism. "Islam can very well tolerate secularism, but secularism can never tolerate Islam, " he added. Zakir is hopeful that if the Westerners understood the true teachings of Islam they would be the first to accept Islam, "because it presents the best solutions for their pressing problems."

Dr. Zakir's dialogue with Vedic scholar and editor of Arya Marg Patrika created headlines in Indian papers. Quoting the scriptures, he proved that the Vedas affirmed the oneness of God.

Zakir's video cassettes are being distributed by the Islamic Research Foundation, which has one of the largest and most broad-based collection of video cassettes on Islam and comparative religion in the world. The more than 1,600 titles (more than 1,150 in English, 450 Urdu and a few Arabic and French) are available for free hire. The Video titles including films, interviews, television programs and documentaries. IRF can be contacted on : 56/58 Tandel Street (North), Dongri, Bombay 400-009, Tel # 376-4968, Fax: 91-22-3730689.

A PROMINENT preacher from India told his fellow Muslims that they should not shy away from practising Islamic teachings in their day-to-day life and should not be apologetic towards them.

Dr. Zakir Naik, Secretary-General of the Bombay based Islamic Research Foundation, urged them to acquire in-depth knowledge of Islam and try to gain the wisdom behind each command. This will enable them to remove the misunderstandings about Islamic belief and teachings in non-Muslim minds, he said.

Addressing a jam-packed gathering of different nationals at the Islamic Education Foundation here last evening, Dr. Naik said it is not impossible for Muslim girls to study in the colleges and universities without abandoning their hijab. There are so many Muslim girls in veils studying medicine at the Bombay University and at different colleges of Karnataka and Kerala. "To adhere to the Islamic culture, it is compulsory to educate our children irrespective of their sex," he said.

Dr. Naik was delivering a lecture on "Education in Islam", sponsored by the Saudi Gazette, at the Foundation auditorium here. "Our beginning was from 'Iqra' (read), but, unfortunately, we are the most illiterate community in Indian today. Muslim parents can be the best teachers of their children. It is only possible when they are themselves educated."

Dr. Naik cautioned the Muslims against sending their children to Christian missionary schools where in the name of education innocent minds are being poisoned. If there is no choice, they should provide their children Islamic education alongside the regular school education.

Dr.Naik suggested that the authorities religious schools in India should abandon the centuries old syllabi and include science and modern education which will disclose the wisdom of Islamic teachings to Muslim children and strengthen their faith.

Replying to a question on the proposed uniform civil code in India, Dr. Naik said intellectuals from all religious communities should sit down and discuss the civil codes of all religions, and choose the best one, which is the nearest to human nature, free from personal prejudices and more practical.

ZAKIR Abdul Kareem Naik, a young Indian who is scaling the heights of popularity not as a professional medical doctor, as he is, but as a true Islamic preacher, is now-a-days on a visit to Saudi Arabia to perform Umrah. He delivered lectures on various aspects of Islamic beliefs and teachings before the crowded audiences of different nationalities and religions at different venues in Jeddah.

At a reception in his honour sponsored by Saudi Gazzette at Abdul Raouf Khalil Hall last week, Dr. Zakir emphasised the need to understand the 'Religion in the right perspective', which was also the topic of the day.

The Qur'an ordains to establish a debate with the people of the Book- the Jews and the Christians. Show them that the Muslims worship non but Allah and associate no partners with Him. (Chapter 3. verse 64) And if this formula works use it for Hindus and Buddhists, too.

Islam is the only non-Christian faith which makes it imperative for Muslims to believe in Jesus(pbuh). No Muslim is a Muslim if he does not believe Jesus(pbuh) as the son of Mary and messenger of Allah. A Muslim believes in all the miracles of Jesus. He was a

195

messenger of Allah. His birth was miraculous and he brought dead to life by Allah's permission.

What Muslims do not believe is that Jesus was the son of God. In fact, Jesus himself repeated what Moses had said in the book of Deuteronomy that God is one. Jesus also said in the Gospel of Matthew (Chapter 5, verse 17-20) that he did not come to destroy the laws of the previous prophets but to continue them. By reading the scriptures, Old Testament and the Bible, one will be in a better position to understand the religion in the right perspective.

The concept of God in all the main religions - Judaism, Christianity, Hinduism and Islam - is that God is universal and He is the only one. But if the common Hindus are asked about the God they worship, one Hindu would say he believes in three gods, some say Hundred and others even say that they believe in myriads of gods as they believe in the theory of Pantheism.

The Hindu's holy scriptures - Vedas and Bagwat Geeta - provide the better understanding to those who want to know about Hinduism in the right perspective. In Bagwat Geeta it mentioned in chapter 7 verses 19-21 that all those who worship idols are materialistic people. The most authentic of all the Hindu scriptures are the Vedas. In chapters 3, 32 and 40, verse no. 32, 3 and 8, it says that no one can make the image of God. That God is imageless and bodiless. That God is formless and bodiless. And in chapter 40, verse 9, it says that all those who worship Ahambooti (The natural things like, Earth, Water, and air etc.) they are in darkness, and those who worship man made things like, chair, table and machinery are Sambhootis and are more in darkness. But in the same Veda (Vol 2, Chapter 1, verse 3 - 11) it says God has several human attributes which contradicts with its previous verses. In the Qur'an there are 99 attributes given to God All-Mighty but not a single of them gives human form to Him.

The Qur'an warns the Christians who argue about the Trinity of Jesus Christ (PBUH). It says "O People of the Book! Commit no excesses in your religion. Jesus Christ is the son of Mary who was no more than a messenger of Allah. So believe in Allah and in His

196

messengers. Desist yourself from committing a sin by believing in 'Trinity'. For Allah is One God". (Holy Qur'an; chapter 4, verse 171)

A man of any faith whether a Jew, a Christian or a Hindu, let them prove their claim if their god fits into the four lines definition on Chapter 112 of the Qur'an. "1. Say: He is Allah, the one; 2. Allah, the Eternal Absolute; 3. He begetteth not, Nor He is begotten; 4. And there is none like unto Him."

While arguing with the non-Muslims it is necessary to keep cool and adopt the best possible way to preach Islam. The Qur'an mentions in Surah An-Nahal, "Invite (all) to the Way of Thy Lord with wisdom and beautiful preaching; And argue with them in ways that are best." (chapter 16 verse 125).

All major religions emphasise belief in God. If we ask a Hindu which god he believes in, he will say that he believes in the same God Whom we believe in. The same applies to Christians and Jews. They also believe in the same God Muslims believe in. However, the difference becomes apparent when the followers of other religions, besides Islam, associate so many gods, goddesses or partners with the Creator, a well-known Indian Da'wah worker, Dr. Zakir Abdul Kareem said here at the Jeddah Da'wah Centre on Friday.

Dr. Zakir, who came to the Kingdom to perform the Haj, was invited by the centre to deliver a lecture on "The Concept of God in major religions".

Citing the reference from the Torah, he said that Prophet Moses(pbuh) preached to his people to follow only one God. He told them categorically that their Lord is only One Who is their Creator and Sustainer. "Ye Children of Israel! Your Lord is one Lord."

Addressing the Children of Israel at another place in the Torah, God states: "Thou shall have no other God besides Me," he said.

While referring to the Bible, Dr.Zakir said that Prophet Jesus (Pbuh) informed his followers that he had not come with something new. He (pbuh) said in the Gospel of Matthew :I have

197

not come to destroy the Law; I came to prefect it." Prophet Jesus (pbuh) came to propagate the same neglected and forgotten lesson of worshipping only one Lord Whom Prophet Moses (pbuh) had worshipped and instructed his followers to worship.

Dr. Zakir said that Muslims also believe in Prophet Moses and Jesus (pbuh) and the books which were revealed to them. "A Muslim is not a Muslim if he does not believe Moses and Jesus as Messengers of God, and the Torah and the Bible as the books of God," he said emphatically. However, the difference between Muslims, Jews and Christians is that Muslims do not associate with God anything or anyone while the Jews and Christians do so.

While talking of the Hindu religious Book Bhagwat Geeta, Dr. Zakir said that if Hindus have taken a quality of God (Sifat) and turned that into a "god". But the difference is also that they associated millions of deities with Him which we believe to be an unpardonable sin.

Citing the reference from the Vedas, Dr. Zakir said that it is mentioned that no image of God can be made. He is bodiless and imageless. "If you worship asambhooti (which cannot be personified) you are in darkness. And if you worship sambhooti (created things) you are in more darkness." Now, if Hindus make an image of God, they are themselves deviating from their own religious doctrines.

There are four features of God which clearly identify Him. First, He should be only One; secondly, He should be Absolute; thirdly, He should not beget or be begotten, and finally none should be like Him. The God of Muslims possesses all these features.

Unfortunately, the children of Israel made their God as someone who begets and there are so many persons like him. The same is the case with Hindus. They believe in Rama who had parents and was begotten and also had a wife. His wife was abducted but he could not save her. How can such god/gods save their followers from the wrath of others, asked a dismayed Dr. Zakir.

198

Analyzing the word Jew, Christian, Hindu and Muslim lexically, Dr. Zakir said "Jew" means someone who loves and praises God. In this way he is a Jew because he does so. But, if it is meant someone who believes in Judaism then he is not a Jew. "Christian" means someone who practises the teachings of Prophet Jesus (pbuh). "I also practise Jesus's teachings" Zakir said. "In this way I am also a Christian."

Similarly, the word "Hindu" has a geographical meaning. It means someone who hails from the Indus valley - in the Indian Sub-continent. Since, he hails from that region of the world, he is a Hindu. But, if it means someone who is an idol worshipper and believes in millions of gods and goddess, then absolutely, he is not a Hindu.

Finally, "Muslim" means someone who surrenders himself to the law of Allah and the Constitution He sent down to His Prophet (pbuh) as a guidance for the entire mankind for all the time to come.

Questioned why Allah chose the Arab nation for sending His last messenger for the whole mankind and for all the time, Dr. Zakir said that in those days Jews were the most advanced nation. They used to laugh at and make a fun of Arabs who were illiterate and uncultured. Arabs even used to circumambulate the Holy Ka'aba naked. If the Qur'an can change such an uncivilised nation into the most advanced and cultured nation within a short span of 23 years, why can't it change the situation of the people who live in the Indus Valley or the Amazon jungles or the Nile Valley, he asked.

****

A Voyage to Faith!

The following is Dr. K.S. Zubair's story of his 'Voyage to Faith'. Dr. Zubair was previously a staunch communist worker but after embracing the True Islamic Faith, he has become a strong advocate and propagator of the 'Religion of Allah'. In the beginning he was not interested in Islam, but when he read some Christian missionary books written in the Kerala Language of Malayalam which quoted some verses from the Holy Qur'an, he was impressed to study them. After going through the verses of the Holy Qur'an, he came to the conclusion that the Christian missionary were wrongly quoting the Qur'anic verses to prove certain beliefs such as Trinity, whereas the Holy Qur'an strongly condemned Trinity[1].

Being a Medical Practitioner, Dr. Zubair was greatly impressed by the Qur'anic scientific details, especially embryology in Surah Al-Muminoon which reads :

" Man We did create from a quintessence (of clay); then We placed him as (a drop of) sperm in a place of rest; firmly fixed; then We made the sperm into a clot of congealed blood; then of that clot We made a (foetus) lump; then We made out of that lump bones and clothed the bones with flesh; then We developed out of it another creature. So blessed be Allah, the Best to create! after that, at length ye will die." (Qur'an Surah Al-Muminoon 23:12-15) - Editor.

Dr. Zubair is very much impressed by the scientific facts quoted in the Holy Qur'an and believes that these facts will attract more and more people to Islam.

---

[1] "They disbelieved indeed those that say that Allah is Christ, the son of Mary. Say : Who then hath the least power against Allah, if His Will were to destroy Christ the son of Mary, his mother". (Quran Surah Al-Mai'da : 5: 17; see also Quran Surah Tauba 9:30). - Editor.

He has written a booklet dealing with biology of man and another booklet comprising the modern inventions with dealing with the scientific facts mentioned in the Holy Qur'an.

We feel pleasure in reproducing his 'Voyage to Faith' interviewed by P.K. Abdul Ghafoor with the courtesy of the Islamic Voice1, Bangalore - Editor.

Faith is a great blessing from God. One has to implore the Almighty to take him to the right faith and path, says Dr. K.S. Zubair, a former Communist worker and presently a strong advocate and propagator of Islam. He said negation of faith had nothing to do with education or thought of a person.

Dr. Zubair made the above comments in the light of his own experience. He was not interested in Islam until he read some Christian missionary books written in the Kerala language of Malayalam quoting Qur'anic verses.

"I was wondering why these Qur'anic verses were in Christian books , "Dr. Zubair, a general practitioner at Al-Rayan Polyclinic in Sharafiyyah, Jeddah told Arab News, while explaining his voyage to real Islamic faith. The missionaries were wrongly quoting the Qur'an to prove certain Christian beliefs such as trinity. "They use the Verse N. 171 in Al-Nisaechapter to prove trinity. Actually the verse disproves trinity" he said.

Zubair said he was greatly impressed but the embryology in Al-Mueminoon chapter of the Qur'an. "The stages of embryological development explained in the fifth verse of this chapter is similar to what we have learned at the medical college," said Zubair, who has prepared a book-let on the subject.

Dr. Zubair believes that the scientific facts in the Qur'an could attract a large number of people to Islam, especially the intellectuals. He has written another book-let comparing modern inventions with scientific facts in the Qur'an.

---

[1] Islamic Voice, August 1994. page 18.

The creatures in the universe including human beings are a strong proof for the existence of God, says Zubair. Why are electrons running around nucleus in a hydrogen atom? Instead of joining together and forming neutron, they rotate keeping a certain distance. This means an external force is working here".

"Blood produced in the brain goes to lungs for purification before circulating through the artery. A man produces millions of sperms but only one sperm contacts with ovum, which is quickly covered by a tissue to prevent entry of other sperms. Who is the power behind this? Surely it's God. In the absence of God everything becomes meaningless. According to Dr. Zubair, proving the Qur'an as the word of God is the best way to propagate Islam among non-Muslims.

He said the Qur'an had given strong warning to homosexuals by repeatedly narrating the plight of the people of Prophet Looth (Alaihissala). The land of Looth, now called Dead Sea, was turned upside down as a punishment for practising the most despicable acts including homo-sexuality and oppression.

Geographers and historians say that nothing can live or survive in the Dead Sea. The water is unimaginably bitter and oily, rendering it totally useless. Crops will be destroyed once it comes into contact with this water. Therefore, there are no plants or animals. The area surrounding the Dead Sea is the lowest on the face of the earth, 13,000 feet below sea level.

"Even Hiroshima, which was totally destroyed by an atom bomb, has become a sprawling city. But the land of the people of Looth remains the same even after the passage of 4,000 years. Effects of that punishment exist up to this day as a reminder to man and a sign of Allah's power."

He said AIDS cannot be stopped without ending sexual licentiousness. "Calicut Medical College Professor Jayaram Panikkar has said at a Medical seminar on AIDS that the killing virus is a punishment from God", he pointed out. AIDS would spread quickly in the Third World due to lack of medical facilities.

202

Speaking on the divorce system in Islam. Dr. Zubair said: "Islam discourages divorce by instructing people to do it in three stages.

The wife will stay with the husband during the first two pronouncements of talaq. If pronounced talaq for the third time, the husband should wait until the wife is married to another person. These instructions will certainly prevent a person from divorce unless there is no way to continue marital life with his wife," he said.

Zubair says the destruction of Babri Mosque was one of the factors for his change of mind.

When I understood the truth I prayed God to strengthen faith. If we pray God he'll certainly guide us to the right path. God will not force anybody to accept Islam. He will show you the right path. But if you implore him, please take me to correct faith. He will surely help you," he concluded.

****

203

Islam has become a part of my life!

Dr. Aminah Coxon, formerly Ann Coxon, a British lady, who resides in the 'heart of London' is a Neurologist and she embraced Islam after a deep and thorough study. Her clinic is located at Harley Street, known as 'Medical Road, London. Sister Waheda al Mikdadi, health and Features Editor of Sayidaty (Arabic) magazine, the Arab family magazine) took a detailed interview from Dr. Aminah which appeared in 9th December 1994 issue of the said magazine. We wrote a letter to sister Waheda Mikdadi requesting her to supply us the address of Dr. Aminah. She very kindly provided us the address on 11.1. 1995. After getting the address of Dr. Aminah, we sent her a letter alongwith a 'questionnaire' on 24.1.1995. Dr. Aminah, inspite of her engagements and pre-occupations, replied to our request and disclosed that she was going to perform Hajj. We prayed to Allah, the All-Mighty to bestow His favours on her and give her health and strength to perform the 5th Pillar of Islam. We also prayed to Allah her safe return to her homeland. Consequently, we wrote an other letter to Dr. Aminah on her performing Hajj alongwith some additional questions, regarding prayer, fasting and Hajj.

Dr. Aminah very kindly replied to our letter and sent the answers to our additional questions.

Dr. Aminah spent 2 years of her childhood in Egypt with her father who was working in a Tobacco Factory between 1945 to 1953. She was impressed by the social life, manners and customs of Egypt. She was also affected by the streets, beautiful Mosques and sound of the Azaan in particular. With the result, she was inclined slightly towards Islam.

She came back to England in 1947 and got admission in an elementary school in Reading. Owing to the political and revolutionary situation, her family returned to England in 1953. She worked hard day and night and came out with flying colours in every examination. She got married but her marriage was a failure because her husband was a materialistic person and being a wife and mother of her kids, she did not get any sort of help from

204

him. When their marriage ended in a divorce, Dr. Aminah felt herself free. She happily quotes Imam Al-Ghazali by singing:

"A person cannot discover the world unless and until he discovers himself and his needs".

In 1978, Dr. Aminah specialized in Neurology and started her clinic in London. During the eighties she had the chance of meeting large number of Muslim patients and got acquainted with their habits, life and customs. Moreover, she came to know the attitude of the Muslims in miseries and hardships. At this moment a young girl happened to come to her clinic with ailing mother who belonged to an Arab country. This young girl looked quite well by her appearance. it seemed that she was not suffering from any disease but when Dr. Aminah examined her as a precaution, she found that the girl was suffering from Breast-cancer. When Dr. Aminah told her that she was suffering from breast-cancer, she said, 'Al-Hamdu Lillah'! Praise be to Allah! (the Cherisher and Sustainer of the Worlds). The young girl told Dr. Aminah that it was the will of Allah that she came to her and discovered the 'unseen disease'. Dr. Aminah was wonder-struck because the attitude of the young lady was quite surprising. She neither wept, nor cried or frightened. Dr. Aminah was very much impressed by her attitude and felt a sort of relief.

With the passage of time, Dr. Aminah got acquainted with a large number of Arab Muslims and her relations grew with them.

In 1983, she had the privilege to treat the mother of Sultan Qabus bin Saeed, king o f Oman, who was a patient of sugar diabetes but she did not complain of the disease. She was very beautiful and charming lady. Dr. Aminah had meetings with this family firstly in London, later on in Oman. So she was greatly impressed by their behaviour and for the first time she felt about Islam, and Islam became a source of her spiritual feelings. It is a fact, that she cannot live without spiritual feelings because it is a part of her nature.

The above-mentioned two experiences compelled Dr. Aminah to embrace Islam. With this soul-inspiring introduction, we

205

reproduce hereunder the details of Dr. Aminah's 'Reversion to Islam' along with her views about Islam, the Holy Qur'an, the Noble Prophet Muhammad (PBUH), Prayer, Fasting and Hajj and their importance in our day to day life.

Thank you for your letter of 24.1.1995. I should have acknowledged its arrival but Ramadan came soon after, and I have a hard time in even keeping up with basic work so my less urgent correspondence got indefinitely postponed. I am now, inshallah, hoping to go on Hajj, so I must complete everything!

I was interested in your letter, and your research. I would, of course, be happy to be included in your book. Not because I am a personality, but if reading about me helps anyone to make their own decision about taking the path of Islam, then I would be happy to be used in that way.

I will answer your questions as best as I can.

1) Date of Birth: 11th October 1940.

2) Educational Qualifications: M.B.B.S D.H.M.R.P.: Graduate and postgraduate qualifications in medicine from the British Royal Colleges of Medicine and the University of London. Postgraduate accreditation in Neurology . Psychoanalytic training.

3) Family: My name is Saxon. Coxo was King of England North of Northumbria before the Normas invaded in 1066. This makes me something like the North American Indian as a member of original tribe of Britain. My father was a Director of British American Tobacco, and my mother the daughther of a self made American Millionaire. They were both Catholics, and my brother and I went to Catholic boarding schools. My fathers sister never married, but was an artist of great talent, as were several cousins, and my paternal grandfather. My brother is an eminent financier in the US, who is married with three children. He still follows the family tradition of worshipping God as a Catholic.

4) Previous religion: My life as a Catholic was central to my education. I went to a Catholic school where my great-aunt

206

(my fathers aunt) and several cousins were nuns. I think it was thought possible that I might follow in this family tradition, but obedience was not one of my virtues! I had no doubts about this religion until my mid twenties. I struggled hard, sometimes with some success until I discovered Islam in the early 1980s.

5. Reasons for leaving Christianity:
(The other questions were easy to answer .. these are more difficult)
I had come to question Catholicism over a long time. I wondered if this was a form of rebellion about the demands of the religion, and blamed myself. I felt oppressed by the feeling that my sins had been so bad that they contributed to the brutal execution of Christ on the cross. I did not understand why this had to be celebrated in the form of eating human flesh and drinking human blood, even in a spiritual sense. I thought the concept of the Trinity was confusing, and that God could not be limited to an identity of three parts. Mostly, I had problems in feeling the deep love of Jesus because of my existential sense of guilt. I would have carried on this struggle but for three clear dreams. They were quite unlike ordinary dreams. I can remember every detail of them, and woke knowing that their message was direct. The message was no of my own thoughts and terrified me.

(I am not sure if it is haram to talk about the details of dreams, but have just indicated that they formed a powerfully strong guidance. They told me directly that 1. I did not need a priest to love God 2. that my straight path was Islam. 3. that Eissa (PBUH) and our beloved Prophet (PBUH)were together in heaven in complete harmony, and Eissa had given my care to our Prophet (PBUH).

6. The circumstances that led me to Islam
This question is so difficult to answer. I have always thirsted for truth, and for a way to Allah. I was restless and miserable in my religion, but not looking for another one. In my work I

207

came across Muslims as patients. Some, of course, were flawed humans, but in general I saw a different quality amongst them to my Western friends, even those who were sincerely Christian. I noticed a greater serenity, and acceptance of all happenings, good and bad, as the Will of Allah, for which he must be praised. (In the West we tend to claim credit for the good things, and blame God for the bad things!) This was particularly true of my patients who were suffering significantly in their illnesses. One of these patients was the mother of the ruler of Oman, Sultan Qaboos al Said. Bibi was a shining example of a Muslim woman. I remember her true majesty, which was the infinite respect for all of whatever rank (or lack of it). She gave of her material wealth with overwhelming generosity , but more important she gave of herself, her time and her love, to a degree that not always helped her health. She never complained of her illness which she accepted completely was the will of Allah, even though she had great suffering. When asked by me who supported her to live so powerfully in all her activities, she always said she was nothing without Allah. Her God (unlike mine) was 'al Rahman arraheem', and she radiated her love for him. She told me it was permitted for all who worship God to follow the month of Ramadan, so I started fasting for this month, in addition to following my own religion. The dreams that I had had showed me that Islam was my true path, but it still felt crazy to think of myself as a Muslim so I thought this was the compromise that would satisfy the meaning of the dream. One year, just before Ramadan, a Kuwaiti patient, whose family I knew well, was in London with a family member for treatment. I was visiting them regularly, and they were always happy, teasing, but totally committed to Islam. This family showed me also the strength of a close family, united in adversity. The patient, Yousuf al Zawawi, asked me if he could give me anything to repay my kindness (he teases a lot : he offered me all his sons in marriage, his total wealth etc..) I

208

told him that what I wanted was even more precious than what he had offered, but when he knew what I wanted he would have to refuse because I was not worthy of the gift.. so I couldn't ask him. He persisted and eventually I told him that I wanted him to sponsor me in Islam. He burst into tears of joy and summoned all his family. I took shahada next-day. I had asked him because I suddenly knew that I wanted to follow Ramadan as a Muslim.

7. What are my views about Islam

It is impossible to answer this question. Islam is the path to heaven for fallen man. How can I have a 'view' when my vision is obscured by my own failings. I know that this is the true path, and I pray for guidance.

8 The Holy Qur'an

As a Catholic I studied widely, and passed many exams in Catholic theology. The power of Jesus was obvious from the Gospels, and the Bible had evidence that his life was predestined. I long to meet Him in Heaven: there is a line from the first Chapter of St. John about Jesus 'the light shone in the darkness and the darkness did not understand it'. I started to wonder why my understanding of Jesus was so different to what I was being taught in the Churches. I never at that time read Qur'an. Discovering the Qur'an was a bit like being in a big old house, and going from room to room. The rooms were small and dark but in each room there were little interesting things : never enough to satisfy so I went onto the next room. Suddenly I opened a door and.. eternity .. a vast white light that dazzled me. It is impossible to describe the power of the Holy Qur'an unless you have been deprived of it. This is the direct word of Allah. It is obvious. But I shut my eyes because it is too much for me. I find myself opening my eyes a little bit and daring to take in something of its power. But I am only a beginner, and will never be more than that. I can only ask Allah's mercy and compassion, to allow me to understand

209

according to my limitations. But one drop of its knowledge is worth more than all the other Books.

9 The Holy Prophet Muhammad

I want to know more and more about him. I feel such love for him, for his example, and for the great gift in being chosen to carry the true message of Allah. I feel he is with us, in a practical way, patiently teaching and guiding us to understand the message that was given to him. His life had desperate trials, and the example of so many details of his patience and faith are totally relevant today. I have heard that there is to be a special Institute for the study of the life of the Prophet and I want to join to learn more.

I feel that he would have loved Jesus had they met in human life. They spoke with one voice and shared the same love for Allah. Their love for all people reflects this.

10 Is Islam going to be the religion of the future?

The dominant world religion now is the worship of Shaitan (Satan).We have lost our way in materialism and self indulgence. naked greed and ambition have replaced the old fashioned virtues of love of family and community, mercy, justice etc. Allah can overturn all of this when He wills .. but there will have to be a major confrontation and possibly a major war and loss of life. I think of a time then when it will be obvious to the Jews and the Christians that the Qur'an was the true message of Allah following the earlier revelations, and all will be united. But this cannot be accomplished by man's will. It is enough for each person to try to show through example something of the teaching of our beloved Prophet (PBUH).

I hope all this makes a little sense. I did not want to take up too much room in your book, but would be happy for you to identify me in case anyone reading it would like to talk through their questions. It is somehow easier for a 'convert' to help others on the same path, than someone who has never made that journey.

210

What didn't come in under any of the questions was what it feels like to be a Muslim. Had you asked that question I would simply say 'unbearably happy.

Please let me know if what I have written is clear, and has not offended in any way. I am not a scholar, or anything but a beginner, and my 'view' inevitably still has components of my past which might seem shocking to a traditional Muslim. I cannot repudiate Jesus to become Muslim. He is a great prophet of Islam, and becoming Muslim has enabled me to understand that more.

It was good to receive your letter and to know that you got my confused and badly typed letter safely. I like to type freely, so that at least you know that what I write is not rehearsed or corrected but represents my understanding (and lack of it!) accurately.

I was glad to receive your CV from Who's Who in the World. My own from the same publication is a lot shorter! It is good to have a list of your publication (or some of them). I am already collecting quite a Library, but will try to get hold of some of them or get them from the Central Mosque library. My main problem is that my work takes a lot of my time, I feel it is important to keep in touch with my many Muslim friends, and then there must be time for prayer. Then I have to perform some daily survival chores, and there is too little time for reading. I know that I must learn Arabic and at least to read Koran in Arabic with understanding .. I wish that there were 48 hrs in the day, or that Almighty God would decide that I should stop work..! But the patients are still there for the moment so I have to accept the humbling situation of my illiterate state .. good training !

Some more answers to your questions ..

My experiences of prayer in the two Holy Mosques of Mecca and Medina

First Medina .. just because I started there.

I was told that Medina was beautiful, powerful, words like that, but I was still unprepared for what I experienced. The mosque itself was stunning. The recent extension is flawless in its taste and elegance, and supported, rather than distracted

211

from, prayer. I quickly decided that I wanted to spend as much time as possible in the mosque and developed a routine of 02.30-08.00 : 10.30-14.00 : 15.30-22.00 in the mosque, reading Koran, praying, making zikrs etc. The ladies were allowed into the area close to the Prophet(PBUH) tomb twice a day, and I visited at least once if not twice. In the evening I went across to the graves of the Companions.

I don't usually pray so much, but in Medina, I couldn't stay away. In the mosque you felt so close to Rasoullallah (PBUH). In the area close to him I would cry not knowing why, feeling his love, and understanding. I felt the presence of a tough practical loving person, who saw through all my pretensions and faults, and was completely 'on my team' to change me into the person I should be with Allah's guidance. I know that for some scholars, a personal relationship with Rasoulallah (PBUH) is not considered 'necessary', but for a beginner like me it is essential.

In Medina I had such a strong sense of his life and his work. The trials and difficulties, the people he had changed, all sorts and different kinds of personalities that had dedicated their life to the cause of Allah and Islam through his teaching. But I was unprepared for the sense of his love, here and now, for each one of us. And when I asked for his help (in prayer, to concentrate more, things like that) it was received immediately with a power that was unexpected. That personal relationship is still there, and I feel that I do not want to let him down. I can understand the human dimension of a man chosen by Allah to be the vehicle of His revelations, who gave everything of himself, and inspires others by his example to do the same. I saw how important it is to really understand hadith, and I plan a lot more reading to know more details about the example of the Prophet (PBUH) in our lives.

Leaving Medina was very hard. I wanted to stay forever.

I forgot to comment on the tombs of the Companions. I loved the barren plain desolate silence of the area in the moonlight ,

212

and loved praying there at night. The simplicity is a powerful reminder that they, too, gave everything. I hoped that the y would look in wonder at the millions who have come to Islam through their dedication and thanked them, and Allah, for such blessing.

To Mecca :

We left at 9 am and arrived at 11 pm. It was difficult to get through Tawaaf and Saie by 08 am. I was worried about a friend who was with me who was 76, but he has done several Hajj pilgrimages .. even so he said it was hard. That first night I was mainly concerned with survival. I have never been in a crowd so dense, and by the end of Tawaaf my feet were bruised and bleeding. I thought that the 'prayer' value of being in such a struggling scrum would be negligible, and during Tawaaf itself I felt nothing, although I was concentrating as hard as I could on the powerful mystical message of such an ancient prayer. I just think of the story of Man, his inner jihad, and his thirst to return to Allah. The whole of civilization over all races, all times, is a swirling mass, accelerating in momentum to the vortex of Tawaaf, and the prayers go straight to Allah., I imagine angels doing Tawaaf endlessly above. but it was difficult to be completely aware of this while trying to stand up, or find your balance, and not being irritated by people who pushed and shoved and prodded you unnecessarily ! of course, this is a mirror of real life, so this earthy gritty mass of people reflected London at its worst and reminded me that Allah is with you in the most material nightmares, which is all still Tawaaf! Anyway, by the end when I limped to the side to do my two rakaats, the sense of peace was overwhelming, and made me realize that Tawaaf is not and ordinary prayer.

I started talking about Tawaaf and not the architecture of Mecca, because it was so powerful, it is the essence of Islam, and even if the place was horrible, the prayer of Tawaaf would be the same.

213

Of course, the modern extensions at Mecca are beautiful. The way that people are fitted in three levels, still with a sense of the harmony of the Haram, is remarkable. I did not discover the air conditioned bit until sorely before I left (after Hajj) and so got heat stroke (mildly), but am glad that I was in the 'old area' because I liked the sense of history etc., until the heat overwhelmed me!

The call to prayer at Mecca was elegant and beautiful, and I particularly liked Fajr with the bodies of the dead brought out for prayer and remembrance. I don't know why it was less easy to pray there than at Medina .. other than Tawaaf. May be it was the heat. But even in the air-conditioned , there was not the sense of a loving warmth pulling you on. There is more a sense of awe and intense sorrow at ones failings. In Mecca you encounter Allah directly.

I liked Saie. I liked the fact that the first thing that is celebrated after Tawaaf (the mystical and existential statement of Man's search for his return to his divine nature), is the frantic search of a slave woman abandoned by the father of the child, for basic sustenance in an inhospitable valley. I liked the celebration of woman (why is it that people are always saying that Islam is bad for women?) I liked the fact that this example is chosen because there is no search more focused than a woman fearing for her child's life, searching for basic sustenance. We are dying of spiritual malnutrition, and must experience the same determined search. Islam is not a religion which encourages you to believe that angels will come along and make it easy. We are human, and the wok of human, and the work of humanity is to fight for the spiritual survival of our true nature. Saie reminds you that it is not easy and it takes work. Of course by time I did saie, my feet were very painful, and that added to the prayer.

2) My views about Hajj, and its importance from the spiritual, cultural, religious and political point of view.

This was my first Hajj. For three-weeks before I felt terrible. I had constant thoughts about my own inadequacy, fears that I

214

would be unable to change, that I would be unable to accept the forgiveness of sins implicit in Hajj, fears that I was unworthy, ill prepared etc. I think Shaitan doesn't want people to do Hajj !!

The concept of Hajj is awesome. To contemplate the single mindedness of a man obeying God's will to sacrifice the life of his beloved miraculous child after clear instruction from Allah is terrifying (I like the story of his desperate attempt to placate Allah with the sacrifice of camels ..!) And yet we have the example of our Prophet (PBUH), his wife Khadija, his companion Abu Bakr who gave all his wealth etc. I did not want to return one of the hypocrites.. to have made Hajj but carried on as if nothing had happened . Even to think about doing Hajj makes you realise the extent to which one is less than whole hearted in your dedication to Allah, and the work of Allah. (In Christianity there is a prayer "Lord, make me good, but not yet..!

Hajj follows Tawaaf and Saie : You start with the reminder of the purpose of man on earth, to return to his divine nature : You are reminded that you must search for your spiritual sustenance with the frantic energy of a mother for a starving child, and then you are asked to sacrifice the attachment to the very child, because no material concerns can come between you and the will of God. Nothing can be more clear, or radical than that.

But thinking about it makes you so sorrowful for the pathetic sins that one clings to, the Luke warm inadequacy of your jihad etc.

I was glad that Hajj was tough physically, but I was not prepared for the 'Hajj tourists'. In my group, there was only one other woman who was making a serious attempt at prayer. On the holiest day of Arafat, there was a stampede to be the first in tent to get nearest to the air conditioner, and the women never stopped gossiping and talking about shopping. Fortunately I was able to see through a gap in the tent to an African who had found a corner by some rubbish outside, and spent the whole afternoon in the sun in deep prayer reciting Qur'an. I came to understand that for some people Hajj was a cultural norm, devoid of real meaning.

215

But the deep faith and sincerity of others made me see that even on the Holiest Day, humans continue to be pathetically preoccupied with their own comforts. I think I had imagined something of the discipline of my Christian background, but although this romantic view was shattered it only emphasized (as with Tawaaf) that this is the reality of the 20th Century : the man of God is a rarity, even in the group of people who 'claim' culturally, to be religious.

The religious theme is Abrahamic, and made me feel one with all of the 'People of the Book'. My Jewish friends were remembered by me on Arafat particularly. I like the links with all the prophets and the sense of continuous revelation that is central to Islam, and the essence of Hajj. I longed for the arrival of Mehdi who will unite all people in one religion.

Political: Islam celebrates all people. Is Haggard, a slave woman : is honored. Bilal was one of the Prophets (PBUH) most faithful companions. All people are called to return to their origin in the one God, the Creator. We are one Ummah. Why is Muslim fighting Muslim? Why are Muslims ignoring the needs of their brothers in other countries, The day that Islam wakes up from its slumber of self interest it will rule the world. But I do not believe this can be achieved by wrapping women up in black tents and murdering tourists in Egypt. Our beloved Prophet showed us that the political example is unity through love and respect, and he led by example.

Sadly, even in the holiest days of Hajj I saw little of the real unity that should be there. In Mina, where the conditions outside our hotel were really difficult, the waste of food was shocking. No-one was interested in taking it 100 yds to desperately hungry fellow Hajjs. In this atmosphere, national characteristics became parodies of human behaviour. We were stoning Shaitan, but he was still having a field day!

Returning to Mecca for five days to give thanks was a time of great peace. I slowly realised that I had lived in a time warp, where I had not thought one about my family and friends, my work, or

216

anything 'back home', and only how to live closer to understanding the will of Allah. Even with the blessing of Tawaaf again (and I did realise that, undeservedly, I had been forgiven) I felt unsure about the practical details of how I must change.. I was leaving the Haram for the last time when I saw an old man lying on the table, in old clothes, but he had a peaceful face. I asked my companion (who speaks Urdu etc.) to give him some Zakkat for me but he came back to say that the man had thanked us and refused the little gift saying that he had no needs. I realise that my prayer had been answered. The details are still not there, but the example is . T.S.Eliot in the Four Quarters quoted and English mystic, Dame Julian of Norwich who described that the spiritual journey is

'to seek a condition of complete simplicity, costing not less than everything'. I hope that I have made my first step.

I was inspired by an old man from Bangladesh, an African praying at Arafat, and an Arab woman who gave me her earrings in friendship. We were all just Muslims, submitted to God, undivided by race, culture, class or wealth. I long for Heaven where this will all be easy.

One more detail.. how is it possible on Hajj to cope with such little sleep. From 2.30 am on the morning we left to Mecca, to the afternoon at Mina 2.½ days later, I had no sleep. I never need more than 3 hours, and survived on catnaps very happily. I think I understand a little about why angels never sleep.

3 **The sacred month or Ramzan .. and the spiritual and medical aspects of fasting.**

I started to fast the month of Ramzan when I was still a Christian in 1985. The issue was self denial, keeping to the proscribed times, but it was a test of will and discipline rather than a prayer to Allah. It was a test of ego because my friends (Muslim and others) laughed at me, but I couldn't give it up, and began to understand that the spiritual path means choosing loneliness.

To fast Ramzan as a Muslim is completely different. The fast is to enable you to appreciate more the gifts of Allah, not to congratulate yourself on your capacity for self denial. It is only when we realise how dependent we are on clear water, on the simplest foods, that we start to appreciate the miracle of all His creation. Ramzan is a hymn of praise, and the fasting helps you to experience your need for him, and all his blessings.

Ramzan is very much needed by 20th Century man. We are greedy, corrupted by self-interest and lost in aspiral of excess and addictive desires. In Ramzan we allow ourselves to focus more clearly on how little we need of material things which makes us think how much more we need of our true spiritual food.

Medically, Ramzan is a great blessing. In this Century most of us eat too much and sleep too much, and are preoccupied by work. In Ramzan you eat less, you sleep less, and have clear mental energy to spend praising Allah and not chasing the dollar! to deepen your spiritual nature is to gain detachment from material needs. This is the best tranquilizer and antidepressant that there is, cancels the need for a psychiatrist and lowers the blood pressure. The heart rate lowers, the stress hormones settle, and there must be a lower rate of heart attacks.

For diabetics the weight loss helps to stabilize sugar, and normalise cholesterol. For smokers there is a brief respite from a dangerous habit which can hopefully be broken completely. In short, the news is all good. We should fast at least twice a week. I try to but sometimes forget. The thirst can be difficult as I have to talk a lot in the day, so I do a 'modified fast' from food only.

****

218

I know that I am being rational as I see logic in my daily life. The rules and regulations guide my moves. The reasons given by the Qur'an and hadith reaffirm the rationale. There is a discipline in Islam!

Hereunder, we reproduce the story of Dr. Ayesha Abdullah formerly Chandra Leela how she reverted to Islam. She was born to a Hindu family of Bangalore, India. She was not taught any principles of Hinduism by her parents. She was disgusted with the beliefs of Hinduism, i.e. Ravana had Ten heads, Krishna had sixteen thousand wives, because no one gave her convincing answers regarding the authenticity of these stories. She did not believe in hundreds of gods, which are grouped into good gods and bad gods.

During her education in pr-university, she was impressed by Darwin's theory of evolution. It was this atheistic period that she fell in love with a Muslim and married him without changing her belief whatsoever.

While she was a 3rd year Medical student, she came in contact with Dr. Zia ul haq who was her classmate. It was through his persuation, she met his mother who taught her the 'Strength of Islam', i.e. within one month all the basic principles of Islam and helped her in removing all her doubts. Although her marriage took place in 1966, she entered the fold of Islam in December 1973. She was greatly impressed by the 'Uniformity' of prayer and 'Equality' of Islam. She has given examples of the 'Caste System' of Hinduism and tells us how it is playing 'havoc' with its followers.-Editor.

I was born in a Hindu family though I was not taught any principle of Hinduism by my parents. My father never believed in going to the temple but until today I could not remember them telling any lie. His moral standards bore a great effect on my later

219

perception of Hinduism and religion in general. My mother, on the other hand, visited temples frequently and I used to accompany her on and off. During examination periods my visits were more frequent and much money was spent on coconuts and joss sticks.

Like the majority of Hindus in Bangalore, India, my belief was based on tradition and unquestioned following of the religion held by my forefathers and the society that engulfs my personality and choice. I would not call it 'blind following'. It was the most natural for her to do.

Krishna and his Sixteen Thousand Wives.

During my school days I learnt stories of Ramayana and Mahabharatha. The stories were interesting and have strong moral values. But some of them were hard to believe even for a gullible little girl like me. For example, Ravana had ten heads, Krishna had sixteen thousand wives, and so on. At times I doubted whether they could be fabricated or real stories. Nobody gave me convincing answers regarding the authenticity of the stories.

To question is tantamount to bring extremely rude and a sign of lack of conviction. Later I found out that it was mainly because the elders themselves did not know the answers and such 'interrogation' only revealed their ignorance and illogical stand.

At this point of time, I was made convinced that there are hundreds of gods, each in his own specialized field. These gods are grouped into good gods and bad gods. The threats of punishment and rewards by different gods resulted in feeling of fear and hatred to the bad gods and thankfulness to the good gods only. I had always felt the conflict of character in these gods but afraid to be rude, I buried in the feeling deep inside me.

Atheistic Period

While I was studying in pre-university I learnt Darwin's Theory of Evolution. It made great impact on me. It totally affirmed my suspicion on the numerous gods. I then felt liberated from the clutches of the bad gods. No more gods to fiddle with my life. For the next few years I was an atheist.

220

During this atheistic period, I fell in love with a Muslim and without much fuss, married him. I did not give much attention to his religion. As an 'educated' person, I still adhered to the scientific proofs and Evolution Theory.

Islam Stepped In

While I was in my third year at Medical College, one of my classmates (Dr. Zia-ul-Haq, presently practicing in Saudi Arabia) curiously inquired why I have not changed my name even though I am married to a Muslim. With great confidence, I explained to him that I did not want to embrace Islam until all my doubts are cleared. Not only was I doubtful about Islam, I was apprehensive to accept any kind of religion. I was still feeling cheated by Hinduism. He then invited me to visit his mother who was a religious teacher (Ustazah Latifunnisa, may Allah bless her.)

Alhamdullilah!, just within a month she taught me all the basic principles of Islam and its importance in daily life. She gave me convincing answers to all my doubts. She took me to religious class every week wherever it was held. I even learnt Arabic to enable me to recite the Holy Qur'an.

The Tree as a Point Operation

Ustazah Latiffunnisa taught me the strength of Islam. We would go to a certain district to propagate Islam. Our operation usually started under a tree or at bus-stop. Any Muslim woman that passed by will be approached. Their Hijab distincted them from the Hindus. Some would kindly invite us to their house and offer their services. Others would ignore or give a polite 'no'. But her perseverance marvels me.

In December 1973, I embraced Islam even though my marriage was held in 1966.

Fear of Ostracism

Life as a Muslim convert in a sea of Hindus was not pleasant at all. I could not publicise my conversion for fear of ostracism from all parties. A Muslim convert would not be invited to a Hindu wedding and treated worse than a leper.

221

As I began to understand Islam further, my fear of rejection from the society lessened. I know that I am being rational as I see logic in my daily life. The rules and regulations guide my moves. The reasons given by the Qur'an and Hadith reaffirm the rationale. There is a discipline in Islam.

My scientific background helps to convince me that Qur'an is God's Word. Living under hundreds of gods was claustrophobic, living under none was destructive to my moral development. Islam provides me the feeling of coherence in the belief of the Oneness of God.

I can approach Allah directly. I don't have to carry coconuts and flowers and have the priest as my intermediates.

There is no superstitious belief in Islam. In Hinduism, if you want to go out, they will check whether it is an auspicious day or not (Rahu Kalam). Their daily life is centered around wrong beliefs., superstitions and traditions, not with reasons.

Widows equal criminals

There is a place for widows in Islam. The Hindu society reduces the status of a widow to that of a criminal. She cannot play an important role in functions such as marriage ceremony. If a person was so unfortunate to have his path crossed by a widow, he will have to stop, perform prayers for blessings and only then carry on his journey. In some remote areas, a widow who refused to jump into the fire during her husband's cremation is considered unfaithful. A widow is literally doomed. She cannot even redeem her status as remarriage is forbidden.

The most important factor is uniformity in prayer. Everybody recites the Kalimah Shahadah, faces the same direction and performs five times daily prayers. This gives me a feeling of equality among fellow human beings. Prior to Islam, I was not equal to fellow Hindus. As a non-Brahmin, I was considered lower (Despite my position as a Medical Degree holder). It is customary to see a generous Brahmin pouring water into the cupped palms of a non-Brahmin who asked for a drink. The sharing of glasses is considered degrading. Only Brahmins study the 'vedas' and

222

become priests. The caste system is naturally repelling to any rational human being.

****

223

After Studying and reading about ISLAM for four years, I realised that it was the TRUTH!

This is the 'Reversion story' of sister Bilqis Ramjanee, formerly Hazel d'Offay. She hails from Seychelles but at the present, she has been residing in England for the last 9 years. She belonged to a Protestant family. She was, as she puts it, more a blind person searching for the light, which she has finally received. But when Allah the Al-Mighty wills one comes to the Right Path. So sister Bilqis reverted to Islam almost in 1993. She got married to a Muslim form Mauritius but her Christian family did not accept Islam. She is preaching them and hopes that Allah will guide them, Inshaalah! to the Straight Path! We produce hereunder her 'Road to Islam' with the courtesy of Iqra. - Editor. 1

I am a Seyhelloise and I have been living in the UK for almost 9 years. I come from a Protestant family and 2 years ago, I reverted to Islam, as everyone is born Muslim. It's their parents that bring them up to believing in another faith. I am striving very hard to become a better Muslim and also giving Dawah to the rest of my family. I am married to a Muslim who comes from Mauritius and it was my husband who introduced me to Islam.

At first, Islam didn't strike me as a major important role in life but, after studying and reading about Islam for four years, I realised that it was the truth. I was also influenced by my husband's family and by their way of life. This way of life seems perfect, peaceful, and realistic and led me to recite my Shahaadah and accept my role as a Muslim wife. I now have a son, called Hisham. He is two.

My parents are Christians although they are not that strict in belief. My mother has firm belief in the trinity and is just following what her parents did. I was not a practising Christian, but I was

---

[1] Iqra February 1995 (Ramazan 1415. page 37

224

more a blind person searching for the Light, which I have finally received.

I am still seeking for more knowledge in Islam, to increase my Iman. I do meet up with a lot of Muslim sisters for Circle Talks at the Islamic Cultural Centre in London. I do read a lot of Islamic articles that I can lay my hands on. I also try hard to make it for all the Islamic activities that I know of.

Alhamdulillah!, I can now read the Holy Qura'n in Arabic. I took lessons at the Islamic Centre, 3 days a week. I am now learning Classical Arabic which is held every Sunday at the same venue.

Insha Allah, my son will carry the light of Islam. I now understand the importance of Islam and why it is obligatory, (Fard) upon all Muslim women, the importance of hijab and the importance of giving Dawah and passing on the flag of Islam on to the rest unfortunate, i.e. my family, who have not any understanding about Islam, whatsoever.

****

225

Haj is part of a journey back to Allah, a withdrawal from the world. It is life and movement of life, and a renewal of a Muslim's covenant to Allah!

This is the 'Road to Islam' story of sister FAREEDAH CARTER who entered the fold of Islam eight years ago. She hails from Capetown, South Africa and is, at present, associated with the Islamic College of Southern Africa. Like other devout Muslims, she had an earnest desire to perform the 'FIFTH PILLER OF ISLAM, HAJ' and there was no such arrangement whatsoever. But where there is a 'WILL', there is a way. Allah, Most Gracious, Most Merciful, paves the way for those who strive for the right cause, as the Holy Qur'an says:

"As for those who strive hard in Us (Our Cause), We will surely guide them to Our Paths (i.e. Allah's Religion ---Islamic Monotheism). And verily, Allah is with the Muhsinun (good-doers)1 (SurahAr-Rum 30: 69)

As she was true and sincere to her 'Faith', so Allah, The All-Mighty, paved her way and with Allah's help, she performed Haj in February 1994. Hereunder, we reproduce the story of her 'Haj: a journey of Fulfillment' which was published in Arab News and Islamic Horizons.-Editor.

As 1993 was drawing to a close, I had a yearning to perform Hajj although I did not have the adequate finances, nor any thought from where I would get the money. Suddenly, things started falling into place and I was Makkah bound in February 1994.

---

1 Al-Muhsin (a good doer who performs good deeds totally for Allah's sake, without any show off or gaining praise or fame etc., and does them in accordance with the Sunnah (legal ways) of Allah's Messenger Prophet Muhammad (pbuh). The Noble Quran, page 622.

Upon seeing the Ka'abah, I felt that it was standing tall and strong, decked in black and gold, waiting to welcome me. This a sight that brings forth a sudden awareness of the pilgrim's frailty and insignificance.

As I stood there on the cool white marble-covered area encircling the Ka'abah, surrounded by hundreds of thousands of Muslims from around the world, I felt alone. I felt that I was on a secret journey of my soul to its source. At that moment, I was reminded of my daughter, Carolan's poem:

> I look for You
> on mountain sides
> through summer trees
> Where do You hide?

What is Hajj? It is part of a journey back to Allah, a withdrawal from the world, a gathering, a movement, a reawakening, humanity's essential link with Allah, and a baring of the soul. It is life and movement of life, and a renewal of a Muslim's commitment to Allah. As such thoughts raced through my mind, I was againg reminded of my daughter's poem:

> I look for You
> on moonlit lights
> through endless stars
> Where do You hide?

When I was able to feel the atmosphere around me, I was confronted with other experiences. A young man and his friend stepped out from the ever moving wheel of thousands in tawaf (circumambulation around the Ka'abah), his face lit up in ecstasy. He cannot see, yet he has experienced the closeness of Allah. My eyes rest upon a new-born child lovingly held in her father's arms. I wonder if the beneficial energy absorbed by the infant on this first journey around the Ka'abah will be sustained as she walks on her path through life? An old man leaning heavily on his staff, despite his disability, walks with a lightness of step for he is reaching out, gaining strength from his vulnerability, sensing the entire universe truly filled with the glory of Allah.

227

Mina, the battlefield to come, where we secure our places outdoors. As I quietly meditate in preparation for the day on the plain of Arafat, I again repeat my daughter's poem:

I look for You
on silent thoughts
through empty days
Where do You hide?

I think will Arafat be the beginning of my birth to this world? I pray to Allah to break down barriers so I can experience inner love, and let me reach out and trust, with such ideas still on my mind, our restless army marching on foot and in every form of transport, approaches Arafat. The cries of pilgrims resound through the air and echo to eternity! Labbayk, Allaa humma labbayk... (O, Allah here I am, present, answering Thy call.)

The pilgrims, searching for the return to Allah, bare their souls in humble submission to the will of Allah. I ask myself have they dug deep enough, have they cared enough, and are they thankful enough? The road back to Allah is very long and difficult, yet very precious. It is a fight and a struggle and the inner peace creeps in so quietly, you scarcely know it's there.

As I crouch on a hillside beneath a huge umbrella, finding no escape from the enveloping dry heat, I feel a closeness of Allah pervading the atmosphere. A life-long dream is now a reality, yet the pilgrim is only too aware of his insignificance and frailty. Again a cascade of questions comes forth. Will I be able to break the barriers that have kept me chained through life. Will I be able to continue life afresh and renewed? Will I have a deep commitment to make a difference in time to come and be worthy and free?

With these thoughts in mind, I eye the Jabal al Rahmah (the Mount of Mercy). It is a shimmering mirage of white and as far as the eye can see there is movement. There are millions of pilgrims, each making contact with their Creator in their own way.

Soon the voice of the muezzin breaks the relative silence. I walk down the hill and join a group of pilgrims from the

228

Philippines. I do not know them, yet I feel a part of them and welcome. All of us are one in our communion with the Almighty.

The lone lizard skitters silently across the soaring heat of the Arafat sand. He is a creation of Allah. I wonder, what is his experience on this day of Arafat? He shelters beneath the small shadow of drooping tree, whilst small birds sing in what was an arid desert space. I ask myself, is this the beginning of the Garden of Eden?

Dusk has come and it is time to move from that plain to pause in Muzdalifah where we arm ourselves, ready for the battle yet to come. The pilgrims on foot move ever quietly forward, like the rolling waves on the ocean deep. There is more speed by foot than in the massive army of vehicles that creeps inch by inch.

The pilgrims return to Mina to battle Satan. It is a day of struggle and rapidly flying pebbles. There is dust and the crush of the crowd. I ask myself where is the peace gained at Arafat now? The answer comes that war must go on, even after the victory. The war never ends for the end is the beginning.

We return to the Ka'abah for Tawaf and Saai, where the turning wheel of humanity swells, and the mass of moving bodies seemingly blur into one. The frail and weak move on biers around the outer perimeters.

Upon our release from the state of Ihram, we wash and change rest and slowly wind our way through the throngs in Makkah. The crowds surge from the Haram after prayers, more crowds surge into the Haram for tawaf and Saai. It is a continuous movement, as in life, a never ending circle after circle. Thousands choose to walk back to Mina for the Eid al Adha to commemorate Prophet Ibrahim's resolve to sacrifice his son on Allah's command.

One we have fulfilled this commemoration, we return to battle. The pilgrims march forth, armed with their specific number pebbles, chanting Allhau Akbar (God is the Greatest).

It is the sixth day of the Pilgrimage, millions have streamed out of Mina for the return to Makkah. The pilgrim walks quietly and peacefully through the mountain tunnel to Makkah. I decided to

229

remain here for the day after the crowds had left, feeling compelled to continue the battle in relative solitude. It would provide me with the opportunity for soul-searching, for quiet reflection, while still moving in this sea of life. I felt deeply thankful, committed and ready to continue my journey in life. I was alone, yet not alone. With Allah in my heart, how could I ever be alone? Once again, I remembered my daughter's words:

> I look for You no more
> For on mountain sides
> and moonlit nights
> my silent thoughts
> bring You to life
> Hidden things are revealed
> and with all life I share
> the knowledge and eternal light
> of knowing You are everywhere

I pray that all Muslims may have the chance to commence their sacred journey to the Holy City of Makkah[1].

****

[1] Islamic Horizons. March-April 1996 (Vol 25 no. 2) Pages 14-15
(Australian News, 10th April 1996 page 12)

My rocky road to Islam!

This is the reversion story of sister Fatima I. Tutay. In her opinion, her acceptance of Islam is the 'best blessing', the greatest event that ever happened in her life, comparing it to the past Christian life, which was so confusing, materialistic and unrealistic.

When she reverted to Islam, she had to face bitter opposition. Her own family opposed her. Her sons were ousted from the school. Her eldest son rebelled against her and even left her and denied her as his mother. Many of her friends, relatives and neighbours gave her the title as 'crazy'. Her real sister, a physician, advised her to consult a Psychiatrist. In her own words, it was a self-revolution, transformation and self-education. With the courtesy of 'Islamic Future', we have the privilege to produce her heart-rending, thought-provoking and wonderful journey to Islam for the benefit of the esteemed readers. Editor.[1]

Alhamdulillah, though I had been in those rough times, Islamizing is the best blessing I have now! Al-hamdulillah, the greatest that ever happened to my life, comparing it to the past Christian life, which was so confusing, materialistic and unrealistic. I also realized that my prime duty as a wife and mother was my family and children.

Islamizing my life, my dress, my ways and holding fast the primary obligations of a Muslim were totally weird and strange to the members of my family. Above all, the most loneliest and hurting was the fact that my sons who are studying in a Catholic school run by the Church whose directress is a Nun, almost ousted my sons from that school, but Alhamdulillah, after explaining my

---

[1] Courtesy : Islamic Future, August 1995, vol 11, no, 49, page 6.

Islamic faith to her, she allowed them back to school, even if it was the policy of the school not to enroll non-Catholics.

My eldest son rebelled and even ran away to live with my sister and even denied me as his mother because many of my friends, neighbours and relatives thought that I was going crazy. To ease the predicament of my son, my sister who is a physician urged me to see a Psychiatrist. However, I know that Allah (SWT) controls every human mind, Alhamdulillah, for not so long, my son came home, begged for forgiveness and joined in our prayers. He also inquired me the teachings of Islam which I was practicing. Alhamdulillah, he now defends me when people give bad comments on our Islamic way of life out of their ignorance.

Residing in a predominantly Christian community here in Metro Manila, both friends, neighbours and relatives are curious seeing always in Islamic attire, everything is covered except the face, hands and feet and most of the time in my "chador" or "abaya". In the market place some vendors even mistake me for a nun and usually ask me to what denomination do I belong. In the bus, in school, in the supermarket and almost everywhere it is a common experience to be looked upon, or asked, "sister, among denomination po kayo?" (Sister, what religious denomination do you belong?) Usually, I reply that "I am with the Islamic denomination or simply, I am a Muslim!" Some contested why should I dress like a nun. Even the school directress commented that I should refrain from using such attire. However, I explained to her that I am different from that of a nun, that I don't wear belt, only my hands, face and feet are visible, the same with that of Virgin Mary. I go on explaining that this Muslim attire is a manifestation of our love for Virgin Mary who is the ideal of all believers. It follows that when we idealize or we admire someone we must adopt her ways otherwise we don't really love her.

With this Christian oriented explanations, I have won the acceptance of most people whom I meet or came to associate with. My parents and kins always make food halal when we visit them, and my father who is not yet a Muslim, always prepares a

232

prayer place for us and he also reminds my kids to say their prayer on time. Alhamdulillah! The school directress who is a nun is friendly and herself seemed to be curious rather than offended. A friendly market vendor insists on calling me "sister" and usually gives me special discount claiming that my purchases bring them good luck and easy sale. My neighbours and family friends keep their good ties with us, and they always lend a hand when I need help. Sometimes, they even entrust their children to my care at home and then later on, relate me about their children persuading them to perform their prayer the way I perform my "salat".

For this, I claim that the acceptance I enjoy now before the Christian society is credited to my being a Muslim in an Islamic way.

It has been related in the Hadith that Prophet Muhammad(Peace be upon him) has mingled with the Christian, Jews and unbelievers. This must be so, otherwise, there should be few Muslims to date. Although he did not present Islam on a Christian point of view, definitely he did not treat him with aggression. Sometimes, he even turned to the Christians for refuge from the idolaters. (Refer to the Book on Life of Prophet Muhammad(pbuh).

Many Muslims scholars agree that the true teachings of Jesus Christ (pbuh) are similar as that with the last Prophet (PBUH) and doctrine of all the prophets (Peace be upon them) for that matter. (See reference in the Qur'an about Allah (SWT) warning mankind about the misgivings of the ancestors who did not heed their prophets). Also by deductive reasoning, how can a fair God tell one doctrine to one prophet and then another doctrine to the others. Obviously, what had been revealed to Jesus Christ (pbuh) must be the same and a part of that revealed to Prophet Muhammad (pbuh). Hence, all Muslims must believe that all the teachings of Jesus Christ (PBUH) are correct one-hundred percent. But the vital practices of Christendom of today are neither found in the Bible or the Qur'an.

If the prophets are intended by Allah (SWT) to be our teachers and models, Muslims, therefore, follow only the teachings of prophets. Contrary to practices of the so-called Christians of today, Muslims cannot find any line in the Bible where Jesus Christ (pbuh) asked his followers to pray to Virgin Mary, nor did virgin Mary prayed to Jesus. All of them including Jesus Christ (PBUH) has shown in the Bible that they all pray to ONE GOD, the Creator. Would Jesus Christ (PBUH) be offended if these so-called "Christians" pray to the Creator the same way, his mother, his apostles and he himself did? So does the Muslims, they pray the same way Jesus, Virgin Mary, and all the prophets and saints (peace be upon them) did.

What would you say if the picture of virgin Mary wears a dress just below the knee instead of the usual length? This will be a big surprise and denial that this is not Mary, the mother of Christ. Allah (SWT) is well pleased with the way of Virgin Mary (pbuh). Would a believing woman hesitate to dress up like Virgin Mary if it is one way to please Allah (SWT) Al-hamdulillah, only Muslims are able to follow this.

234

The more I learned about Islam, the more right it seemed to me. Islam has given me my dignity as a woman!

We feel much pleased in presenting the 'Acceptance of Islam' story of sister Ms. Georgina Noueiri, who was brought up in a strong Anglican (Christian) atmosphere. She had a secure faith in God, or in her own words: "I had always believed in the first part of the 'Kalimah', i.e. there is only One God". Despite this strong faith, she was not satisfied with the certain dogmas of Christianity, for instance, 'TRINITY'. She firstly encountered with Islam, when she met Mr. Muhammad, a fellow-student of the University of Swansea who had arrived in U.K. from Lebanon a year before. During her discussion with brother Muhammad about Islam, she came to know the reality of Islam, the True Religion of Allah. The more she learned about Islam, the more right it seemed to her. Consequently, on impulse, she recited the 'KALIMAH', i.e. 'There is only One God, and Muhammad (pbuh) is His Messenger".

After embracing Islam, sister Ms. Georgina Noueri is feeling herself secure and leading a peaceful life. Her contact with the Muslim Community, has strengthened her deep conviction in Islam, and Islamic teachings. While going out from her house, she wears the traditional head-scarf and long coat and feels quite safe and secure. In reality, Islam has given her the dignity of a women! Sister Syeda Aniqa Tazein interviewed sister Ms. Georgina Noueiri which was published in the Saudi Gazette. With the courtesy of Saudi Gazette, we reproduce her interview. - Editor. [1]

My first in-depth encounter with Islam came about when I met Muhammad, a fellow student at the University of Swansea. He had arrived in Britain one year earlier from war-torn Lebanon. Despite a strong (Anglican) Christian background and a secure faith in God. I had unresolved questions of faith, to which Muhammad's religion seemed to have the answers. I'd never understood about

---

[1] Saudi Gazette. 12th April, 1996, page 7.

235

the Trinity, for instance. Then when Muhammad said there are no partners with God, it just seemed very pure and beautiful to have a religion which puts Him alone.

Islam corresponded with everything I had always felt deep down inside, even when I was a child, that Jesus (pbuh) was a wonderful prophet with a wonderful message of forgiveness, but he was not to be worshipped as God. I was searching for spiritual clarity. But I didn't realize I could find it classified under Islam.

The more I learned about Islam, the more right it seemed to me. But conversion was not an easy step to take. I was intensely longing to do it, but I didn't know if I had the courage. I was afraid of what my family would think, the culture difference, my role change in society.

Then one night as I was talking to Muhammad about Islam, I had a feeling of having found my right place in the universe. Now was the time to stop holding back and to follow my instincts. On impulse, I recited the "Kalima" i.e. "There is one God, and Muhammad (pbuh) is His Messenger," to my then fiancé. I said this before him from my heart. I had always believed the first part. Now on that special night I had the courage to say the second part. When I wake up the next morning, I knew I had taken the right step. I felt relieved, I had freed myself.

I was well aware of the risk I was taking. Islam is a massive subject - supposing I discovered something I didn't believe in - but the more I learned, the more I felt it was everything I wanted to believe in.

Marriage to a Muslim was not the reason for my conversion, but had to do with an internal process. Since childhood, I had visited Lebanon and Egypt with my family. For a reason I can't explain, I felt at home there. It hurt every time I had to leave.

Muhammad, and I moved to Lough-Borough so that he could continue his studies. There we made contact with the Muslim community. For the first time, I was exposed to the practices of devout followers. It gave me a desire to adhere more strictly to the laws enshrined in the Qur'an. I welcomed its disciplines, such as

236

praying five times a day: at first light, noon, the first shadow, twilight and night. In a technological age it keeps you in tune with nature; its like meditation, your mind is re-directed.

I also welcomed the Islamic rule of separating the sexes, it leads to a much more peaceful life. The wives are more relaxed because they know their husbands are not going to be tempted by other women. People think we don't trust our wives or husbands, but as Almighty Allah created us as human beings capable of giving in to temptation, so He has also given us this rule as a precaution.

That precaution gives women an enormous sense of well-being when they are together. There is no tension, no showing off to the opposite sex. They can enjoy each other's beauty without feeling threatened by it.

When I go out, I cover myself with the traditional head scarf and long coat. It was hard at first. I was brought up in a western society wanting to be attractive. Then vanity started to drop away from me and I became a little purer. I was glad! Suddenly I felt safer on the streets and I felt happy that men wouldn't whistle at me or have personal thoughts about my body. I was no longer just an object; Islam has given me my dignity as a woman.

****

"Every page of the Book -- Qur'an, was, for me, a 'Revelation' giving me great spiritual satisfaction I have never known before".

It was during the month of July 1995 when brother Abul Hassan Atique of Dar-ul-Hadyan, Riyadh, told me about Dr. Hassan Ko Nakata. Though it was late, but it was not too late because Dr. Hassan had left Riyadh for good and joined the Faculty of Education of the University of Yamaguchi, Japan, after serving for a number of years in the Embassy of Japan. Brother Atique very kindly gave us the postal address of Dr. Hassan and on the 29th July, 1995, we wrote a detailed letter along with a 'Questionnaire' requesting him to favour us with the answers. Sister Khaula Hassan Nakata was so kind enough as to send us reply and favoured us with the answers to our questions on behalf of Dr. Hassan who was very busy and pre-occupied and could not reply to our letter soon. She very graciously sent a copy of her 'Road to Islam', which was published in the 'Minaret'. [1]

Sister Khaula Hassan Nakata was born in 1961. She embraced Islam in 1990 in France before she met Dr. Hassan. She got married to Dr. Hassan in 1991 in Egypt at the end of his 6 years' student life in Cairo. Sister Khaula spent a number of years in France. While recollecting her memories she writes :

"When I returned to Islam, the religion of our inborn nature, a fierce debate raged about girls observing the hijab at schools in France. It still does. The majority, it seemed, thought that wearing the head-scarf was contrary to the principle that public - that is the state funded - schools should be neutral with regard to religion. Even as a non-Muslim, I could not understand why there was such a fuss over such a small thing as a scarf on a Muslim student's head.

In Japan, it may be seen and understood as conservative traditionalism, or the result of anti-Western feeling, something

---

[1] The Minaret, published by Daar Adh Dhikr, Dept. of Da'wah and Islamic Education for Non-Arabic speaking women, Riyadh vol.2 no.1, issue 7 page 4.

which the Japanese themselves experienced following the first contact with Western culture during the 'Meiji era; The feeling still persists amongst the non-Muslims that Muslim women wear the hijab simply because they are slaves to tradition, so much so that it is seen as a symbol of oppression. Women's liberation and independence is, so they believe, impossible unless they first remove the hijab.

My hijab is not a part of my racial or traditional identity it has no social or political significance. It is purely and simply, my religious identity. I have worn the hijab since embracing Islam in Paris. In France, I wore a simple scarf which matched my dress and perched lightly on my head so that it was almost fashionable! Now, in Saudi Arabia, I wear an all-covering black cap; not even my eyes are visible. Thus I have experienced the hijab from its simplest to its most complete form.

When I decided to declare my Islam, I did not think whether I could pray five times a day or wear a hijab. Maybe I was scared that if I had given it serious thought I would have reached a negative conclusion, and that would affect my decision to become a Muslim. Until I visited the main mosque in Paris, I had nothing to do with Islam; neither the prayers nor the hijab were familiar to me. In fact, both were unimaginable but my desire to be a Muslim was too strong "ALHAMDULILLAH" for me to be soberly concerned with what awaited me on the other side's of my conversion.

My hijab made me happy; it was both a sign of my obedience to Allah and a manifestation of my faith. I did not need to utter my beliefs, the hijab stated them clearly for all to see especially fellow Muslims, and thus it helped to strengthen the bonds of sisterhood in Islam.

Two weeks after my return to Islam, I went back to Japan for a family wedding I took the decision not to return to my studies in France; French literature had lost its appeal and the desire to study Arabic had replaced it.

239

As a new Muslim with very little knowledge of Islam, it was a big test for me to live in a small town of Japan completely isolated from Muslims. However, this isolation intensified my Islamic consciousness, and I knew that I was not alone as Allah was with me. I had to abandon many of my clothes and, with some pantaloons, similar to Pakistani dress. I was not bothered by the strange looks people gave me.

After six months in Japan, my desire to study Arabic grew so much that I decided to go to Cairo, where I knew someone. None of my host family there spoke English (or Japanese) and the lady who took my hand to lead me into the house was covered from head to toe in black. Even her face was covered.

Before becoming a Muslima, my preference was for active pants-style clothes, not the more feminine skirt, but the long dress I wore in Cairo pleased me; I felt elegant and more relaxed.

My father was worried when I went out in long sleeves and a head cover even in the hottest weather, but I found that my hijab protected me from the sun. Indeed, it was I who also felt uneasy looking at my younger sister's legs while she wore short pants. I have often been embarrassed, even before declaring Islam, by the sight of a woman's bosoms and hips clearly outlined by tight, thin clothing. I felt as if I was seeing something secret. If such a sight embarrasses me, one of the same sex, it is not difficult to imagine the effect on men. In Islam, men and women are commanded to dress modestly and no be naked in public, even in all male or all-female situations.

In Islam, a wife will try to look beautiful for her husband and he will try to look good for his wife. There is modesty even between husband and wife and this embellishes the relationship.

Just as a short skirt can send the signal that the wearer is available for men, so the hijab signals loud and clear: 'I am forbidden for you'.

Those who consider it permissible for women to leave their faces and hands uncovered at all times cite the saying of

240

Prophet Muhammad (PBUH), who told the sister of his wife 'Ayesha (Asma'), when he saw her in a thin, transparent dress, that a women who has reached the age of menstruation should not show anything except these, indicating the face and hands.

The Prophet Muhammad (pbuh) once asked his daughter Fatima 'What is the best for a woman?! and she replied, 'not to see men and not to be seen by them'. The Prophet Muhammad(pbuh) was pleased and said, "You are truly my daughter".[1] Now, we, with great pleasure reproduce the 'Road to Islam' story of our esteemed sister Khaula Hassan :

As most of the Japanese, I'd followed no religion before I embraced Islam in France. I was majoring in French literature at the university. My favorite thinkers were Sartre, Nietczhe and Camus, whose thinking is atheistic. At the same time, however, I was very interested in religion, not because of my inner necessity but of my love for the truth. What was waiting for me after death did not interest me at all; how to live was my concern. For a long time I had a sort of impression that I was not doing what I should do and I was wasting my time - to live with God or without God.

I started to read books on different religions except Islam. I had never thought that Islam was a religion worth studying. It was for me, at that time, a sort of primitive idolatry of the simple mind (how ignorant I was!). I made friends with Christians, with whom I studied the Bible, to come to realize a few years later the existence of God. But then I had to face a dilemma because I could not feel God at all, in spite of my conviction that He should exist. I tried to pray to church, but in vain. I felt nothing but the absence of God.

I then studied Buddhism, hoping I would be able to feel God through Zen or Yoga. I found as many things in Buddhism that seemed to be true as I had in Christianity, yet there were many things I could not understand or accept. In my opinion, if God exists, He should be for everyone and the truth should be simple

---

[1] Courtesy : Iqra (February 1996), pp. 42-45 and impact International, U.K.

and clear to everyone. I could not understand why people should abandon ordinary life to devote themselves to God.

I was really at a loss for what to do to reach the end of my desperate quest for God, it was then that I met an Algerian Muslim. Born and raised in France, he didn't even know how to pray and his life was quite far from the ideal of a Muslim; nevertheless, he had very strong faith in God. However, his belief without knowledge irritated me and made me decide to study Islam. To start with, I bought a French translation of the Qur'an, but I could not read more than two pages. It seemed so strange and boring. I gave up my effort to understand it alone and went to the mosque in Paris to ask someone to help me. It was a Sunday and there was, by coincidence, a lecture for women. The sisters welcomed me warmly. It was my first encounter with practicing Muslim women. To my surprise, I felt myself very much at ease with them, although I'd always felt myself a stranger in the company of Christians. I started to attend the lecture every weekend and to read a book given to me by one of the Muslim women. Every minute of the lecture and every page of the book were, for me, a revelation, giving me great spiritual satisfaction I've never known before. I had an excited feeling that I was being initiated into the truth. What was wonderful, Subhaanallah (Praise be to Allah), was my feeling the presence of God very close to me while in the posture of Sajdah (prostration). I had found God at last ! One month later Al-Hamdulillah (Thanks be to Allah), I professed the Shahaadah (declaration of belief in Islam).

As soon as I started to learn Arabic, I became fascinated with the beauty of the Qur'an and realized that I had not been able to understand it at first because I had read a translation.

I regret much that we, the Japanese, have few chances to know Islam, as shown by the fact that many of the Japanese Muslims embraced Islam abroad. I regret it all the more because the morality of Japanese people and life style of discipline are very similar to that of the Muslims. May Allah guide my nation to the right   path.

I realized that Islam was what I had been looking for being a Muslim does mean that for every challenge I come across, the solution lies in following the 'Path of Truth'.

Sister MaDonna Johnson is an American lady who was brought up in Christian environment and remained a Christian all her life. She found it very hard to look outside the Church even though her heart was not totally Christian. After the death of her daughter (who was only 5 months) and died of 'Sudden infant death syndrome' (SID), she was a changed women. She was not satisfied with Christianity because she had too many un-answered questions. Hence, she was looking for 'One True Religion'. At last, Allah, Most Gracious, Most Merciful, guided her and she found Islam. With the courtesy of Islamic Horizons, we feel pleasure in reproducing her soul-inspiring and thought-provoking story - Editor.1

Looking back on my past, I would have to say that the turning point in my life was without doubt the birth of my daughter.

Before she was born, I spent my life on a day to day basis, concentrating my time and attention to whatever crisis I could get my hands on. If there wasn't one, then I made one.

When I became pregnant, I knew I would be raising my child alone. If it weren't for the love, devotion, and determination of my mother, things would have been different.

When my daughter was 5 months old, she died of "Sudden Infant Death Syndrome" (SID), which is a medical term for "Not known cause".

I had never experienced such pain, panic, and complete emptiness. However, throughout the funeral, I was consoling other people, telling them I believed with all my heart that God would not cause me such pain if He didn't have something incredible

---

1 Islamic Horizons, January/February 1996 (Volume 25, no. 10 pages 14-15.

waiting for me in future; all I had to do was stay on the right road, and God would show me when I was ready.

Friends would say "You'll see her again someday." I would question them openly; how does anyone know that I'll be going to Heaven? Just because I was a Christian was no guarantee, since I couldn't bring myself to swallow all of Christianity. There were too many unanswered questions.

So my quest for the "One True Religion" began out of desire to insure that I would indeed see my daughter again.

I went through all the Christian religions diligently. Having been a Christian all my life, I found it very hard to look outside the church, even though my heart wasn't totally Christian.

People would say things to me like, "Jesus spoke to me today," or "Jesus is with you, all you have to do is invite him into your heart and you will see your daughter in heaven."

I was beginning to think I was doomed. I looked at Tarot cards, crystals, and even entertained the thought that all religions would take you to heaven, if you followed their beliefs.

Eventually I put my search on hold for a while and got a job at a bar in Indianapolis. It was there that I met a girl, who later turned out to be a good friend for a while. She had three or four business running out of her home, none of them doing very well, and some of them questionable.

One day, she asked me if I wanted to go to Malaysia. She said she wanted me to buy some Malaysian style clothes, get pictures taken of them, and find an importer-exporter to handle the business. Without thinking I said "I'm there!"

I arrived in Kuala Lumper during the middle of Ramadan. I'd never heard of Islam before, and had no idea that Malaysia was an Islamic country. Almost every women I saw had a scarf on her head in 95 degree heat!

I also noticed that people went out of their way to be nice to me. It took a very special friend (plus, he was one of the few who could speak English fairly well) to explain that Malaysia was an Islamic country, and Muslims believe that whenever we do

244

something nice for someone for the pleasure of Allah (SWT), then we will be rewarded for that deed on Judgment Day, Insha Allah.

However, all I could see were the negative aspects of Islam, the same things others see, who are ignorant about Islam; so I bought some Islamic books (Including a Qur'an) and began studying Islam.

I asked many questions, such as why do women cover their whole body, except for the face and hands? Why is everyone so happy and willing to fast throughout the day? How could anyone be happy about starving themselves? It seemed suddenly that no one could speak English well enough to satisfy me, so I turned to the Qur'an.

Ever since I can remember, I have felt out of place in Christianity, like I was the only one in the whole church who didn't know the joke was on me.

The more I studied about Islam, the more I began to wonder if this was the road to my daughter; would this religion get me into Heaven?

Although my biggest obstacle was the Islamic concept of Jesus (pbuh), and how I would explain this to everyone at home, I found the answers to some of my questions and realized that Islam was what I had been looking for.

But I had a problem, should I take the challenge ... become a Muslim and walk the straight path to heaven? Or deny the Truth I knew in my heart out of fear of disapproval and persecution from family and friends ... only to abide in the hellfire forever?

I constantly carried with me a feeling of doom and anxiety. This was my state of mind everyday while I was deciding whether I should revert to Islam or not.

For me, this decision was not as easy. Islam is not a part time religion; a true Muslim doesn't practice Islam one day a week. Islam is a full-time challenge with enormous struggles, as well as benefits. The more you learn and understand, the more you realize you have only just begun to scratch the surface, which makes you strive even harder to learn more.

245

One day I woke up with the words, "OK, I believe, I will go and revert to Islam," and from the moment on, all my turmoil and anxiety was gone Alhamdulillah.

All the pain I had felt from my past experiences, including my daughter's death, were gone. The nightmares stopped, and I felt the most incredible peace.

I went to PERKIM, the Malaysian Muslim Welfare Organization, and took my Shahadah, filling my life with the peace and love of Allah (SWT) Alhamdulillah.

Looking back, I can say all the things I experienced on my path to Islam were well worth the effort and pain, because now, Insha Allah, I will be able to see and hold my daughter again, if I can stay on the right path.

Sure, I still have challenges, being Muslim doesn't mean I won't have problems. But being a Muslim does mean that every challenge I come across, the solution lies in following the path of Truth. And at the end of that path lies Heaven, my daughter and numerous other pleasures that the human mind can't begin to comprehend.

All praises are due to Allah for bringing me to the Truth and for His grace in making me a Muslim.

****

246

The basic feeling that I had was that Islam was the TRUTH!

The following is the autobiographical sketch, i.e. story of 'Reversion to Islam' of sister Maryam Ahmed. She knew nothing about Islam in the beginning. She came into contact with Islam through her friends. Later on, she started reading Islamic history and the more she read, the more she wanted to know about Islam, until she read several books which were available to her. Having close relationship with some Muslim families she became an 'Adopted Aunt'. The Islamic way of life impressed her and she felt very comfortable. As a result, she began to learn how to pray and tried to learn to write and speak Arabic. Consequently, she entered the fold of Islam. Although after accepting Islam, she faced opposition from different quarters even then, one of her daughter and her family have recently accepted Islam. She is preaching her other family members and is quite hopeful that they will join the fold of Islam, Inshaallah!

In fact, Islam has given her so much more than what she had lost from giving up her Western way of Life. - Editor. 1

I was looking for a religion. I certainly knew nothing about Islam. I had a vague idea of what a Muslim may be but was not particularly interested. Through my work I came in contact with some people who were Muslims and after we became friendly I decided to go to the local library and see if I could find some books to explain Islam to me, so I could understand them (my new friends) a little better.

So I started to read the history of Islam and the more I read the more I wanted to know until I finished the several books that were available in the library. The library even ordered books from other

---

[1] Iqra February 1995 (Ramazan 1415), p.39.

247

libraries for me when I requested them. I remember one book was stolen out of a friend's car and I felt sad about that and hoped it hadn't been thrown into a garbage can somewhere. I paid the library the cost of the book which was only $10 but the loss was more relevant.

As I became braver I reached out further to other Muslims and began my quest for Islam by attending a group at the Islamic Women's Center at Lakemba and gradually I became friends with Australian Converts who were married to born Muslims and also some Muslims who had come to Australia to find a better life.

I found all these women to be very supportive, encouraging and accepting. I was invited into their homes and to a few families I became an "adopted aunt." The Islamic way of life felt very comfortable to me and I began to learn how to pray and tried to learn to write and speak some Arabic.

The basic feeling that I had was that Islam was the TRUTH and that "Alhumdulillah" (praise be to Allah) I was led to this truth and the peace of mind and practical solutions to the problems associated with living in this confused world.

I accepted Allah Subhana wa Tala's word sent to Muhammad (PBUH), without hesitation. In six years it has been a gradual process but with salat and practice I have found my way.

Islam has given me so much more than what I had lost from giving up my western way of life. It hasn't been easy to change one's complete way of life so family and friends became in a way alienated as they became hurt, bewildered and angry at a former partner in their activities embracing a way of life which was often abhorrent to them Alhumdulillah, my children have also become interested to learn about Islam and one of my daughters and her family have recently accepted Islam as their religion, Alhumdulillah.

At work I am virtually isolated by being "different" as I am not mixing socially with my colleagues as I used to. I am further isolated as I now wear a scarf and wear loose modest Islamic clothing and not the revealing fashions that my peers wear. Their

248

language and behavior is also different to mine as we have differing moral and value systems. So now I am the "foreigner" in the country in which I was born.

In the fasting month of Ramadan Muslims are more exposed as we do not partake of food in the work breaks and we can attend but can't eat at the office parties. It is a time of explaining why and wherefore of our practice in an attempt to break down their fear and distrust of Muslims.

So what I gained..., certainly more peace of mind within myself, the courage to live at last the right way and the friendship and sense of family from my brothers and sisters in Islam. I have a bonding and understanding with others as we travel the same spiritual path and face the same problems and Alhumdulillah I have found a devout husband who completed my Iman and who is helping me to understand further Allah Subhana wa tala's message to Muhammad (pbuh), and to all mankind, given to us in the Qur'an.

My advice to other converts would be to go slowly, read the Qur'an when you can, pray when you can, in Arabic even if the pronunciation is not correct and don't be hard on yourselves. Dress in the style you feel comfortable, don't force yourself to look different too soon. You will be able to wear the head cover when it is the right time for you, inshallah. Ask Allah Subhana wa tala's help to guide you and show you the way, remembering that Allah knows your intention. Contact other converts for friendship and help through the difficult times, they have been there too.

May Allah Subhana wa Tala guide you and help you in your quest for the truth.

****

How did Ms. Maryam Jinnah (Quaid-e-Azam Muhammad Ali Jinnah) Embrace Islam?

by Muhammad Haneef Shahid

The marriage of Miss Ruttenbai Petit to Mr. Muhammad Ali Jinnah (later on Quaid-e-Azam) has historic importance and will be remembered as an 'historical event' in the annals of Indo-Pak Sub-Continent history. She was the only daughter of a Parsee [1]textile magnate Sir Dinshaw Petit (1873-1933)[2] and a member of the Legislative Assembly.[3] He was one of the richest persons in Bombay and his full name was Sir Dinshaw Manockjee Petit. The first meeting between Miss Ruttenbai Petit and Mr. Muhammad Ali Jinnah took place in 1916. It was also an historic event because the Sessions of the congress and All India Muslim League were held in Lucknow. Muhammad Ali Jinnah not only presided over the Session of the All India Muslim League but also led the Congress. Sir Dinshaw Petit alongwith his daughter Ruttenbai attended the session. It was for the first time that Ruttenbai saw Muhammad Ali Jinnah.

According to Hector Bolitho 'Among Muhammad Ali Jinnah's friends was Sir Dinshaw Petit, one of the proud, self-confident Parsees who had helped to make Bombay into a prosperous city. Jinnah liked to escape from his desk, and his duties, now and then, to dine with the Petits in their elegant house, or to stay at their country place in Poona. Ruttenbai, twenty four years younger than Jinnah, was an enchanting girl: today - a quarter of a century after her death -- there are gallant old gentlemen in Bombay who recall her, and say, "Ah, Ruttie Petit! She was the "Flower of

---

[1] Parsee : a member of a Zoroastrian religious sect in India descended from a group of Persian refugees who migrated to India during the 7th and 8th Century. New World Dictionary page 1035.

[2] In Memory of Mohtarma Maryam Jinnah, by Dr. G.A. Chaudhry. The Pakistan Times, Oversees Weekly, January 3, 1992, page 12.

[3] Quaid-e-Azam's Married Life (Urdu), by Aqeel Abbas Jafri, page 31.

Bombay". Then, "She was so lively, so witty, so full of ideas and jokes".[1]

Sir Dinshaw was the client and friend of Mr. Muhammad Ali Jinnah and they enjoyed cordial relations. Commenting on the relations between Mr. Jinnah and Sir Dinshaw's family, Prof. Stanley Wolpert writes :

"From his meeting in Allahabad, Jinnah went North to Darjeeling to escape the next two months of intense Bombay heat by vacationing at the summer home of his client and friend, Sir Dinshaw Manockjee Petit. The Petits were one of Bombay's wealthiest Parsi families, textile magnates, whose vast fortune was begun by Sir Dinshaw's enterprising great grandfather, who came to Bombay from Surat in 1785 and worked as a shipping clerk and dubash (two language interpreter) for the British East India Company. French merchants who dealt with this bright, very small Parsi clerk dubbed him 'Le Petit Parsi'. The nickname became his descendant's surname. His son Manockjee Petit founded Bombay's first successful cotton mill, which grew into the sprawling Manockjee Mills Complex in Tardeo. The first baronet Sir Dinshaw started Bombay's powerful Mill Owner's Association in 1875, which he chaired from 1879-94. He also served as one of the five trustees of the Bombay Parsi community's most sacred matters -- marriage, succession laws, and proper disposition of the dead upon the Towers of Silence. the elder Sir Dinshaw had been instrumental in securing British legal recognition and public promulgation of the Parsi Succession and Marriage Acts, which he personally helped administer. The Petit family was thus not only among the richest, but also one of the most devout, orthodox Parsi families in Bombay by the end of the nineteenth century.

With the death of the first Sir Dinshaw in 1901, his entire name, fortune, and religious duties and responsibilities passed on to his

---

[1] Jinnah; Creator of Pakistan, by Hector Bolitho. London, John Murray, 1957. page 74.

son, whose first child and only daughter, Ratanbai, had been born the previous year, on February 20, 1900. Ruttie, as she came to be called, was a thoroughly enchanting child, precaciously bright, gifted in every art, beautiful in every way. As she matured, all of her talents, gifts, and beauty were magnified in so delightful and unaffected a manner that she seemed a "fairy princess," almost too lovely, too fragile to be real. And her mind was so alert, her intellect so lively and probing that she took as much interest in politics as she did in romantic poetry and insisted on attending every public meeting held in Bombay during 1916, always sitting, of course, in "the first row", chaperoned by her "multimillionaire philanthropist" maiden aunt, Miss Mamabai Petit".[1]

It is said that she was extraordinarily charming, elegant and possessed uncountable qualities. She was beautiful in every respect. In other words, she had the qualities of head and heart. In short, she was considered the 'Princess of Fairies'. She was brought up in 'poetical environment'. She was still 11 years old when her father, Sir Dinshaw Petit, gave her the 'complete poetical works' of Lord Tennyson as a gift. When she met Mr. Jinnah, she had studied deeply Shelley[2], Keats[3], Browning[4], Burns[5] and other poets. Moreover, she had read numerous

[1] Jinnah of Pakistan, by Prof. Stanley Wolpert. New York, Oxford University Press, 1984. pages 43-44.

[2] P.B. Shellay; a poet of repute, born on 4th August, 1792 and died on 8th July, 1822. for more details see Comptions' Encyclopaedia, Vol. 13. page 23.

[3] John Keats; a well known British poet, born on 1795 and died in Rome in 1821 For further details see Comptions' Encyclopaedia Vol. 14, page 23.

[4] Robert Browning ; an English poet of repute, was born on 7th July, 1812 and died in 1889. For more information about his life and works see Comptions' Encyclopaedia Vol. 4, pages 347-48.

[5] Robert Burns; Scotland's greatest poet, born on January 25, 1759 and died on 21st July, 1796 at a young age of 37 years. For more information see Comptions' Encyclopaedia, Vol 4, pages 383-84.

novels and dramas. She had become romantic and she met Mr. Jinnah in this 'romantic atmosphere'.[1]

Muhammad Ali Jinnah was a tall, handsome youngman and possessed a dignified personality, and was considered 'first rank lawyer (barrister) and politician'. Sir Dinshaw Petit used to invite him at his residence where Ruttenbai took part in discussion with him on various subjects.

Sir Dinshaw Petit's family was accustomed to go to "Matheran hills' (Bombay) in summer and stay at their bangalow namely 'Petit Rose'. Muhammad Ali Jinnah also used to go either to Simla, Mussoorie, Naini tal or to Darjeeling. and spend summer holidays there. When relations grew between Mr. Jinnah and Sir Dinshaw, the later forced Mr. Jinnah to accompany him to Matheran hills. In this way, Mr. Jinnah used to spend a few weeks in 'Petit Rose'. Mr. Jinnah as well as Ruttenbai loved horse-riding and enjoyed riding together on their horses

In 1917, Sir Dinshaw's family decided to go to Darjeeling instead of Matheran and Mr. Jinnah also became ready to accompany them on their invitation and persuasion. They spent summer holidays together. It was here in Darjeeling that the situation took a new turn for which Mr. Jinnah was not ready at all. Miss Ruttenbai proposed to Mr. Jinnah that she wanted to marry him.[2]

Mr. Rizwan Ahmad writes :

"Mr. Jinnah tried hard to tell Miss Ruttie that there was a great difference in their ages[3], but it was of no use. Mr. Jinnah turned a deaf ear to her, on the contrary Ruttie, considering it apathy, coldness and indifference from his side, warned him of her decision saying:
"If you refuse to marry me, I will commit suicide".

---

[1] Quaid-e-Azam's Married Life, by A.A. Jafri. page 35.
[2] Quaid-e-Azam's Married life, by Aqeel Abbas Jafri. pages 36-37.
[3] Miss Ruttenbai Petit was twenty-four years younger than Mr. Muhammad Ali Jinnah. - Editor.

It was, undoubtedly, a very critical situation for Mr. Jinnah, but he knew to overcome every sort of situation successfully, because 'Failure was a word unknown to him'.

After his return from Darjeeling, Mr. Jinnah went to the residence of Sir Dinshaw Petit one night and asked him about his opinion regarding marriage between the people of different sects and religions. Sir Dinshaw who was totally ignorant of the situation gave his view clearly by saying : "Such kind of marriages prove very useful in strengthening the ties of national unity fraternity, and moreover, these marriages might be the solution to sectarian problems in the long run". Mr. Jinnah could not expect such reply from his old friend. So without loosing any time and indulging into any sort of discussion, he told him frankly that he wanted to marry his daughter, Ruttenbai Petit. Sir Dinshaw was wonder struck. Becoming furious, he refused this marriage saying that it was absurd and funny.

On the contrary, Miss Ruttenbai Petit informed her parents about her marriage with Mr. Jinnah. They told her that it was impossible because of the great difference in their ages and religious customs, but Ruttenbai had decided once for all to marry Mr. Jinnah and no force on earth could persuade her to change her decision[1].

According to Mr. Zain Noorani :

"Jinnah possessed a dignified personality. So he talked to her parents directly, but they did not accept the marriage proposal due to the reason that they were Parsees, hence, they could not marry their daughter to a Muslim. They clearly told him that they did not have any conflict with him. Neither they thought age-difference between them any hindrance in their marriage. But keeping in view their Religion, they would never agree to the marriage. Inspite of the fact, they knew that Mr. Jinnah was honest, Member of the Legislative Council, Barrister of repute,

---

[1] Qaid-e-Azam's Married Life, by Aqeel Abbas Jafri. pages 40-42.

254

dignified person and an outstanding politician, they warned him that they would not spare any effort to prevent the marriage. [1]

Legally Ruttie had not come of age and could not marry without the consent of her parents. Consequently, Mr. Muhammad Ali Jinnah had to wait. Ruttie was young, kind-hearted and possessed a strong will power. None could prevent her from taking decision. She had decided to marry Mr. Jinnah once for all and chose her life partner.

She also waited very patiently till she reached the age of 18 years. At this point, she could marry according to her own wish. So on the morning of 18th April, 1918, she left her parent's house and on the same day she entered the fold of Islam in the Grand Mosque of Bombay voluntarily.

Her father was a millionaire who enjoyed great respect, honour and dignity. She did not care for the religion, honour and wealth. She sacrificed her all for the sake of Mr. Jinnah. Dr. Ghulam Ali Choudhry commenting on her sacrifice, writes :

"Mohtrama Maryam Jinnah sacrificed for the sake of Quaid-e-Azam Muhammad Ali Jinnah, her religion, her family, her patrimony --- her all." [2]

In short, this fearless and daring Miss Ruttie embraced Islam in the Grand Mosque of Maulana Khair-ud-din (father of Shams-ul-Ulema Maulana Muhammad Hussain Azad) at the hands of Maulana Nazir Ahmad Khajandi and she took the Islamic name 'Maryam'.

On this historic event, the world press published the news of Miss Maryam's acceptance of Islam. An English daily namely "The Statesman" published the following news :

"Sir Dinshaw Petit's only daughter Miss Ruttenbai accepted Islam yesterday and she will be married to Hon. M.A. Jinnah today". [3]

---

[1] Weekly Akhbar-e-Khawateen, 25 to 31 December, 1976. page 9
[2] In Memory of Mohtarma Maryam Jinnah, by Dr. Ghulam Ali Chaudhry. The Pakistan Times Overseas Weekly. January 3, 1992. page 12.
[3] Quaid-e-Azam's married Life, by Aqeel Abbas Jafri. page 47

Times of India published the following news:
"Sir Dinshaw Petit's daughter Rattie Petit has embraced Islam and married to Mr. Muhammad Ali Jinnah according to the Islamic rituals".[1]

The 'Nikah ceremony' was held in a very simple manner at the residence of Mr. Muhammad Ali Jinnah called 'South Court' situated at Mount Pleasant Road, Bombay. Maulana Hassan Nafji led the 'Nikah ceremony', and Rs. 1001 s 'Mehr and Rs. 125,000/- as 'Gift' was decided. Haji Sheikh Abul Qasim Nafji appeared as witness from Miss Ruttenbai's side whereas Hon. Muhammad Ali Khan Raja of Mahmoodabad was witness from Mr. Muhammad Ali Jinnah's side.

The following statement was recorded in the 'Nikah Register' :

"Item No. 118. Date April 19, 1918. Rajab Seventh 1349 A.H. Meher : Rs. 1001/- Gift: Rs 125000/- Pesh Imam Maulana Hasan Najafi.[2]

Talking about the marriage of Miss Ruttie to Mr. Muhammad Ali Jinnah and the 'gift' which the latter gave to the former Mr. Stanley Wolpert writes :

"Jinnah married Ruttie on Friday, April 19, 1918, at his house, South Court, on Mount Pleasant Road atop Malabar Hill in Bombay. She had converted to Islam three days earlier, though she remained a nonsectarian mystic all her life. None of Ruttie's relatives attended her wedding. She had fled from her father's palatial prison less than a mile away on the day she turned eighteen and was mourned as if dead by Sir Dinshaw until she and Jinnah separated less than a decade after they had married. The Raja of Mahmudabad and just a few other intimate Muslim friends of Jinnah attended the quiet wedding. "The ring which Jinnah gave to his wife on the wedding day was my father's gift,' Mahmudabad's son and heir recalled." [3]

---

[1] The Weekly Akhbar-e- Khawateen. 25th December, 1976, page 9.

[2] Quaid-e-Azam's married Life, by A.A. Jafri. page 48.

[3] Jinnah of Pakistan, by Prof. Stanley Wopert. New York, Oxford University Press, 1984. page 53. For more details regarding marriage and news,

Giving details of the second marriage of Mr. Jinnah, Hector Bolitho, author of Jinnah: Creator of Pakistan, writes :

"Jinnah waited, and Ruttenbai devoted. When she was eighteen, her father had to reconcile himself to the cold announcement in 'The Statesman; on April 19, 1918, that 'Miss Ruttenbai, only daughter of Sir Dinshaw Petit, yesterday underwent conversion to Islam, and is to-day to be married to the Hon. Mr. M.A. Jinnah'

The lovely young bride moved into the sombre bachelor house, with her books, her ornaments, and her multitude of pretty dresses. She sent to her husband's mustyrooms in the Law Courts and enlivened them with bright paints, elegant furniture, and flowers."[1]

Mr. Hamid jalal, in his 'Jinnah; the man remembered', gives the following details of the marriage:

"Jinnah's historians record that he married Ruttic (who took the formal name of Rattanbai on her conversion to Islam), when he was forty-one and she was about twenty two years younger. Their love was deep enough for her to walk out of her multi-millionaire father's house taking only the clothes that she was wearing. Jinnah saw to it that she lived in the style to which she was accustomed. There is a descriptive inventory in his papers listing his gifts to he --- nearly a hundred items of jewelry with diamonds, emeralds, pearls, rubies and agates: all these in only nine years of married life!" [2]

---

editorials and comments by different newspapers, please see Islam & Quaid-e-Azam, by Muhammad Haneef Shahid. pp 22-29 and Quaid-e-Azam's Married Life, by A.A. Jafri. pp. 50-55.

[1] Jinnah: Creator of Pakistan, by Mector Bolitho. page 75.
[2] Pakistan : Past and Present, London, Stacey International 1977. page 56-57

Mr. Jinnah, unlike some other secular Muslims[1] did not like 'civil marriage', and it was not difficult for him to undergo 'civil marriage'. Civil marriage act, in those days, had become outmoded and obsolete. According to this act no person could marry who was a follower of any Religion. On the contrary, he/she had to declare that he/she was an atheist, and Mr. M.A. Jinnah, could never think of declaring such an affidavit. He was representing the Muslim Constituency in the Central Assembly. As a result of this marriage, he was not deprived of this right of Representation. This is a vivid proof of his strong belief in Islam.

Moreover, "his family had a great regard for their religion, the tenets of which they observed faithfully. They were neat, clean, sober, thrifty, ambitious and in trade enterprising and cool and resourceful. Muhammad Ali Jinnah was an outstanding exemplar of that inheritance keenly competitive, sober, thrifty, enterprising, cool and resourceful in all emergencies, whether professional political or physical and ambitious".[2]

Mr. Muhammad Ali Jinnah was a great lover of the noble Prophet Muhammad (PBUH) and Islamic teachings. He was a 'Muslim' first and 'Muslim' last. He possessed the noble qualities of head and heart. In the words of Mr. Farouk Luqman, Managing Editor of the 'Arab News',

"Mr. Jinnah was a born leader, brilliant advocate, a shrewd debater and parliamentarian, a single-minded devotee of principles, honest to the marrow of his bones, financially independent, incorruptible, unpurchasable, fearless and

---

[1] They were : Mr. Humayun Kabir (1906-1969), author of Indian Heritage, Education in New India ; Britain and India, etc. and Mr. Salman Khursheed, Ex-Deputy Minister and a member of the family of Dr. Zakir Hussain, former President of India.
[2] Bombay Gazettier, vol. 9, part 2, page 112 and Pakistan; Past and Present, page 14.

disdainful of flattery. He was by all accounts and on all counts a rare breed of leader unlike anybody else".[1]

He always used to say what he meant. Talking about 'Islam as a code of life', he made it clear in a public meeting by saying :

" Islam is not only a set of rituals, traditions and spiritual doctrines. Islam is also a code for every Muslim which regulates his life and his conduct in politics economics and all other affairs. It is based on the highest principles of honour, integrity, fairplay, and justice for all. Unity of God is one of the fundamental principles of Islam, and there is no difference between man and man. The qualities of equality, liberty and fraternity are the fundamental principles of Islam."[2]

From the above-mentioned statements, one can fully understand what kind of 'Muslim', Mr. Muhammad Ali Jinnah was! In short, the marriage ceremony was finalized, but the Parsee community of Bombay was out-raged. Same was the case of Sir Dinshaw Petit, father of Miss Ruttanbai Petit. They would have no objection if they (i.e. Mr. Jinnah and Miss Ruttie) would have performed 'civil marriage.' But miss Ruttie's conversion to Islam was unbearable and unpardonable crime in their eyes. with the result, a case of 'abduction' was filed against Mr. Muhammad Ali Jinnah, but he did not appear before the court as a Barrister but as respondent/defendant. He knew the law and honoured the law. In her statement to the court, Miss Ruttie, said : 'My Lord! As far as abduction is concerned, Mr. Jinnah has not abducted me, on the contrary, I have abducted him, I love him and I have embraced Islam with my own free will and not under any compulsion. As regards, wealth, neither me nor Mr. Jinnah want it."[3]

---

[1] Jinnah: The Founder of an Ideological Islamic State, by Muhammad Haneef Shahid, page 2.
[2] ibid. page 6.
[3] Islam and Quaid-e-Azam, by Muhammad Haneef Shahid. page 26.

259

Consequently, the case was dismissed and Mr. Jinnah was acquitted with dignity and honour!

After marriage, the Jinnah lead a lovable and happy life. Mr. Jinnah was zealous after books. She took keen interest in autobiography, history, astronomy and current history. Usually, she bought first edition of the book, she was interested in. She had a good collection of rare books. Besides this, she used to collect diamonds and paintings. She proved a stimulating force for Mr. Muhammad Ali Jinnah and always encouraged him in his political pursuits. Although she did not take active part in politics, yet she showed great interest in the affairs of the Muslims. She participated in the political debates in the company of her friends and had strong belief in the freedom of the Muslims!

She breathed her last on 20th February, 1929 and was buried in 'Arambagh Graveyard' of Bombay. It is just a coincident that Mrs. Jinnah was born on 20th February, 1900 and died on the same date, i.e. 20th February, 1929. The following 'tablet' is engraved on her tombstone :

"Here rests the lady who vaulted the Quaid to greatness and thereby fulfilled the ambitions, she nursed of perpetuationg her name in the paragraphs of history"[1]

So, here lies Ruttie in "Arambagh Graveyard' of Bombay, leaving the " Quaid" alone who lies in "Quaid's in Karachi. When his (Quaid's) cherished goal --- Pakistan was achieved, he visited the graveyard, he visited the graveyard of his beloved wife and placed a last bouquet on her tomb. He left Bombay with a heavy heart for good. Mr. Larry Collins, author of 'Freedom at Midnight' gives the picture of the Quaid's mind when he left the Muslim cemetery after placing a bouquet. he says :

As always, he was alone, shrouded in silence, Muhammad Ali Jinnah walked through the early morning sunlight

---

[1] Quaid-e-Azam's Married Life, by A.A. Jafri. page 107

260

towards a simple stone grave in a corner of Bombay's Muslim cemetery. There, he performed a gesture which, in the days to come, millions of other Muslims would perform because of what he had wrought. Before setting off to his promised land of Pakistan, Jinnah placed a last bouquet on the tomb he was leaving behind forever in India."[1]

After the sad demise of Mrs. Maryam, the Quaid was, though, left alone, but her memories always reminded him of her presence in one way or the other. A former Chauffeur of the Quaid-e-Azam recalls :

"Sometimes my Sahib would give orders that a big cabin trunk be opened. It contained his dead wife's clothes and those of his daughter when she was a child. They would be taken out of the trunk and spread out in and airy room. He would look at them in silence, and grief would crease his fine and sensitive face. Suddenly he would remove his monocle from his right eye and, with both eyes moist, would murmur to himself, "It's all right It's all right," and polishing his monocle with his handker chief walk out of the room."[2]

****

[1] Freedom at Midnight, by Larry Collins and Dominique Lapierre. New Delhi, Vikas Publishing House, 1978. page 224.
[2] Pakistan; Past and Present. Stacey International, London, 1977, pages 54-55.

Among the many blessings bestowed upon me by Allah, I count the one that I found ISLAM as the most valued!

This is the most heart-rending and soul-inspiring story of a sister Nadia Shaukat Ali's 'Reversion to Islam', who is at present living in California, USA and was born into the Russian Orthodox faith. From her very early age she began to oppose and question the ritualistic practices found in the Russian Orthodox Church.

Her father who was a strong professor of the Islamic faith and held great respect for our Noble Prophet Muhammad (PBUH) started telling her a little about Islam. As a result of this teaching she overcame the prejudices strongly ingrained in Christianity and to objecting look for the light of faith she so strongly sought for so long, which, at last, she found in Islam. Among the many blessings bestowed upon her by Allah, she count the one that she found Islam as the most valued.

She had the good fortune of visiting the Islamic Republic of Pakistan and see Islam in practice very closely. She is fortunate that she, after reading the Holy Qur'an and Islamic literature which she could get in the USA and the valued instructions she received from a revert to Islam, she knew that to have not accepted the True Faith of Islam was the same as being shown light and choosing to stay in darkness.

We feel pleasure in producing her 'Voyage to Islam' with the courtesy of the Minaret and Islamic Voice - Editor. [1]

My name is Nadia. I was born into the Russian Orthodox faith. Very early in my life, I started to question the ritualistic practices

---

[1] Islamic Voice (Bangalore, India) September 1993. page 17.

262

found in the Russian Orthodox Church. For instance, the priest in Russian school taught that God had forbidden the making of images, the worshipping of idols. Jesus Christ came to the Israeli peoples and said, "Yet our church was full of pictures: images of saints, pictures of Jesus, the Holy Virgin, the disciples, various angels, and scenes of the crucifixion along with Christ's ascent to Heaven. The "eye" of God was pictured above the altar. Whenever I asked about this discrepancy I was given various answers which no matter how well-phrased, left concern in my small mind that there was inconsistency between what God commanded and what was being done. The more intensely I questioned, the more emphatically I was told to accept as "true faith is blind." Somehow this did not sit well with me. In the Russian Orthodox church the images not only cover the walls and are set up on pedestals, they are regularly kissed in reverence! Czar Nicholas's family is pictured on one of these images (called icons) as martyrs in the name of the church yet they were slain for political reasons. To me this depiction is preposterous. They were slain for purely political reasons and to have them be sainted seems a deficiency in someone's power to reason. Unfortunately this decision is a result of a high Orthodox church authority. Thankfully I do know who.

In my church there were other practices which even as a young girl seemed wrong. As another example I will take the worship of saints. Saints are people who have given their lives in the cause of the Church. Although I revere anyone and everyone who sacrifices in the name of the true God, I in no way can accept worship of a human being. I do not mean to say that these martyrs should not in any way be recognized. I just never felt that these saints should share in man's worship of God, or should be depicted on the walls of the Church. So, saint worship is another thing that bothered me immensely since I was old enough to understand what the word "Worship" meant. My idea was that when I pray, when I worship, I worship God and I was told this was arrogance. Somehow I did not believe this. Is not my prayer more pleasing to God when I say it to Him directly? Perhaps my understanding of the saints depicted in my church as just now described by me will be challenged should any authority of the Orthodox church read this. I can only say that my understandings are the direct result of my inquiries at a very early age. Since my teenage years I could not even bring myself to pray to even Jesus Christ (Peace be upon Him). I held the strong belief that my prayers will be addressed directly to God.

Anyone familiar with Christianity is acquainted with the rituals of communion and confession. Since I first understood the description of communion, I was unfortunately repulsed by it. I say unfortunately, because somehow even to me now it seems unfortunate that I was unable to accept with grace what was told to me was Jesus' behest. The act, explanation of the act, and the part taking of it to me seemed repugnant. Even now, after completely accepting Islam, I am ashamed of this admission. Another thing I found strange concerning communion is the serving of wine representing Christ's blood. Faith, without question, is an intoxicating thing. But the serving of an alcoholic beverage in a place of worship to me is bizarre. The thought of orally receiving something representing Christ's body and blood for consumption was always loathsome to me and on the level of ritualistic cannibalism. This, of course, is my own personal view and in no way should reflect on the representation of the acceptance of Christ's doctrines. Man, unfortunately, according to his nature and with the help of Satan, has a way of misinterpreting / misrepresenting some things that were no doubt meant to be otherwise.

Let me touch upon the ritual of confession. In the orthodox church in order to receive God's forgiveness for sin, you must go to the priest during a church service (not necessarily during the service, but this is how it is ordinarily done), and describe your sin (obviously in hopes of repentance and God's clemency). The priest then covers the head of the confessor with a part of his vestment and says a prescribed prayer asking for God's forgiveness of whatever transgression was confessed. Periodically, the priest imposes

264

certain acts of penance which must be fulfilled before God's clemency will be granted. I always questioned the power of the priest to decide which act must be gone through by the sinner to receive God's forgiveness. I know that the degree of penance is probably dictated by church authorities in proportion to the sins committed, but who is man to judge man in this respect? I've always believed that God and God alone should know man's sins, and God knows beyond the shadow of any doubt or distortion the sinner's intention and desire for true repentance. I quit going to ritualistic confession about ten years ago. Instead whenever I felt I have transgressed, I prayed in private to God telling Him what He already knew and letting Him know that I recognized my sin, hoped for His mercy in judgment, and knew that God knew the degree of remorse in my heart.

That is how strong my own personal faith has been. On my own, without knowing it I was following many of the ways of Islam, for in Islam this is how confession is done. In everything I have said, again let me repeat that although I disagreed with the rituals of my church, my faith in God never wavered. Sometimes I, as everyone else with a sound mind, I am sure, have questioned my own beliefs and the correctness of my actions.

When I was about 9 or 10 years of age and I started strongly questioning many of the things I have just mentioned, my father started telling me a little about Islam. He was a strong professor of the Islamic faith and held great respect for Muhammad (pbuh). Thanks to him I was able to overcome prejudices strongly ingrained in the Christian faith and to objectively look for the light of faith I so strongly sought for so long, which fortunately I have found in Islam. Among the many blessings bestowed upon me by Allah, I count the one that I found Islam as the most valued.

Over the course of the past few years, I have examined the Islamic faith and have found to my great surprise that what I believed has already been professed and the style of worship I believed in was being practised by the Islamic peoples for centuries. This was not a disappointment, but an illuminating relief.

My views of Islam are idealistic since living in America I am isolated from a completely Islamic society. What I know and believe may, however, be somewhat less adulterated since I have not been exposed to any cultural overtones which doubtlessly tend to over-shadow Islam due to the nature of man. Some may criticize this view. I tend to hold it in esteem. My views, by virtue of their idealism at this time, tend to be more pure since I am yet untouched by anything other than the idealism I behold. I do not as yet know all about Islam, and I am still only a student of its practice.

I was surprised to learn recently on my first visit to Pakistan that women are banned from worshipping in mosques. Perhaps I do not fully appreciate the reasons, but to me this seems a corruption of Muhammad's (PBUH) teachings as I at this time understand them. I strongly agree with the separation of men and women as I understand it in the Islamic faith. And this is a view I have held for a long time. There are natural difference which, in order to maintain dignity and order in society, must be respected. But to forbid women's worshipping in mosque I can accept as a cultural eccentricity, but not as a teaching of the revered Prophet (pbuh).

In all the things I saw in my church, my faith in God never faltered. Rather I concluded that what I saw and what was being practiced simply did not correlate. Just because I did not agree with certain ritualistic practices in no way diminished my reverence for the true God, Allah, and my desire to worship Him and Him alone in a way I felt to be pure and right.

After the conclusions which I came to within myself, after reading the Qur'an, after learning the Islamic literature which I have been fortunate enough to obtain in the United States, and after the small amount of very valued instruction I have received from a convert to Islam, I knew that to have not accepted the true faith of Islam was the same as being shown light and choosing to stay in darkness. I am convinced of the righteousness of my decision with every ounce of strength and honour within me.

266

Islam came to me as a 'Modern-day Messenger'. What appealed to me most about Islam was that it allowed no compromise with untruth, antiquated beliefs, superstitions and all kinds of irrationalities.

Sister Sabiha Khan, formerly known as Carole Botes was born and grew up in a Christian home. She attended a Catholic school and led a 'Carefree' Christian life like most white Christian girls in South Africa. She was enjoying life to its full, but she never thought of her Creator and the purpose of her life. During her study, she did not get any sound knowledge of the Bible or the history and origin of Christianity. No mention was made of Islam or our Noble Prophet Muhammad (pbuh) because other religions as a subject, are not included in the South African educational curriculum. Though her life was quite enjoyable yet she was feeling something missing from spiritual point of view. To find the Truth, she started comparative study of religions, i.e. Buddhism, Judaism, Hinduism, etc., but to her great fortune, she 'discovered Islam'. She had intensive study and dialogues with different people for about more than one year. It was then she accepted Islam as final religion (Deen), Deen-e-Qayyam, Religion of Allah and the Noble Prophet Muhammad (pbuh) as the 'Seal of the Prophets'. Syeda Aniqa Tazein interviewed sister Sabiha Khan and with the courtesy of Saudi Gazette, we reproduce her 'Reversion to Islam' story for our esteemed readers. - Editor.[1]

No matter how expertly Christianity or any other religion may be presented, no matter how deeply indoctrinated one might be, it will never make an impression on one who is committed to finding the truth.

---

[1] Saudi Gazette, 15th March, 1996, page 7.

267

I was born and grew up in a Christian home. I attended Catholic school and led a 'carefree' Christian life like most white Christian girls in South Africa. I knew no fear. My life was exciting, eventful and full of opportunities.. but I gave little thought to my Creator and the purpose of my life on this earth. I did, however, feel a desire to have a closer relationship with God, but I conveniently placed this thought last on my list of priorities.

During all my school days spent under the guidance and supervision of nuns at a convent, I could never acquire a sound knowledge of the Bible, or the history and origin of Christianity. Religious lessons consisted of the same old Bible chapters being repeated. No mention at all was made of Islam and Prophet Muhammad (pbuh). In fact, other religions as a subject are not included in the South African educational curriculum. Young minds, thus, are insulated and never given the chance to expand and be ventilated by the refreshing air of liberty and rationality.

I began to realise that though my life was enjoyable, there was a spiritual desideratum (something essential or missing) in my life's make-up. I felt that there had to be a more complete and meaningful way of life, bud did not know how to find it. Eventually, I resorted to an in-depth study of various religions, e.g. Buddhism, Judaism, Hinduism, etc. But to my great fortune, I discovered Islam, as one suddenly finds a scintillating diamond on the road while walking aimlessly along the path of uncertainty.

Islam came to me as a modern-day "messenger". What appealed to me most about Islam was that it allowed no compromise with untruth, antiquated beliefs, superstitions, and all kinds of irrationalities. It was a simple, straightforward, uncomplicated way of life. The most outstanding feature of Islam is that though it evolved to its perfect form some 1,400 years ago, it correlates completely with the scientifically advanced modern world.

My conversion to Islam was not immediate. It took over a year of intense studying and asking questions before I finally accepted it as the final religion (Deen), and Muhammad (pbuh) as the Seal of the Prophets.

One of the first discoveries I made was that I had two different concepts of God. As a Christian, I viewed God as a soft, lenient, undemanding Being, allowing us to do as we pleased, waiting hopefully for us to turn to Him. It was the Doctrine of Atonement that I could never accept. When questioned, I was given circuitous, tortuous, circumambulatory, and nebulous answers that confused me even more.

As I became more inclined towards Islam, I regarded Allah as a Great Power, a loving but firm Being Who demanded discipline, Who was not going to give us the easy way out by alluding us that someone else had died for our sins. Allah, the Only One True God, told us in no uncertain terms that we ourselves are responsible for our own actions and He will reward or punish us accordingly.

What struck me most in my study of the life of Prophet Muhammad(pbuh) was the perfect example he set for his followers who loved him so much that they would have given their lives for his safety.

I drew a comparison between Muhammad (pbuh) and Jesus (pbuh). According to the Bible, Jesus's (pbuh) closest followers denied him after the supposed crucifixion. This was never the case with Muhammad's (pbuh) followers.

Comparing the two prophets, I understood why Muhammad (pbuh) was the Seal of Prophets. Jesus's (pbuh) mission was - as he himself said - for "the lost sheep of the House of Israel," whereas Muhammad's (pbuh) mission was universal, that is, for all mankind. Muhammad (pbuh) gave us a complete code of life which he himself lived according to the dictates of the Qur'an, whereas Jesus's (pbuh) life was incomplete. He did not teach us how to live our lives and conduct our affairs on this earth as Muhammad (pbuh) did. Jesus (pbuh) was emphatic that his kingdom was not of this world.

The Qur'an made a profound impression on me. It is pure, unadulterated Word of Allah, and is not polluted by men as is the case with the Bible which is interpolated, altered, added to and subtracted from by men. The original Word of Allah as revealed to Jesus (pbuh) is not in existence today.

It was not one particular facet or a few aspects of Islam that led to my conversion. It was Islam as a whole, which convinced me and made me decide that there is no religion on earth that can even remotely touch Islam in beauty and simplicity.

It is a bit difficult for a person who has reverted to Islam to practice it successfully in a non-Islamic environment.

I, however, was fortunate that I married into a truly Islamic family - not the kind of people who accidentally inherited Islam and treat it casually and with indifference; nor the kind of Muslims who merely talk as "authorities" about Islam while behind that image indulge in all kinds of evils. I married into a family that has Islam in their hearts; who are disciplined Muslims; who practise what they preach.

Living as a Muslim, I now have a far greater knowledge of Allah. I live in constant awareness of the Day of Qiyamah (Reckoning). Life is a bliss because I now have a purpose for living on this earth. I have discovered a new meaning to life which I did not have when I was a Christian. I found that love and service to fellow humans is the quintessence as an acronym for "I Shall Love All Mankind!"

Yusuf Islam (former singer Cat Stevens) motivated and influenced my desire to discover Islam, after my husband mentioned his conversion to me.

My parents are curious about Islam but show no interest in further inquiry. My friends declare, "We are Catholic born and Catholic to say."

My domestic ambition is to lead my four year-old daughter Taskeen and my two year-old son Siraj to read the Qur'an. I'd like to introduce children to elementary steps of Islamic education and fill them with the fear of Allah to establish sound moral values in a Western, anti-Islamic dominated world.

270

Islam Is For "All People". No Nation Owns Islam!

This is the story of 'Journey to Islam' of sister Sarah Joseph who is the Editor of Muslim Youth Magazine Trends. She is a British Muslim who embraced the Religion of Allah not from the pathway of birth and family, but from a different point of view. In her own words: "She comes from the House of Pharaoh". Before entering the fold of Islam, she read the Holy Qur'an and the Sunnah of the Noble Prophet Muhammad (PBUH) first. She did not follow the Muslims like so many other persons whom she 'had the chance of meeting' and who had accepted Islam. In other words, she did not follow suit. On the Contrary, she was impressed by the marvellous character, patience, honesty and the integrity of the Noble Prophet Muhammad (pbuh) who faced the hardest opposition and brutality. As she was a sincere 'seeker of Truth' in the real sense of the word, so Allah, Most Gracious, Most Merciful, guided her to the "Straight Path" :

"We have made the (Qur'an) a Light, wherewith We Guide such of Our servants as We will". (Surah Shu'ra xlii:52)

With the courtesy of Impact International and Iqra (Ramadan 1416 AH) we reproduce it for our esteemed readers. - Editor 1

I write as a women, inspired by role models too often ignored . Khadija, Ayesha, Sumayya and Nusayba - may Allah be pleased with them all, who fought and battled alongside their brothers in Islam for the creation of a just and God-fearing society. The men and women of Medinan society struggled together, doubling the

---

1 Impact International : Iqra Ramadan 1416 A.H. Page 37.

271

number of those striving for Allah. By emulating that example today, maybe we too can help better our society.

I write as a British Muslim, embracing Islam not from the pathway of birth and family, but from a different world. One can say that I come from the house of Pharaoh; but even in the house of Pharaoh there was Pharaoh's wife, a pious women; the Magicians, who were from Pharaoh, part of his workforce, but as soon as they saw the truth, they followed it, even though Pharaoh threatened them with torture and death; and of course, there was Moses, placed in Pharaoh's house by Allah, to be called upon later to spread His Message.

Likewise, my home, Britain, has many pious and good people in it. It has within it people who, if exposed to truth, would follow it. But all too often the truth is veiled and hidden from them. And not just by the media.

The truth is veiled from them by Muslims, hiding Allah's message in culture, tradition and in anger.

I am not saying that Muslims, in so many cases, do not have the right to be angry. Anger is natural when mothers, fathers, brothers, sisters, husbands, wives, children - so many of our loved ones - are being hurt, injured and ill-treated.

But anger is the opposite of da'wah, the divine invitation to the path of Allah, and da'wah is an obligation upon each and every Muslim; Allah commands us : 'Invite all to the way, of your Lord with wisdom and beautiful teaching' (Al-Qur'an, An-Nahal 16:125). The Prophet (peace and blessings of Allah on him) said that every Muslim has a border to guard. Daw'ah is surely the frontier for Muslims living in the West to guard; it must be considered our primary duty.

And yet, when we utter words such as 'Islam versus the West', then we are basically saying that the West, in its entirety, is our enemy.

Words such as these breed nothing but enmity and hatred in the people, so they end up asking: 'Why should we want to embrace

272

Islam?' 'Why should we want to join with these people who do not like us'?

If I had read many of the leaflets or heard these slogans before I had embraced Islam, I would not have wanted to be a Muslim, but alhumdulillah, I read the Qur'an and the Sunnah first. I am not alone in these sentiments. So many whom I have met who have embraced Islam did so inspite of, not because of, Muslims. How far this is away from the example of the prophet (peace and blessing of Allah on him) who caused so many to enter the faith because of his character: his patience, his honesty, and his integrity even in the face of the hardest opposition and brutality.

Think of a woman who used to throw thorns, fish heads and other vile concoctions over him as he passed by her house, he never got violent or aggressive towards her. Indeed, after some days of passing by her house when he did not have her 'brew' poured over him, he became concerned about her. He visited her - she had been ill and the Prophet (peace and blessing of Allah be upon him) cared after her. So inspired by his love in the face of her hatred, she embraced Islam.

But how do we treat our neighbours and those we meet? Our reaction is gradually one of retaliation in the face of mildest animosity towards us. We cite the premise that self-defense is no offence and immediately attempt to combat aggression with aggression. Granted, self-defense is no offence, but one must consider the context of our situation, and consider all the facets of the Prophet's (peace and blessings of Allah be upon him) character. He did fight back on many occasions, but more often than not his example was one of calm, patience and a firm belief that all pride and honour are from Allah alone. He was discerning in his response, he did not have a blanket response to all situations, even if they seemed similar.

We however, take "The West' as one whole unit, tending to have a negative attitude towards it in its entirety. In this way we are denying what is good and seeing only the bad.

273

Muslims around the world do not want to be associated with or judged by the Muslim governments of the countries they live in. They do not want to be seen as an integral unit with regimes that persecute, and so it is with many in the West. But unlike Muslims, people in the West have no alternative system with which to identify with. They do not have Islam. They cannot say 'we disassociate ourselves from our governments and associate ourselves with Islam'. So whilst we condemn their identity we give them nothing in return, for we are not giving them Islam!

Islam is for 'all people' - no one nation owns Islam, yet still when I say 'I am from England', the immediate response is : 'yes. but where are your parents from?' The idea of a Western, English Muslim is almost unimaginable because of the mental connections that we make between the West and tyranny. We do not divide the individual people from the policies of governments, and as such cannot really imagine an English Muslim.

But every year there are quite a few like me who embrace Islam in Britain alone. Who knows how many more that there would be if we related with them as fellow human beings, who are suffering injustice and inequity and need moral and intellectual support to liberate themselves from their Pharaohs, instead of looking at them with suspicion and judging the many by the actions of a few. People need Islam - I pray that we do not hide it or keep it from them.

****

GLOSSARY
****

Adhan	The call to prayer
Anarchy	The complete absence of government; political disorder and violence; lawlessness; disorder in any sphere of activity.
Ansar	Helpers; title of the people of Madinah who helped the Prophet Muhammad (PBUH) and his companions when they migrated from Makkah to Madinah.
Apostasy	An abandoning of what one has believed in, as a faith, cause, principles, etc.
Apostle	Prophet of Allah
Asar (Asr)	Late afternoon prayer.
Ascension	The Journey by night of the Prophet Muhammad (PBUH) from Al-Masjid-al-Haram (at Makkah) to the farthest mosque in Jerusalem.
Atheist	A person who believes that there is no God
Atonement	The Act of atoning; the effect of Jesus's sufferings and death in redeeming mankind and bringing about the reconciliation of God to man, according to the Christians. The Muslims do not believe in Atonement.
Ayat	Proofs, evidences, verses, lessons, signs or revelations from Allah
Badr	The name of a place and the battle which was fought at a place about 150 kilometer

275

to the south of Madinah between the early Muslims and the infidels of Quraish

Bahai	A believer in Bahaism
Bahaism	A modern religion, developed originally in Iran from Babism, that stresses principles of universal brotherhood and social equality, etc.
Baptism	A baptizing or being baptized; the ceremony or sacrament of admitting a person into Christianity or a specific Christian church by dipping in water or pouring or sprinkling water on him as a symbol of washing away sin and of spiritual purification
Baqi (Baqee)	The cemetery of the people of Madinah, many of the companions of the Prophet Muhammad (PBUH) are burried in it
Bigamy	The act of marrying a second time while a previous marriage is still legally in effect.
Buddha	Gautama; a religious scholar, philosopher and teacher who lived in India 563?-483? BC and was founder of Buddhism
Buddhism	A religion and philosophy, system of central and Eastern Asia, founded in India in the sixth century BC by Buddah; it teaches that right thinking and self-denial will enable the soul to reach Nirvana
Celibacy	The state of being unmarried, esp. that of a person under a vow not to marry

Christian	A person professing belief in Jesus as the Christ; or in the religion based on the teachings of Jesus.
Christianity	The Christian religion based on the Old and New Testament.
Communism	Any economic theory or system based on the ownership of all property by the community as a whole
Communist	An Advocate or supporter of Communism
Conversion	A converting or being converted; a change from lack of faith to religious belief; a change from one belief, religion, doctrine, opinion, etc., to another.
Converter	A person or thing that converts
Crucifer	A person who carries a cross, as in a church procession
Crucifixion	A crucifying or being crucified; the crucifying of Jesus
Deity	The state of being a God; Divine Nature; the Deity God
Dhimmi	A non-Muslim living under the protection of an Islamic Government
Dhul-Hajja	The twelfth month of the Islamic calendar
Dhul-Qa'ada	The eleventh month of the Islamic calendar
Dogma	An opinion that which one believes in; a doctrine tenet; belief.
Faith	A religion or a system of religious beliefs, tenets etc.

Fajr	Dawn or early morning before sunrise, or morning prayer
Fidya	Compensation for a missed or wrongly practised religious ceremony, usually in the form of money or foodstuff or offering an animal
Hadith	The statement or talk, saying of the Prophet Muhammad (PBUH)
Hajj	The pilgrimage to the Holy Makkah
Hajjat-ul-Wada'	The last Hajj of the Prophet Muhammad (PBUH) the year before he died
Haram	Sanctuaries of Makkah and Madinah
Hijrah	Migration in the way of Allah
Hira	A well known cave in a mountain near Makkah
Hindu	A follower of Hinduism
Hinduism	The religion and social system of the Hindus, developed from Brahmanism with elements from Buddhism, Jainism, etc.
Hypocrite	A person who pretends to be what he is not; one who pretends to be better than he really is, or to be pious, virtuous, without being really so.
Hubal	The name of an idol in the Ka'aba in the Pre-Islamic period of ignorance
Idol	An image of a god, used as an object or instrument of worship
Iftar	Breaking the fast; the opposite of fasting

Ihram	A state in which one is prohibited to practice certain deeds that are lawful at other times. The ceremonies of Umra and Hajj are performed during such state.
Imam	The person who leads others in the prayer or the Muslim Ruler or Caliph
Intercession	The act of interceding, mediation, pleading, or prayer on behalf of another or others.
Isha	Late evening prayer
Jew	Member of the tribe or Kingdom of Judah
Jihad	Holy fighting in the Cause of Allah
Jizya	The tax which is levied in Muslim states on non-Muslims living under the protection of an Islamic government
Judaism	The Jewish religion; a monotheistic religion based on the laws and teachings of Holy Scripture and the Talmud; the Jewish way of life.
Jummah	Friday; sacred day of the Muslims
Ka'aba	A square stone building in Masjid-ul-Haram towards which all Muslims turn their faces in prayer
Kafir	The one who disbelieves in Allah, His Messengers, all the Angels, all the Holy Books, Day of Resurrection, etc.
Khums	One-fifth of war booty given in Allah's cause
Khutba	Sermon or Religious talk

279

Masjid	Mosque, prayer place
Mina	A place outside Makkah on the road to 'Arafat
Miqat	One of the several places specified by the Prophet Muhammad (PBUH) for the people to assume Ihram at on their way to Makkah when intending to perform Umra or Hajj
Miracle	A remarkable event or action that apparently contradicts known scientific laws & is thought to be due to ** The Ascent of the Noble Prophet Muhammad (PBUH) to the heavens by soul and body"
Monk	A man who retired from the world and lived in solitary self denial for religious retirement according to a rule and generally under vows, as of obedience, poverty and chastity
Muhajir	Any one of the early Muslims who had migrated from any place to Madinah in the life time of the Noble Prophet (PBUH) before the conquest of Makkah and also the one who emigrates for the sake of Allah and Islam
Mujahid	A Muslim warrior in Jihad
Muzdalifa	A place between 'Arafat and Mina where the pilgrims while returning from Arafat, have to stop and stay for the whole night between the 9th and 10th of Dhul Hajja and to perform the Maghrib and Isha prayers there together

280

Orthodox	Confirming to the usual beliefs or established doctrines as in religion, politics.
Pagan	A heathen, a person who is not a Christian, Muslim or Jew; a person who has no religion.
Pilgrim	A Muslim who travels to the Holy Makkah and Madinah to perform pilgrimage and visit the Tomb of the Noble Prophet Muhammad (PBUH)
Pilgrimage	Peformance of Hajj in Makkah
Prophet	A person who is inspired divinely
Polytheism	Belief in or worship in many gods
Qiblah	The direction in which all Muslims turn their faces in prayers and that direction is towards the Ka'aba in Makkah.
Quba	A place of the outskirts of Madinah. The Noble Prophet Muhammad (PBUH) established a mosque there which bears the same name.
Ramadhan	The month of fasting; the 9th month of Islamic calendar. It was the sacred month of Ramadhan in which the Holy Qur'an started to be revealed to our Noble Prophet Muhammad (PBUH)
Reversion	A reverting or returning as to a former state, custom, or belief.
Sacerdotalism	The character, system, methods, or practices of priesthood.

281

Salvation	Spiritual rescue from the consequences of sin; redemption
Skepticism	The doctrines of the ancient Greek Skeptics; the philosophical doctrines that truth of all knowledge must always be in question and that inquiry must be a process of doubting; doubt about fundamental religious doctrines.
Tauhid	Islamic Monotheism; Oneness of the Lordship of Allah
Tawaf	The circumambulation of the Ka'aba.
Thaur	A well known mountain in Makkah
Theism	Belief in a God or gods; belief in one God; monotheism opposed to pantheism, polytheism; belief in one God who is creator and ruler of the universe and known by revelation; distinguished from deism
Trinity	The condition of being three or threefold; the union of the three divine persons: Father, Son, and Holy Spirit or Holy Ghost in One Godhead
Uhud	A well known mountain in Madinah. One of the great battles in the Islamic history took place at its foot, called by its name.
Umra	A visit to Makkah during which one performs the Tawaf around the Ka'ba and the Saie between Safa and Marwa.
Unitarian	A person who denies the doctrine of the Trinity accepting moral teachings, but

rejecting the divinity of Jesus, and holding that God exists in only one person.

Ushr	One tenth of the yield of land to be levied for public assistance, i.e. Zakat.
Yoga	A mystic and ascetic discipline by which one seeks to achieve liberation of the self and union with the supreme spirit.
Zakat	A certain fixed proportion (i.e. two & half) of wealth of every Muslim to be paid yearly for the benefit of the poor.
Zen	An anti-rational Buddhist sect.
Zuhr	Noon or mid-day prayer.

PERSONAL PROFILE

Name:	Muhammad Haneef Shahid
Country:	Islamic Republic of Pakistan
Place of Birth:	Lahore, Pakistan
Date of Birth:	1st January 1939
Address:	(i) In Saudi Arabia
	King Saud University
	P.O. Box No. 22480, Riyadh 11495
	Kingdom of Saudi Arabia
	Tel: Office 4676118; Res. 4011822.
	(ii) In Pakistan
	170, Jehanzeb Block, Allama Iqbal
	Town, Lahore - 54570, Pakistan

Education:

One) M.A. (Punjab University, Lahore) - 1970

Two) Diploma in Library Science (Punjab University, Lahore) - 1963

Three) B.A. (Punjab University, Lahore) - 1962

Four)Certificate in the French language and literature (Punjab Univers Lahore) - 1965

Five)Research Scholar, Punjab University, Lahore, doing Research Work on the "Life and Works of Sir Sheikh Abdul Qadir" for Ph.D.

Honours:

One)Participated in the "The Allama Dr. Sir Muhammad Iqbal International Congress" held at Lahore from 2nd to 8th December, 1977 and contributed a paper entitled "Iqbal & Government College, Lahore" and awarded God Medal by General Zia-ul-Haq, President of the Islamic Republic of Pakistan.

Two)Participated in 'A Dialogue on the Political Views of Allama Dr. Sir Muhammad Iqbal & Quaid-i-Azam' - a programme

284

telecast by the Pakistan Television Corporation, Lahore in 1977.

Three)Participated in different programmes conducted by the Pakistan Broadcasting Corporation, Lahore from 1972 to 1977.

Four)Participated in "A Guest and A Dialogue; Dr. Muhammad Iqbal; Poet of Islam", a programme broadcast by the Saudi Arabian Broadcasting Service, Riyadh on the 10th November, 1985.

Five)Participated in "Views & Thoughts; Dr. Allama Muhammad Iqbal; Poet of Islam" a Television programme telecast on the 20th and 27th December, 1986 respectively by the Saudi Arabian Television, Second Channel, Riyadh, K.S.A.

Six)Presented a paper entitled "Allama Muhammad Iqbal & the Arabic language" at International Iqbal Congress held under the auspices of Association Marocaine Pour la Solidarite Musulmane, Rabat, Morocco, held from 28th to 30th March, 1988.

Seven)Participated and presented a paper namely "Educational Philosophy of Allama Muhammad Iqbal" at the Iqbal International Symposium held on 9th April, 1987 at Riyadh, K.S.A.

Eight)Participated and presented a paper namely "Allama Muhammad Iqbal & Imam Muhammad bin Abdul Wahab's Contribution to Islamic Thought" at the International Symposium held on the 19th February, 1990 at Riyadh, K.S.A.

Nine)Participated and contributed a number of papers in various "Allama Iqbal & Quaid-i-Azam Seminars" held in Riyadh, K.S.A.

Moreover, written and published more than 300 articles on different subjects. These articles, papers, and lectures were published in newspapers and journals of repute in Pakistan and abroad.

Distinctions:

285

a) Life Member of the Pakistan Library Association

b) Member of the Punjab University Library Alumni Association

c) Life Member of the Punjab Public Library, Lahore.

d) Life Member of the Iqbal Academy Pakistan, Lahore.

e) Life Member of the Pakistan Writers' Guild, Lahore.

f) President of the Bazm-i-Iqbal, Riyadh, K.S.A

g) Secretary General of the International Islamic Research Institute, London (Riyadh Branch Office).

Tributes:

1) It would not be out of place to mention that the Editor's life-sketch (bio-data) is included nearly in all the Reference Works published in Pakistan.

2) It is noteworthy that nearly all the important publications of the Editor are processed and preserved in the Library of Congress, Washington, U.S.A.

3) It is creditable that a life-size photograph -- Portrait of the Editor has been placed in the "Hall of Fame" - Conference Hall, Pakistan Academy of Letters, Islamabad - as a recognition to the contribution and services rendered for the cause of Art, Literature, and Pakistan Movement.

4) It is also worth mentioning that the Editor has been named in the "Who's Who in the World" of Marquis Who's Who, U.S.A.; and his detailed curriculum vitae has been published in its 13th edition of 1996.

PUBLICATIONS ON:

One) Allama Dr. Sir Muhammad Iqbal: Poet of Islam

- *Mufukkar-i-Pakistan;* comprehensive biography of Allama Iqbal (Urdu), Lahore, Sang-i-Meel Publications, 1987. Big size, pp. 720

- *Allama Iqbal Aur Quaid-i-Azam Ke Siyasi Nazriyaat*; (Urdu), Lahore, Shaikh Ghulam Ali and Sons, 1976, pp., 416.

286

- *Iqbal Aur Anjuman-i-Himayat-i-Islam*; (Urdu), Lahore, Anjuman-i-Himayat-i-Islam Press, 1976, pp. 200.

- *Iqbal Aur Punjab Council*; political and active role of Allama Iqbal in the Punjab Legislative Council (Urdu), Lahore, Maktaba-i-Zareen, 1977, pp. 160

- *Iqbal Ki Kahani, Iqbal Ki Zabani*; autobiography, compiled and edited from Alamma Iqbal's writings (Urdu), Lahore, Maktaba-i-Hafeez, 1977, pp., 160

- *Nazar-i-Iqbal*; collections of articles, lectures and writings on the life and works of Allama Iqbal written by Sir Shaikh Abdul Qadir, compiled and edited (Urdu), Lahore, Bazm-i-Iqbal, 1972, pp., 214.

- *Iqbal Ki Barghah Main;* selections of articles written by the contemporaries of Allama Iqbal compiled and edited (Urdu), Lahore, Universal Books, 1994, pp., 260.

- *Iqbal; the Great Poet of Islam;* writings of Sir Sheikh Abdul Qadir, compiled and edited (English), Lahore, Sang-i-Meel Publications, 1995, pp., 160.

- *Tributes to Iqbal*; critical essays on the life and works of Allama Iqbal written by his contemporaries, compiled and edited (English), Lahore, Sang-i-Meel Publications, 1977, pp., 320

- *Hayat-i-Iqbal Ke Mukhtalif Pahloo*; written, compiled and edited (Urdu), Lahore, Al-Faisal Publications, 1994.

- *Documents on Iqbal*; Punjab Government Gazette Notifications on the life and works of Allama Iqbal (English), Lahore, Iqbal Academy, 1996.

- *Iqbal Aur Abdul Qadir*; an historical survey on the relationship between the two Shaikhs of Punjab (Urdu). (Nearing Completion).

- *Saudi Arab Main Iqbaliat*; a survey of Iqbalian studies in Saudi Arabia (Urdu). (Under Print).

287

- *Un-Compiled writings of Iqbal, (Baqiat-e-Iqbal)*, Lahore, Iqbal Academy, 1996.

- *Iqbal wa Saudi Shu 'ra wa Udaba*; Iqbal and the Saudi Scholars (Arabic), Lahore, Bazm-i-Iqbal, 1994.

- *Iqbal Ka Paigham, Tulabah Ke Naam*; Iqbal's message to the students (Urdu), International Islamic Research Institute, London. (Under print)

Two)Quaid-i-Azam Muhammad Ali Jinnah: Founder of Pakistan

- *Islam Aur Quaid-i-Azam*; views of the Quaid about Islam, the Prophet, Noble Qu'ran and the Muslim World (Urdu). 2nd ed; Introduction by Dr. A.R. Khalid Alvi, London, International Islamic Research Institute, 1991, pp., 244

- *Punjab Ki Kahani, Quaid-i-Azam Ki Zabani*; a collection of speeches and statements of the Quaid regarding Punjab's political, religious, cultural and educational aspects (Urdu), Introduction by Hakim Aftab Ahmad Qarshi, compiled and edited, Lahore, Sang-i-Meel Publications, 1976.

- *Quaid-i-Azam Par Qatilana Hamla*; the story of assault on the life of the Quaid-i-Azam (Urdu), Lahore, Sh. Ghulam Ali & Sons, 1976. Big size, pp., 44

- *Quaid-i-Azam Muhammad Ali Jinnah*; speeches, statements, writings and letters of the Quaid-i-Azam (English), Introduction by M. Nusrat Ali, compiled and edited, Lahore, Sang-i-Meel Publications, 1976, pp., 232. Reprinted under the title : 'The Quaid-i-Azam on Important Issues' in 1989.

- *Tributes to Quaid-i-Azam*; a selection of speeches, articles and writings by his contemporaries on the life and services rendered by the Quaid (English), compiled and edited, Lahore, Sang-i-Meel Publications, 1976. pp.

- *All India Muslim League Aur Urdu*; role of the All India Muslim League in the defense, development and promotion of Urdu from December 1906 to December 1947 (Urdu +

288

English). Introduction by Dr. Jameel Jalibi, translated by Ijaz Ahmad Farooqi, Islamabad, National Language Authority, 1991, pp., 42. Second edition; Preface by Dr. Waheed Qureshi, Introduction by Dr. Saleem Akhtar, and views by Amjad, Islam Amjad, Riyadh, International Islamic Research Institute, March 1992, pp., 58+54.

Three)Islam

- *Why Islam is Our only Choice* (Part One); (English), compiled and edited, Dar-us-Salam Publications, Riyadh, 1996, pp., 328.
- *The Sovereignty of Allah and Other Writings of Syed Suleman Nadvi*; (English), compiled and edited, Lahore, Bazm-i-Iqbal, 1995, pp., 250
- *Why Islam is Our only Choice* (Part Two); compiled and edited, Dar-ul-Hadyan, Riyadh, 1997, pp., 280.
- *Why Islam is Superior to all other Religions*; (English), Lahore, Taj Mahal, 1995, pp., 300.
- *Islam*: The Religion of the Future; consists of : the Noble Qur'an; the Prophet; Islam in the light of the Noble Qur'an; Islamic teachings; also includes Comparative Study of Religions, i.e. Islam, Christianity, Judaism, Buddhism, Hinduism, Anti-Islam Propaganda in Europe & America, Ways & Means of Propagation of Islam in Europe & America, Proposals by the Reverts; and Islam: the Religion of the Future (English). (Nearing completion).
- *Islam in the Eyes of the Reverts*; (English). (Nearing completion).
- *The Noble Qur'an in the Eyes of the Reverts*; (English) (Nearing completion).
- *The Prophet Muhammad in the Eyes of the Reverts*; (English). (Nearing completion).
- *The Commentary of the Noble Qur'an & Other Writings (relating to Islam, Noble Qur'an and Prophet Muhammad (*Õài

289

Çááå Úáíå æ Óáã) *of Muhammad Marmaduke Pickthall*;
(English). (Ready for printing).

Four)War Heroes of Pakistan

- *Captain Raja Muhammad Shaheed, N.H.*; story of his life and services rendered for the cause of Islam and defense of Pakistan (Urdu), Foreword by Maqbool Jehangir, Lahore, Sunrise Publications, 1972, pp, 240.

- *Major Tufail Muhammad Shaheed, N.H.;* life and services (Urdu), Foreword by Major General Sarfraz Khan, Lahore, Sh. Ghulam Ali & Sons, 1969, pp, 400.

- *Nishan-i-Haider*; collective biography (life and services) of the 8 Shaheed soldiers, who, after martyrdom were awarded Nishan-i-Haider, the highest military award, by Government of Pakistan (Urdu), Foreword by General Tikka Khan, poetic tributes by Abul-Asr Hafeez Jullundhuri, Lahore, Technical Publishers, 1972, pp., 392.

Five)Sir Shaikh Abdul Qadir, Editor Punjab Observer, Makhzan, etc.

- *Miqalat-i-Abdul Qadir*; biographical, literary, and critical articles, speeches and writings of Sir Shaikh Abdul Qadir, (Urdu), compiled and edited, Lahore, Urdu Development Board, 1986, pp., 345

- *Sir Shaikh Abdul Qadir*; a biobibliography (Urdu), Islamabad, National Language Authority, 1992, pp., 48.

- *Sir Shaikh Abdul Qadir Aur Urdu*; a collection of Urdu and English writings, speeches and lectures of Sir Abdul Qadir on the Urdu Language (Urdu+English), Foreword by Dr. Waheed Qureshi. Islamabad, National Language Authority, 1987, pp. 44+32.

- *Sir Abdul Qadir on Urdu Literature*; a collection of speeches, statements, lectures and writings (English), compiled and edited, Lahore, West Pakistan Urdu Academy, 1994, pp., 136.

Six)Other Publications

- *Mashriqi Pakistan Se Bangladesh*; political history of the fall of East Pakistan (Urdu), Lahore, Lahore Law Times, 1976, pp., 270.

- *Saudi Arab Main Urdu*; literary & cultural activities in Saudi Arabia (Urdu), Foreword by Dr. Waheed Qureshi, Islamabad, National Language Authority, 1986, pp., 27.

- *Haqooq wa Faraiz*; Islamic teachings & ethics (Urdu), Foreword by Dr. Syed Abid Ahmad Ali, Lahore, Technical Publishers, 1972, pp., 112.

- *Kitab-i-Akhlaq*; Islamic teachings & ethics (Urdu), Foreword by Dr. Syed Abid Ahmad Ali, Lahore, Technical Publishers, 1972, pp., 112.

- *Mauj-i-Zarafat*; literary wit & humour of famous poets and writers (Urdu), Foreword by Maqbool Jehangir, Lahore, Technical Publishers, 1975, pp., 80.

- *Seerat-i-Raza*; a biography of the saint - Syed Hakim Ali Abul-Raza (Urdu), Lahore, 1966, pp., 80.

- *Aurat Mashaheer-i-Alam Ki Nazar Main*; views and quotations of political and literary personalities about the woman (Urdu), Lahore, Maktaba-i-Hafeez, 1966, pp., 168.

- *The Role of Sir Shaikh Abdul Qadir in the Indo-Pakistan Politics*; (Urdu). (Ready for the press).

- *Waqiaat-i-Iqbal*; stories & incidents of Iqbal relating to his life and works (Urdu), (Nearing completion).

- *Shams-ul-Ulema*; historical survey of the life & works of the literary figures who were awarded the title of 'Shams-ul-Ulema" by the British Government (Urdu). (Manuscript ready for the press).

****

291

OUR ISLAMIC PUBLICATIONS IN ENGLISH.

S#	TITLE OF BOOK	AUTHOR
1.	An-Nawawi's Forty Hadith with Comment	Seikh Sidheeque M. A. Veliankode
2.	An-Nawawi's Forty Hadith with Comments. (Pocket size)	Seikh Sidheeque M. A. Veliankode
3	Vital Herald to Pilgrims : On Rites from Authentic Hadiths	Seikh Sidheeque M. A. Veliankode
4	Pearls of the Truth : On the most beautiful names of Allah.	Seikh Sidheeque M. A. Veliankode
5	Doomsday : Portents & Prophecies	Seikh Sidheeque M. A. Veliankode
6	Encyclopedia of Names: From the Quran and The Sunnah	Seikh Sidheeque M. A. Veliankode
7	Quadianis are not Muslims	Muhammad Bashir
8	A guide for Hajj & Umrah	Anis Daud Matthews
9	The Bible led me to Islam	Melvin (Abdul Malik) LeBlanc
10	Why Islam is Our Only Choice	Muhammad Haneef Shahid
11	Science in the Qur'an	Shabir Ally
12	Common Questions People Ask About Islam	Shabir Ally
13	Is Jesus God? The Bible Says No!	Shabir Ally
14	101 Questions to Ask Visiting Jehovah's Witnesses:Volumes 1& 2	Shabir Ally
15	Moon God Myth and other Deceptive Attacks on Islam	Shabir Ally
16	Source of Islam Theories	Shabir Ally
17	An Examination of the Book of Mormon	Shabir Ally
18	How Robert Morey Lost... An Interesting Debate	Shabir Ally
19	What God Said About Eating Pork	Shabir Ally
20	Yahweh, Jehovah, or Allah? Wat is God's Real Name?	Shabir Ally
21	101 Clear Contradictions in the Bible	Shabir Ally

إصـــداراتنا الـحديثــة:

م	اسم الكتاب	اسم المؤلف
١	اشراط الساعة الصغرى والكبرى	د/عز الدين حسين الشيخ
٢	المخدرات وشباب الأمة	د/ عبد المجيد دريقة
٣	رد الإنتقاد على ألفاظ الشافعي	أبي بكر أحمد البيهقي
٤	القاموس الإشاري للصم	ماجدة سيد عبيد
٥	الإعاقة السمعية	ماجدة سيد عبيد
٦	الأخوة الإسلامية	برق التوحيدي صاحبزادة
٧	المؤنس المفيد	صالح سليمان الرشيد
٨	اللقاء الأخير	عبد الله السميري
٩	تعليم العربية والفليبينية في عشرة أيام	عبد الكريم العامر العنزي
١٠	كتاب التوحيد الذي هو حق الله على العبيد	الشيخ الإمام محمد بن عبد الوهاب
١١	الأربعون النووية في الأحاديث الصحيحة	الإمام أبي زكريا يحيى النووي
١٢	زاد المسلم اليومي (أردو) (شب روز كي دعائين)	الشيخ/ عبد الله جار الله ترجمة (أردو):أبوالمكرم عبد الجليل
١٣	التحقيق والإيضاح (أردو) (حج، عمرة اور زيارت)	سماحة الشيخ عبدالعزيز بن باز ترجمة (اردو): الشيخ إيراهيم زاهد

Dar Al-Hadyan
Publishers & Distributors
P.O.Box 15031, Riyadh 11444
Kingdom of Saudi Arabia
Tel.: 4631685 Fax : 4470266

مكتبــة دار الهــديان
للنشـــر والتوزيـــع
ص.ب ١٥٠٣١ الرياض ١١٤٤٤
المملكة العربية السعودية
ت/ ٤٦٣١٦٨٥ فاكس/ ٤٤٧٠٢٦٦

Al-Attique International Islamic Publications
Toronto Ont. Canada
Tel. :(416) 516 3856 Fax : (416) 516 4066
E-MAIL quran @ istar.ca

مطابع الخالد للاوفست
EL-KHALED OFF/ET PRINTING PRE//
ص.ب ۳۰۱۸ الرياض ١١٤٧١ - تلفون ٤٧٩٣٥٦٩ـ ٤٧٩١٠٩٦
P.O.Box3018 Riyadh11471 · Tel.4793569/4791096